ADVANCED
BOWHUNTING
GUIDE

Advanced
Bowhunting
Guide

Roger Maynard

Stoeger Publishing Company

Published by Stoeger Publishing Company
55 Ruta Court
South Hackensack, New Jersey 07606

ISBN 0-88317-115-5

Library of Congress Catalog Card No.: 83-51866

Manufactured in the United States of America

Distributed to the book trade and to the sporting goods trade by Stoeger Industries, 55 Ruta Court, South Hackensack, New Jersey 07606.

In Canada, distributed to the book trade and to the sporting goods trade by Stoeger Canada Ltd., Unit 16, 1801 Wentworth Street, Whitby, Ontario L1N 5S4

Contents

Dedication

To the memory of Duane Holloway, Mark Bock, Ben Pearson and Jack Witt, who belonged to our small bowhunting group.

Acknowledgments

The writing of this book would have been an impossibility without the help of many people both strangers and friends in the industry.

To Bill MacIntosh and Duane Allen of Bear Archery, Acie Johnson and Judy James of Ben Pearson, Mark Bybee of York, Steve Stevens and Steve Callenberg of Total Shooting Systems and to John Graham of Graham's Custom Bows. To Joe Johnston, Ted Bruning, John Martin, Tink Natham, Roger Rothhaar, Bob Barrie, John Zwickey, Stanley Hips, Andrew Simone, Keith Stuart and many other manufacturers who assisted in many ways with advice, photos and technical information.

To Mary Pearson for permission to publish the photos of Ben Pearson. To Bill Clements, Bill Hogue and Dr. J. L. Smith, three wonderful friends and hunting companions, and to two of my sons, Travis and Rayburn, for their advice and field work. To Fereshteh, my daughter-in-law, and Derek Pierkowski for many of the drawings. To Dave Ensminger of the Archery Center and to Jim and Shirley Larch and Mona Garrett of Custom Archery.

To each of you I say a sincere "Thank You."

About The Author

Roger Maynard, as expected of a native son, roots for the University of Arkansas Razorbacks football team, but, advise his friends, don't ask him who the quarterback is or where the team is playing next week. They doubt that he knows the difference between a wide receiver and a fullback — and cares less. Maynard's lifelong passions have always been fishing and hunting, especially hunting with a bow. For over 33 years he has been deeply involved in all aspects of archery from the early beginnings of bowhunting in America to the present sophisticated state of the art.

During the Great Depression of the 1930s the Maynard family moved from Hot Springs to Little Rock, where Maynard's father had found a better job. Shortly after their arrival in Little Rock, young Roger learned of a state smallbore rifle match to be held nearby. His dad had to work on the day of the match and could not provide transportation, so the 13-year-old lad tied his Remington match rifle across the handlebars of his bicycle and pedaled the 14 miles to Camp Pike (now Camp Robinson) and paid his entry fee with hard-saved cash. When the smoke cleared, the youngster had come within one point of winning the match.

The Depression forced choices between buying match ammunition or a box of high brass sixes for the duck woods. The family couldn't eat paper targets, but mallards were always welcome.

World War II saw Maynard serving first as a small arms instructor, then in the Southwest Pacific with the Fifth Air Force, where he was wounded in action. After his discharge, he returned to college to finish his studies and begin a career in civil engineering. Since 1950 he has worked for the Westinghouse Electric Corporation, starting as a machinist and, for the past 22 years, as a production supervisor.

Maynard was able to overcome a crippling war wound through the encouragement of an old friend, Sam Dramer, who urged him to renew his early interest in archery and bowhunting. The spark was rekindled and has never dimmed. Maynard says, "Sam kept my head 'screwed on right' during a very tough time in my life."

Serious bowhunters were scarce in Arkansas in the early 1950s. Like enthusiasts everywhere, they sought each other's company. In a short while a group was formed. Its members included such bow-hunting pioneers as Ben Pearson, Dr. Dave Bosma, Dr. James L. Smith, Dr. Shelby Woodiel, Daniel Boone Bullock, Lewis Rush and Duane Holloway. Maynard's childhood friends, Bill Clements and Mark Block, were also members.

This small group accounted for about 15 of the first 20 deer taken with bow and arrow in Arkansas. By 1956, state figures indicated 5,880 bowhunters; and the author's group bagged a third of Arkansas' bow-harvested deer until the early 1960s.

Bowhunting in those days was not easy. Seasons were short and there was opposition from many quarters to the use of the bow as a weapon for big game hunting, including gun hunters who considered bowhunting a threat to their sport.

To counter these charges, the Arkansas Bow-hunter's Association was formed with Roger Maynard its first president, and Dr. Dave Bosma as vice president. In later years Maynard served as secretary-treasurer, and in 1981 was honored by the Association for his long service and leadership in the cause of archery in Arkansas.

Maynard has three sons, all accomplished archers and bowhunters. When son Travis developed an interest in tournament archery, his father helped him select equipment and coached the boy. They followed the tournament trail for six years, with Travis shooting in 112 events and winning in 90. Under his father's guidance, Travis competed as an amateur in several National Field Archery Association, and Sectional tournaments, along with many state and local shoots. Maynard says that his son was showing real promise until the young man began to be distracted by young ladies, a not altogether unfamiliar pattern among adolescent male archers.

Nevertheless, during those years of competition the Maynard family traveled extensively and met and became friends with many archers and manufacturers of archery equipment. It was an invaluable education in the finer points of the sport, and keeping abreast of all the latest developments in equipment and techniques. In addition, Maynard has made contributions of his own, as well as researching and testing new gear with an engineer's curiosity about what makes things "tick."

Roger Maynard has been there and seen it all, from the longbow to the most advanced compound, and has been successful with all of them. He has watched the shooting glove give way to the mechanical release, and instinctive shooting replaced by the latest in bowsights. This book is the culmination of over four decades of learning and teaching and sharing the pleasures of archery and bowhunting.

Chapter 1
A Little Background

It was duly noted on the flyleaf of our family Bible by my great-grandfather that he, his two infant sons, his slaves and a pack train of mules arrived at Hot Springs, Arkansas, in the spring of 1850.

At the time, Hot Springs was a gambling man's town, and my great-granddad's profession was a Mississippi River Boat gambler. There's no record of what happended to the mules or how he acquired the slaves and what eventually became of them. Possibly he lost them in a poker game. Apparently he wasn't too successful at his chosen trade. Hot Springs is, as the natives say, "a fur piece" from the River Delta country that he knew so well. In a strange, new environment he gambled against the odds and lost his shirt.

The same thing can happen to anyone who jumps in blindly without knowing how deep the water is. Chances are you already own a bow and have missed your first deer. You may be a good gun hunter and are wondering why you can't score with a bow.

Brother, when you started bowhunting you opened up a new barrel of snakes. Like my great-grandfather, you're in a whole 'nother game, and

if you don't have the odds on your side you'll lose every time. Successful bowhunting demands preparation and practice. These essentials will be discussed in detail later on, but first let's spend a few minutes on a little background of bowhunting in America.

The mention of California brings different responses from any audience, but archers agree that the Golden State is the birthplace of modern bowhunting in this country. A native American Indian showed the way in the early part of the century. Ishi, the last known survivor of the Yana tribe, was befriended by Dr. Saxton Pope, a surgeon at the University of California medical school. Ishi showed Pope how to make bows and arrows and how to stalk game. Pope in turn influenced his friend, Arthur Young. Together, they made archery history.

These two men wrote books and magazine articles, but most important they recorded their experiences on film. Howard Hill and Fred Bear were definitely motivated by Pope and Young. Bear went on to start his own archery company and hunted big game with the bow internationally.

Howard Hill was raised in Alabama but moved to California early in his career. Hill made several short movies on archery, and toured the country during the Great Depression putting on demonstrations to anyone who would pay a dime to watch him shoot. He did the shooting for Errol Flynn in the motion picture *The Adventures of Robin Hood*, and if one single act could be credited with starting the postwar interest in archery it would be this movie. *Tembo*, the film of Hill's African hunt in the mid-fifties, proved that the bow was a capable and humane hunting weapon.

Hill once gave an archery exhibition in our high school auditorium. Three students in the audience were infected with archery fever that day: Mark Block, Bill Clements and me. We decided right then and there that if Hill was that good and the Indians could live by the bow then we could also succeed.

Formal education, World War II, and extremely short bow seasons put a damper on my bowhunting until 1950 when an old friend rekindled the fire. It really took a year or two before I built up nerve enough to be seen with a bow, for these were the formative years for archery in Arkansas and the South. These were the years when people driving by would holler, "Yea Robin Hood," and laugh and drive on.

The small group of friends with whom I started bowhunting included quite a cross section of hunters. We all loved to hunt and the bow was another interesting challenge to meet and master.

Bill Clements and I started hunting together when we were grammar school students, and we just marked our 47th year afield. Bill is a two-time president of the Arkansas Bowhunters, and has won the Annual Broadhead Tournament at least five times. Bill is a master with the barebow recurve and the broadhead arrow. He is also a national wild turkey calling champion and is considered throughout the South as an authority on the eastern wild turkey.

Mark Block joined Clements and I as a hunting companion during our high school years after he watched Hill perform in that early morning assembly. Mark was a respected amateur naturalist, a good bowhunter, and twice winner of the National Wild Turkey Calling Championship. Sadly, Mark is no longer with us.

The late Duane Holloway of Technor, Arkansas, was a rice farmer, a professional hunting and fishing guide and a wonderful friend. His home on the edge of the White River National Wildlife Refuge was the focal point of many of our activities.

Ben Pearson, Howard Hill and many other archery celebrities hunted the White River Refuge with Duane. Virtually all the Pearson films on bowhunting were conceived in Duane's small frame home on the Little Prairie of Arkansas. This area was Ben Pearson's testing and proving ground. The idea for the Pearson Deadhead point originated here.

Dr. James L. Smith, a Little Rock opthalmologist, was a hunting companion of Ben Pearson. "Jimmy Doc" Smith first met Pearson on a professional basis and can say that he was Pearson trained from the very first arrow.

Doc was a witness to Pearson's antelope kill. Ben would not complete this film because both cameras were lying on the ground and the shot, arrow flight, and impact with the antelope were not recorded on film. Dr. Smith also witnessed Pearson's javelina kill in Arizona, which is probably the longest filmed shot every made on a game animal with a bow. The javelina was killed by a white arrow shot from the top of a cliff to the animal in the valley below. Johnnie Gray recorded Ben releasing the shot, the arrow arcing and striking the animal, all on the same run of film. The camera was never moved. This fantastic hunting shot may never be equaled.

Pearson, Dr. Smith, and Holloway were the hunters in the Pearson film *The Arrow Is For Lion.* Dr. Smith's mountain lion taken on this Arizona hunt was ranked number one with the Pope and Young Club for many years.

Dr. Smith and I were sponsored by Pearson for membership in the Arkansas City Hunting Club on Choctaw Island in southeast Arkansas. Dr. Smith recently celebrated his 65th birthday and is still a very active leader in his profession, still an enthusiastic and successful bowhunter, and as fine a friend and hunting companion as a man could have.

Dr. Dave Bosma of De Witt, Arkansas, is the man who actually got us off the ground and changed our hunting tactics from those of riflemen to those of bowhunters. He changed us from arrow shooters to bowhunters in a time when taking a deer with the bow was considered almost superhuman. Many early successful bowhunters were accused of having shot their deer with a rifle and then placing an arrow in the carcass.

Dr. Bosma's ideas enabled this small group, and those who hunted with us, to take a third of the bow-taken deer in this state from the early fifties into the early sixties. Don't let me give you the impression that we invented Arkansas bowhunting, but we had the deer and were the most imitated bowhunting group in the state.

Ben Pearson and an Arizona javelina. The shot was well over a hundred yards, and was recorded on film.

Dr. Bosma is credited with being the first bowhunter to develop tree hunting tactics in this region and we all benefited from his expertise.

The exploits of this small group would fill a book. They hunted from the Brooks Range in Alaska almost to the coast of Russian Siberia. They roamed many Rocky Mountain states, Texas, Arizona, Mexico, and did some bowfishing off the Florida coast.

You may say, "Maynard, I don't want a history of bowhunting," and I'll reply that these men took their bowhunting seriously. They did not gamble with their bowhunting. They made many mistakes but also had many triumphs. Much of this book is based on their experiences and how you can improve your own skills because of them.

No scholar can place his finger on a map and say, "Here is where the bow and arrow originated." No doubt archery was developed by many different primitive innovators in many places throughout prehistoric times.

The Middle East and parts of the Far East are credited with the development of the recurve bow, while Europe and the American continents were known for the straight-ended longbow. It is ironic that the most advanced bow designs of antiquity occurred in areas where there were no suitable native woods for bow making. Ancient bowyers shaped, flattened, and laminated animal horn into the short, powerful, deflexed recurve bows that armed the Mongol armies and shot Saladin's arrows at Christians during the Crusades.

The horn recurve bows were very fast but too sensitive to be very accurate. On the other hand, the European yew longbow was a slower bow but much more forgiving and very accurate.

Conservatism in bow design really found a home with the Englishman and his supply of yew wood.

Accuracy was the name of the game and by order of the King every able-bodied English male put in practice time on the village green with his bow.

The Middle East had the bow with the most range and the fastest velocity, and the English had the most stable and accurate bow in the world. A really successful blending of the recurve's speed and the accuracy of the longbow eluded the most skilled bowyers until fiberglass and modern adhesives became available after World War II.

We pride ourselves on our skill and technology but many a modern flight bow was humbled while trying to best the distance mark set by a young Turkish archer with a horn bow many years ago. Modern materials and technology finally paid off for Harry Drake, who shot an arrow 2,028 yards in 1971 while using an unlimited class foot bow.

It would be quite proper to say that fiberglass and modern adhesives together have made it possible for more improvements to be made to archery equipment in the last thirty-five years than in all the centuries since the invention of the bow.

Many bowyers have said that there are no new ideas in archery — only the materials are new. I suspect somewhere in the past few years that the "no new idea" statement is no longer valid.

The bows of today and tomorrow are beyond our wildest dreams of thirty years ago. Holless W. Allen's patent of the compound really started the new look in archery and gave us a more powerful and efficient weapon. More than 80 percent of today's bowhunters shoot the compound and yet the original compound concept is already obsolete. The two-wheeler is king today, but on the horizon loom three new contenders: the Dynabo, the Delta-V and the programmed eccentric cam bows.

Many changes have affected arrow designs. Super-tough aluminum alloys, carbonglass and

Members of the White River Bowmen and friends who hunted with the author (far right) and pioneered the sport in Arkansas.

fiberglass are used to make modern arrow shafts. The traditional barrelled and tapered cedar arrows with their hardwood foreshafts and personalized crests were victims of high production costs, and were surpassed in accuracy by aluminum. These old arrows are the most perfect flying arrows ever produced but they would warp, crack and break. Most of us just take for granted the high quality and performance of the modern arrow without considering their long development process.

It is natural for an archer to talk about his bow and then his arrows and his release, and eventually he may get around to talking about his broadheads. Why this is I don't know, but it's true. The broadhead, within the realm of reason, is the most important archery item you own. Mismatching a broadhead and arrow shaft affects accuracy and its performance on game. If you can't hit and kill with dependability you fail as a bowhunter.

The postwar years produced a flood of broadheads of every conceivable shape, size and material. Many of these points were just plain ridiculous. Thankfully, one of the biggest improvements in bowhunting in the past few years has been the design and manufacture of some really good broadheads.

This country is full of good archery shops, many with indoor shooting lanes. Bowhunters are proud of their method of hunting and are very willing to share their knowledge and skills with a beginning archer. These proshops and experienced archers are the people to turn to for assistance to help you get started. Develop good habits and proper shooting form right from the beginning. Retraining a poor archer can sometimes be an impossible task. The inability to hit their target consistently has caused more bowhunters to quit the sport than failing to take their chosen game, in my opinion.

Author Roger Maynard with a doe taken during the early days of bowhunting. Recurve bows and wooden shafts were state-of-the-art.

Dr. James L. Smith shot this very large cougar while making a bowhunting film with Ben Pearson near Young, Arizona in 1958.

A successful bowhunter continues to seek out improvements in equipment and refine his shooting skill. To shoot better you will have to develop good practice habits and set goals for steady improvement. You also need to be able to recognize and correct the bad habits that sometimes trap both the beginning and the experienced archer. If you think that going out and just shooting will improve your skill, you are wrong. You need to practice the right things, or else bad habits will become ingrained. Recognize this right at the start and don't be too proud or stubborn to seek help if your shooting goes into a slump.

Learn all you can about your equipment and how to utilize its potential. Increase your ability to use this equipment and improve your hunting skills and you are on your way to success.

Archery and bowhunting equipment have come a long way since the early days of longbows and wooden arrow shafts. Shown here is a representative of the new generation of Maynard bowmen adjusting one of the latest sophisticated compound bows.

Notice the mercury capsules taped to Bill Clements' recurve. Photo was taken during the development of the Mercury Hunter bow design.

The author shooting on a field range in the late 1950s. Ben Pearson was the coach and photographer that day.

Chapter 2
Modern Bows

At one time a new fiberglass bow complete with three field arrows, three broadhead arrows, an arm guard, and shooting glove could all be bought for around $21.95, plus tax. That's what I paid for my Pearson 304 take-down, considered a good quality bow in the early 1950s.

The use of fiberglass in bowmaking was spreading rapidly in those days. Bow design was changing almost overnight from longbows to recurves, and the materials from yew and lemonwood to fiberglass and fiberglass/maple laminates. From bows with skinny little straight grips to the graceful hand-filling pistol grip handle risers of exotic imported hardwoods, the progression was steady and swift.

Bow performance improved too—not just arrow velocity alone — but stability and appearance as well. New materials such as fiberglass and epoxy adhesives allowed imaginative bowyers to experiment with new designs and construction methods. Many people got into the act.

Some bow manufacturers suffered severe financial difficulties and went out of business, but they left their ideas and their technology behind and archery profited because of their efforts.

American archers entered the 1960s using the finest bows ever made. Both bowhunting and tournament archery attracted hordes of new enthusiasts. By the end of that decade there were good archers all across this country. Terms such as bow tuning, shooting form, adjustable arrow rest, arrow plates, and similar archery terminology became well known. Field archery scores were improving. Effective bowhunting techniques were becoming widespread. And more important, bowhunting had attained its place as an accepted form of sport hunting for big game.

During the late 1930s Dr. Claude J. Lapp designed the first compound bow. Apparently Dr. Lapp felt that his unusual-looking bow would not be accepted and the idea lay dormant until the late 1960s when H. W. Allen designed and patented his compound bow. It took several years of hard work by archery manufacturers, plus legalization by the National Field Archery Association, before the compound bow was accepted in

The Jennings Arrowstar four-wheel compound bow shown as a tournament model and as a hunting bow with camouflage limbs.

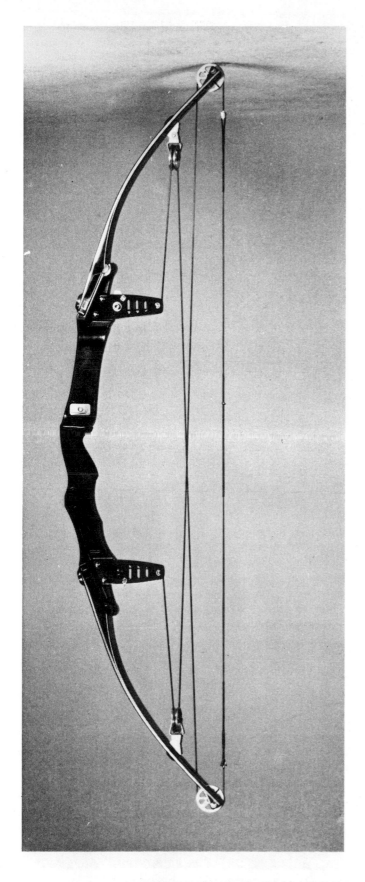

Pearson 440 SS Magnum Pro Staff four-wheel compound.

general and became the dominant bow for the field tournament archer and the bowhunter.

Tom Jennings and his company made many contributions to the development of the compound. Jennings did much of the work necessary to popularize the compound. His efforts were copied by many other manufacturers.

It was just a matter of time and trial until the early four-wheeled compound was simplified to the two-wheel version. The two-wheel compound was the answer to a bowhunter's prayer. It was a much simpler bow and less likely to get out of adjustment. Most important, it placed the compound bow within the price range of the average bowhunter's budget. This was a major step for the increasing popularity of bowhunting.

The four-wheel compound is a very sophisticated design and still popular, regardless of its higher cost. Archery industry officials now report that the majority of tournament competitors have switched to the two-wheel compound.

It would be a very dull world without progress. Where there is a demand you will find competition among manufacturers to capture the lion's share of that market with a better product.

Currently, bowmakers are concentrating on arrow velocity, or as the old archer would call it, "increased arrow cast." This emphasis on speed has resulted in bow designs that not only shoot light arrows fast, but are also an improvement over both the four-wheel and the two-wheel compounds with their ability to handle heavy hunting arrows.

Late in 1981 Bear Archery unveiled the Delta-V. Shortly afterward, York Archery announced a line of Alpha Cam graphite-limbed bows. All of a sudden bowhunters everywhere became eccentric-cam, high performance conscious. The advertisements all claimed increased velocity over the conventional compound bows. Tests with an Arrowmeter verified these claims. Anticipating the future, I foresee some exciting bows. Contemporary bowhunters expect velocity and they will be offered this kind of performance regardless of the bow's shape or configuration.

Martin Archery recognized a renewed interest by archers in the handle riser overdraw setup from the recurve days to increase arrow velocity by shooting smaller arrows. The Martin Jaguar bow is a factory designed overdraw compound. Martin also offers a kit to convert a compound to the overdraw principle.

An overdraw is an extension of the sight window/arrow shelf portion of the handle riser that permits the arrow rest to be moved several inches toward the archer.

Bill Hogue shooting a York Alpha Cam Tracker bow. Notice the high stress placed on the solid matrix limbs.

Bear, Pearson, York, and Indian Archery are now offering high-performance bows equipped with the solid fiberglass limbs.

There has been some call for the return of the wood laminated handle riser. Wood is preferred for its warm feel and beauty. Metal handle risers are strong but cold to touch. Thermogrips alleviate this problem. Despite their aesthetic qualities, wooden handle risers do have stress limitations. Only well designed metal handle risers are capable of the strength necessary for the generous sight window clearances that bowhunters will demand in the years ahead. Look for the handle risers on the high performance bows to be metal and have interchangeable grips of rubber, plastic or some other comfortable, insulating materials.

In slightly over three decades bowhunting has progressed from the longbow to the flat-limbed recurve, from the four-wheeled compound to the two-wheeled compound, and now we are entering the era of the high performance eccentric cam bows.

These three bows are typical of the new high performance eccentric cam bows now on the market:

1. The Dynabo, introduced in 1976, utilizes an eccentric cam unit mounted at the bottom of

This device permits the use of a shorter and smaller diameter arrow thus decreasing overall arrow weight and increasing arrow velocity.

We'll probably see more solid fiberglass matrix limbs on bows. Carbon has been added to fiberglass to create so-called "graphite limbs."

The solid fiberglass limb was once regarded as rough shooting and was used only on inexpensive bows. Due to advances in fiberglass technology these limbs are now appearing on top quality high performance bows.

Another reason for the change to the solid fiberglass limb is the stress to which these new bows are subjected. Compare the York Alpha Cam bow at full draw with the limbs of other laminated limb bows. There is no way that a fiberglass/maple laminated limb can stand this severe stress over a period of time without failure. Next, check the guarantee on the new solid limb bows. Some companies are offering a five year warranty.

Another factor to consider is the cost of manufacturing fiberglass/maple laminated limbs. It takes expensive, highly skilled hand labor to produce these laminates.

Shooting the Martin M-10 Cheetah Dynabo.

the lower limb. This mechanical leverage system is called a "cam-sector."

2. The Bear Delta-V, introduced in 1981, utilizes two eccentric cam units mounted on handle riser pylons. Bear refers to these mechanical leverage units as "programmed cams."

3. The York Tracker has eccentric cams mounted on each end of the bow limbs. The bow has the same configuration as a conventional two-wheel compound. Close examination reveals quite a difference between these eccentric cams and the conventional cylindrical eccentric rollers. York calls their mechanical leverage system "Alpha Cams." This bow was introduced in 1981 and the principle has been adopted by Bear and others.

How do these new mechanical leverage systems produce an increase in arrow velocity?

To better understand how a bow stores energy as it is drawn, study the Overlay Force Draw Chart of the various bow concepts. The charts for the longbow and the two-wheeled compound were not plotted for the sake of clarity.

Notice the smooth steady rise of the recurve from brace height to full draw at 28 inches, and the steeper increase as the bow passes 28 inches. This sudden *increase* in draw weight per inch of

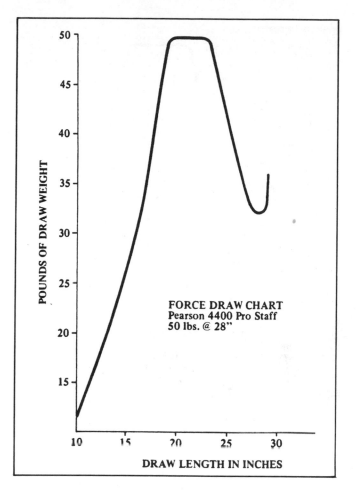

FORCE DRAW CHART
Pearson 4400 Pro Staff
50 lbs. @ 28"

DRAW LENGTH IN INCHES

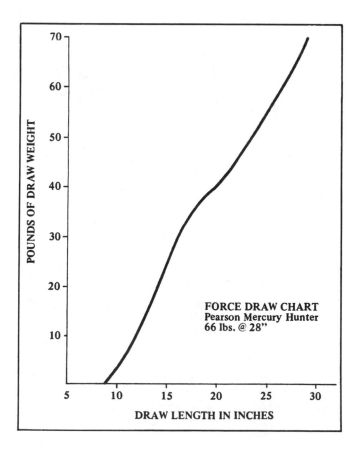

FORCE DRAW CHART
Pearson Mercury Hunter
66 lbs. @ 28"

DRAW LENGTH IN INCHES

draw is known as "stack." This smooth, steadily increasing draw weight is the reason why the longbow and the recurve are favored bows of instinctive shooters.

Now note the more sudden increase from the start of the draw to peak weight of the four-wheel compound. Note the *decrease* in draw weight as the set draw length is approached. This is known as "let-off."

Increased velocity and let-off in draw weight to a lower holding weight is the reason for the compound's popularity. It's fairly easy to draw with the major weight at the start of the draw, then hold and aim while holding at your bow's minor weight.

As an example, a 60-pound compound with a 50 percent let-off means you draw 60 pounds peak weight and then aim while holding only 30 pounds minor weight. The ability to shoot with a heavy bow's flat trajectory yet aim with the ease of holding a light target bow has made the fiberglass/maple laminated compound bow one of the most important developments in archery history.

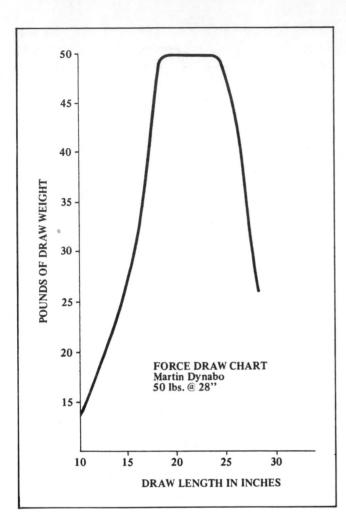

FORCE DRAW CHART
Martin Dynabo
50 lbs. @ 28"

POUNDS OF DRAW WEIGHT

DRAW LENGTH IN INCHES

per second, and the 60-pound Delta-V at 231 feet per second while shooting the same 8.4 metric magnum arrow. Realize that the longbow and recurve archer is holding and aiming with more than 60 pounds draw weight, while the Delta-V shooter has relaxed to 30 pounds draw weight.

It has been estimated that more than 80 percent of all bowhunters use a compound bow. I suspect this estimate to be on the low side. However, there are several small companies manufacturing longbows and recurves exclusively and doing very well at it.

Bear Archery is busy filling orders for the famed Custom Kodiak Take-Down recurve; and the Ben Pearson Company has reintroduced the Mercury Hunter recurve and the Ol' Ben Classic longbow.

Not everybody likes the same thing. Some purists still resist any involvement with compound bows. However, the Professional Archery Association has approved the compound for use in all of its tournaments. Oldtimers may scoff and grumble at the "new fangled contraptions" but there's no

As we compare the charts of the high performance eccentric cam bows focus your attention on the flattened portion of the force draw curve at the top of the chart. This shows you how far an arrow will travel on the bow while being subjected to peak thrust of the bow string. It is also an indication of the bow's potential to shoot a heavy hunting arrow at improved velocity.

It is interesting to note the ability of each bow concept to store energy. Compare the chart of the recurve with the chart of the Delta-V plotted over the recurve line. The shaded area between the plotted lines of the force draw charts shows the progress made in bow design to store energy. Remember that it takes well designed bow limbs constructed of the proper material to release that stored energy quickly and produce a fast bow. Bow limb design is the key factor in how fast a bow will shoot.

Another way of looking at it is to compare the arrow velocities of the 64-pound longbow at 166 feet per second; the 66-pound recurve at 183 feet

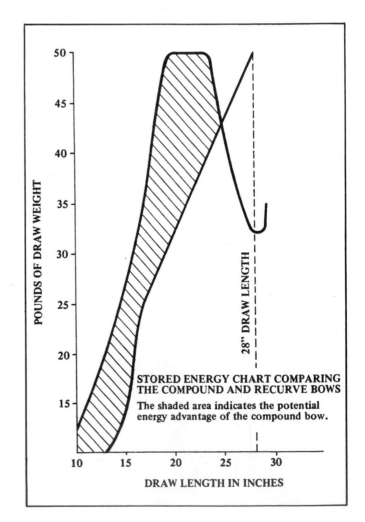

POUNDS OF DRAW WEIGHT

28" DRAW LENGTH

STORED ENERGY CHART COMPARING THE COMPOUND AND RECURVE BOWS
The shaded area indicates the potential energy advantage of the compound bow.

DRAW LENGTH IN INCHES

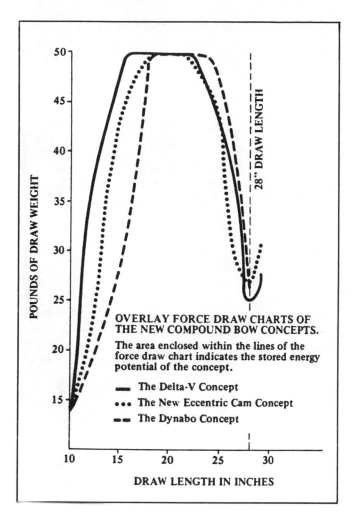

OVERLAY FORCE DRAW CHARTS OF THE NEW COMPOUND BOW CONCEPTS.

The area enclosed within the lines of the force draw chart indicates the stored energy potential of the concept.

— The Delta-V Concept
••• The New Eccentric Cam Concept
- - - The Dynabo Concept

Respecting the revived interest in recurves and longbows, I tested a Mercury Hunter recurve, a Custom Kodiak recurve and a Ol' Ben longbow. It was also felt that many present-day bowhunters would like to see how these early bows compare to today's compound and the new eccentric cam bows.

We also examined and shot two old fiberglass/maple laminated bows through the Arrowmeter. One was Bill Clement's first bow, a Pearson 304, which is still in good shape. The other bow was Dr. Jim Smith's Pearson Bushmaster, the same bow he used in the mountain lion film. This was the first time these bows were tested with modern chronographing equipment. A word of caution about handling old bows is called for. Remember that age may have dried these bows to the point that they are brittle and subject to breakage. They may snap under the strain of stringing and drawing, and should be considered potentially hazardous to the shooter.

Bill Hogue, Bill Clements, and two of my sons, Rayburn and Travis, all well trained archers and

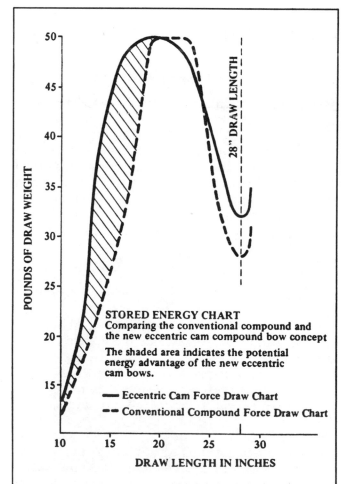

STORED ENERGY CHART
Comparing the conventional compound and the new eccentric cam compound bow concept

The shaded area indicates the potential energy advantage of the new eccentric cam bows.

— Eccentric Cam Force Draw Chart
- - - Conventional Compound Force Draw Chart

denying the mechanical superiority of the latest bow designs. They may lack the grace of a longbow, but they sure work.

There has always been a small percentage of bowhunters that prefers the longbow and recurve. These archers are generally senior shooters with years of experience. Don't ever feel sorry for an old bowhunter with an old style bow. He is most likely using it by choice and knows what he's doing. And many experienced compound bowhunters are taking up the longbow and recurve as a new challenge, and to see how they compare in skill and ability with the early oldtime bowhunter.

TESTING BOWS

Preparation of this book required shooting a number of different bows. As examples of modern bows, I selected a Delta-V, a York Tracker and a Graham Dynabo. Because of its innovative approach to the two-wheel concept, I included a Total Shooting Systems Quadraflex.

experienced bowhunters, assisted me in conducting the tests.

Our objective with the new high performance bows was to go beyond the usual charts and graphs and shake them down for any signs of "bugs" or idiosyncrasies. We tried to determine the areas of bowhunting/archery where these bows are best suited. We shot them with fingers and releases, sights and barebow, used different arrow rests and different arrows, and kept records of our findings.

THE LONGBOW

We had a field day shooting the longbow, in this case a Pearson 5000 Ol' Ben. Clements and I had shot longbows years ago but it was a new experience for Bill Hogue and my sons. It was interesting to watch these young archers receiving basic instructions for instinctive shooting. We all shot barebow with fingers, as this is the way 99 out of 100 longbow archers will shoot. This barebow instinctive shooting is a most enjoyable way to shoot a bow. It's basic, grass roots archery.

Getting acquainted with an early fiberglass bow.

The proper way to string a longbow.

Really, there is very little to test on a longbow except to say that the bow shot well. It had a smooth draw and surprisingly little recoil. Draw was a smooth progression at a steady rate of three pounds per inch out to 30 inches making the bow almost stack free. This bow weighed 64 pounds at a 28-inch draw. It shot an 8.4 Bear metric magnum arrow through the Arrowmeter at 166 (average) feet per second.

Specifications of the Pearson Ol' Ben:
Draw Length—28 inches.
Draw Weights—50, 60, 70 pounds.
Bow Length—70 inches.
Bow Weight—1 pound, 9 ounces.
Handle Riser—elm, right or left-hand grip.
Limbs—laminated maple.

Longbows are available through the Ben Pearson Company, Bear, Martin Archery and also from the custom shops of Howard Hill Archery of Hamilton, Montana, and Don Sturges Custom Longbows of Moab, Utah, among others.

A word of caution: do not use a string type bow stringer on the longbow because the leather tip pods can slip off the bow tips and injure you. Instead, learn to place the lower bow tip on top of your inside shoe sole and brace the bow by sliding the string up the top limb into the string grooves. The long length of the longbow makes this a reasonably safe procedure.

Do not use this procedure on the shorter recurve bows. The string may slide past the string grooves causing the bow tip to strike you on the face. Always use a bow stringer with a recurve bow.

THE RECURVE BOW

The Mercury Hunter by Ben Pearson was the brainchild of Jack Witt and John D. Sanders and is noted for its smooth, recoil-free shooting and its stability.

This bow has two stainless steel, mercury-filled capsules embedded in the handle riser to absorb the shock of shooting.

The old original handle riser of beautiful Brazilian rosewood has been replaced by an unknown hardwood. Realizing the scarcity and expense of rosewood I can easily understand the substitution, and the bow is still a handsome recurve. The arrow shelf is radiused and equipped with a carpet type rest. The bow is set up as an instinctive archer's bow.

Hogue, Clements, Rayburn and I shot this bow. Hogue and I shot instinctively while Clements used his variable anchor point style of precision shooting.

Our only criticism is minor. Clements and I would have preferred the longer 64-inch length of the original Mercury Hunter, and instead of a stabilizer bushing I would have preferred that the bow be drilled and tapped for a cushion-plunger or other adjustable rest.

Another possibility would be the use of a Hoyt adhesive-backed rest should you prefer a precision style of shooting.

The force draw chart shows a gain approaching four pounds per inch of draw for this 66-pound bow at 28 inches. Drawing the bow to 29 inches showed the bow to be almost stack free.

This bow shot an 8.4 Bear metric magnum through the Arrowmeter for 183 (average) feet per second.

A word of caution: always use a bow stringer to string a recurve bow; any other way may cause damage to the bow or injury to yourself.

Specifications of the Pearson Mercury Hunter:
 Draw Length—unlimited.
 Draw Weights—45, 50, 55, 60, 65, 70 pounds.
 Bow Length—60 inches.
 Handle Riser—hardwood, sight window 5 inches

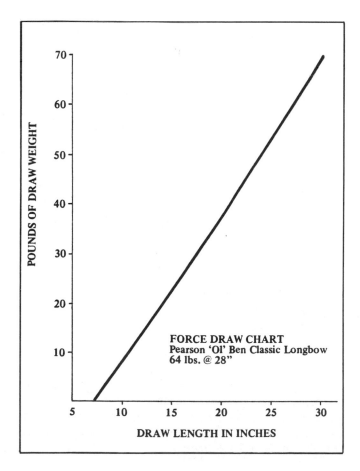

FORCE DRAW CHART
Pearson 'Ol' Ben Classic Longbow
64 lbs. @ 28"

(Y-axis: POUNDS OF DRAW WEIGHT; X-axis: DRAW LENGTH IN INCHES)

Bill Clements shooting a Bear Custom Kodiak recurve.

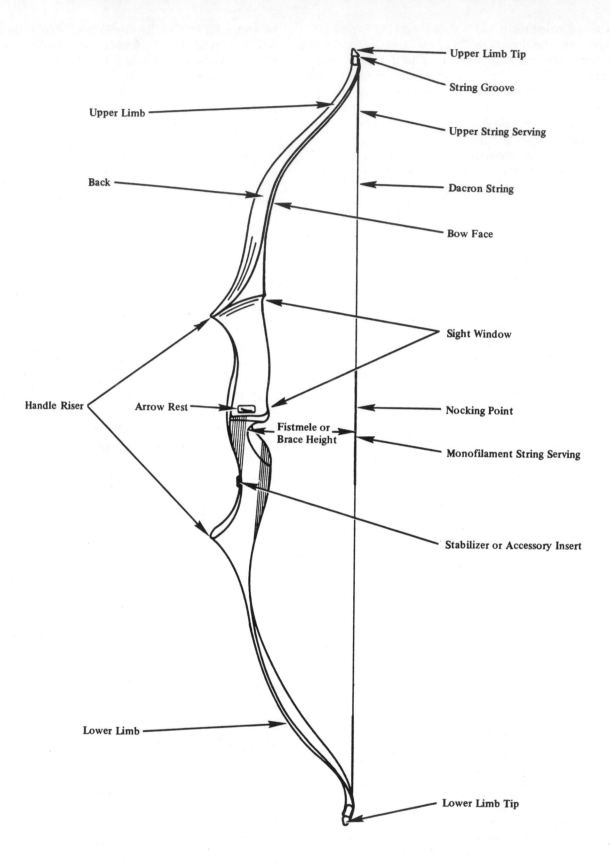

Upper Limb Tip

String Groove

Upper String Serving

Dacron String

Bow Face

Upper Limb

Back

Sight Window

Handle Riser

Arrow Rest

Nocking Point

Fistmele or Brace Height

Monofilament String Serving

Stabilizer or Accessory Insert

Lower Limb

Lower Limb Tip

BASIC PARTS OF THE MODERN RECURVE HUNTING BOW

long with beveled edge carpet arrow rest and stabilizer insert, right or left-hand pistol grip.
Limbs—laminated with fiberglass and maple, reinforced tips.
Other Features—two built-in mercury recoil cartridges.

The early Bear Kodiak was the favored bow of Dr. Dave Bosma. Actually, Dr. Bosma had little choice for this was just about the only bow available at the time in a left-hand model that could handle his 30-inch draw length. Dr. Bosma's bow was 69 inches long and pulled 63 pounds at 28 inches.

The Bear Custom Kodiak is available as a take-down model today. It was developed in 1965 and has killed big game from Alaska to Africa and is Fred Bear's personal favorite.

Clements and I shot this 57-pound bow both instinctively and by using a variable anchor point. I was not able to make a velocity check or force draw chart before having to return the bow, unfortunately. My only modification of this bow would be a bushing for an adjustable arrow rest, and an increase in length to 64 inches.

The bow is a three-piece, take-down bow by the use of a latch and microgroove keyway. You can change draw weights by changing to a different set of limbs. The bow can be packed into a short, compact case for easy transportation on a pack horse or airline.

Specifications of the Bear Custom Kodiak Take-Down:
Draw Length—unlimited.
Draw Weights—50, 55, 60, 65 pounds.
Bow Length—60 inches.
Handle Riser—Laminated hardwood, right or left-hand grip.
Limbs—laminated with fiberglass and maple.

The Mercury Hunter and the Bear Custom Kodiak are excellent factory produced bows but if you prefer a custom-made bow, you might consider a recurve from Bighorn Bowhunting Company in Lafayette, Colorado. Rumor has it that the famed Jack Howard hunting bow is still in production and so far behind in filling orders that they don't advertise anymore. Try Jack Howard Hunting Bows in Nevada City, California.

THE FOUR-WHEEL COMPOUND

At the Arkansas Bowhunter's Annual Spring Broadhead Tournament Acie Johnson, president of the Ben Pearson Company, announced that the firm was contributing the "pick of the Pearson catalog" as a door prize. My son Rayburn was the lucky winner. When Johnson asked the young man his choice he didn't hesitate in picking a 50-60 4400 Pro Staff four-wheeler.

Later I asked Rayburn why he chose a four-wheeler and he replied that he wanted it for broadhead tournament shooting and as a hunting bow. The great adjustability of the 4400 appealed to him very much.

The bow shot well at the fifty-pound setting but as draw weight was increased this bow really came to life. This is typical of any adjustable compound. Peak performance always comes at peak weight.

Velocity at 50-pound major and 32-pound minor weight was 179 (average) feet per second with an 8.4 Bear metric magnum arrow. Let-off figured to be 36 percent at the 29-inch draw.

Velocity at 60-pound major and 33-pound minor was 196 (average) feet per second. Notice the difference in let-off at 50 pounds—36 percent, and 60 pound—45 percent.

These figures point out the necessity of re-weighing and measuring your bow whenever you make any changes. Changing weight affects draw length and let-off. Changing draw length affects your draw weight and let-off. Always check and be sure.

Arrows used were 308 Bear magnums, 8.4 Bear metric magnums, Easton 2016 Gamegetters, Easton 2114 Game Getters and Gilmore #7 Super-shafts.

Specifications of the Pearson 4400 Pro Staff:
Draw Lengths—27 to 29 inches, adjustable by changing draw length slots in eccentric wheels; and 30 to 32 inches, adjustable by changing to another set of wheels.
Draw Weights—all popular weights, adjustable.
Let-Off—approximately 40 percent.
Handle Riser—cast magnesium, rubber grip, sight window 7 inches long, right or left-hand grip.
Other Features—drilled and tapped for accessories, laminated maple limbs, adjustable arrow pressure point with fold-away arrow rest, replaceable self-lubricating wheel bearings.

The 4400 is offered as a hunting bow, but the same bow can be had in a tournament model as the 4401.

May I point out that this bow has a large seven-inch sight window. This permits the use of any anchor point desired. It also makes it easy for any release, either mechanical or hand.

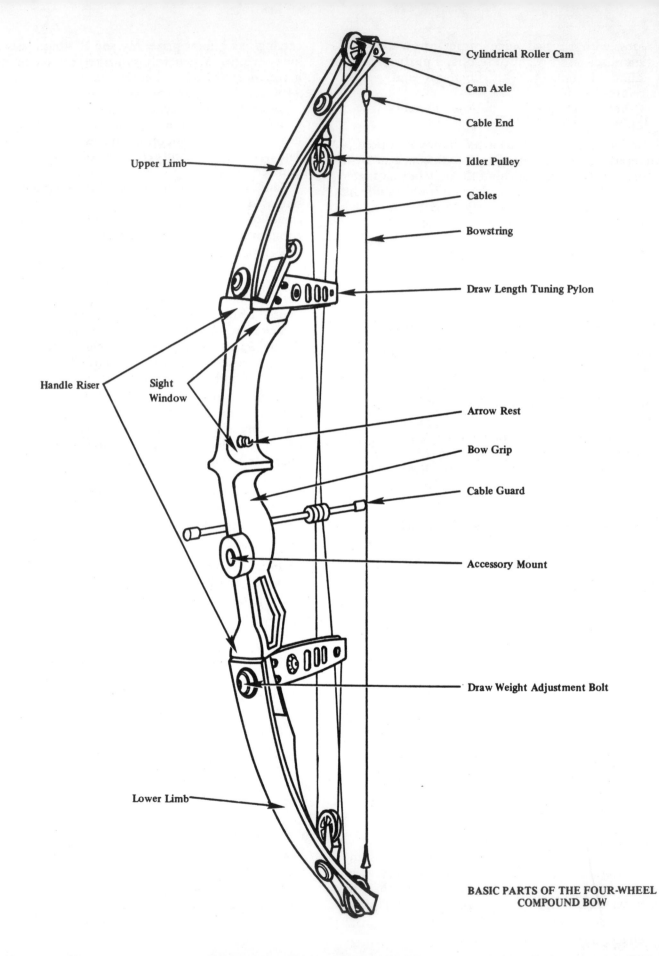

Cylindrical Roller Cam

Cam Axle

Cable End

Idler Pulley

Cables

Bowstring

Draw Length Tuning Pylon

Upper Limb

Handle Riser

Sight
Window

Arrow Rest

Bow Grip

Cable Guard

Accessory Mount

Draw Weight Adjustment Bolt

Lower Limb

**BASIC PARTS OF THE FOUR-WHEEL
COMPOUND BOW**

Excellent four-wheel compounds are available from Bear, Jennings by Bear Archery, Martin, Browning and Precision Archery, among others.

THE TWO-WHEEL COMPOUND

Not long after the four-wheel compound was on the market someone wondered what would happen if they did away with the idler pulleys on the four-wheel arrangement, and the two-wheel concept of the compound bow was born.

The first two-wheelers were not fast bows but they were almost trouble-free and considerably less expensive than the four-wheel compound. This cost reduction placed the compound bow within the price range and consideration of the inexperienced archer.

It didn't take long until two-wheel speed and accuracy were competitive with the four-wheeler, and the two-wheeler has been the bowhunter's popular choice ever since.

THE QUADRAFLEX

Joe Caldwell of Total Shooting Systems took the two-wheel compound a step further. Starting with handle risers, Caldwell forged the riser for his bow from aircraft landing gear aluminum alloy, instead of die casting aluminum or magnesium. Instead of a paint job his riser received a good anodizing. These unusual steps produced a long, very strong, and exceptionally durable handle riser. This handle riser has a lifetime warranty covering material and workmanship.

The limbs are laminated wood and fiberglass. They are slotted almost full length to the weight adjustment assembly. In effect, this created two upper and two lower limbs and allowed each limb half to flex independently and reduce limb torque. These limbs are mounted on a bracket at each end of the handle riser, which allows the entire limb to flex as the bow is drawn and fired. This is the action that gives the bow it's name "Quadraflex." The limbs are mounted in rubber to help quiet the bow.

Instead of a narrow eccentric wheel, the Quadraflex Omega wheel is 11/16 inch in width and grooved to move the cables toward the center of the wheel as the bow is drawn. These cables move in harmony, always balancing the limb load and preventing any possible limb torque. There is no fletch/cable interference with this design.

The 6½-inch sight window is cut ½ inch past center accommodating any type of anchor or release. There will be no problem with either vanes or feather fletch clearance. The riser is drilled and tapped for bowsights, adjustable arrow rest and stabilizer.

Specifications of the Total Shooting Systems Quadraflex:

    Draw Lengths—25 to 33 inches in one-inch increments, adjustable by changing the Omega wheels.

    Draw Weights—30 to 100 pounds in 10-pound increments, adjustable.

    Let-Off—50 percent.

    Bow Length—axle to axle, 47½ inches.

    Bow Weight—3 pounds, 8 ounces.

    Color—two-color anodized camo, black, gold, blue and green.

    Handle Riser—forged aluminum, cushion grip, right-hand only.

    Manufacturer—Total Shooting Systems, 419 Van Dyne Rd., North Fond du Lac, Wisconsin 54935.

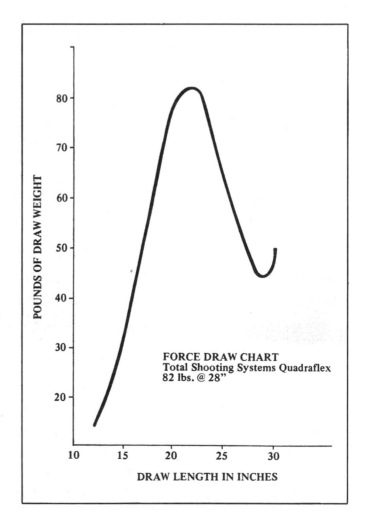

FORCE DRAW CHART
Total Shooting Systems Quadraflex
82 lbs. @ 28"

POUNDS OF DRAW WEIGHT

DRAW LENGTH IN INCHES

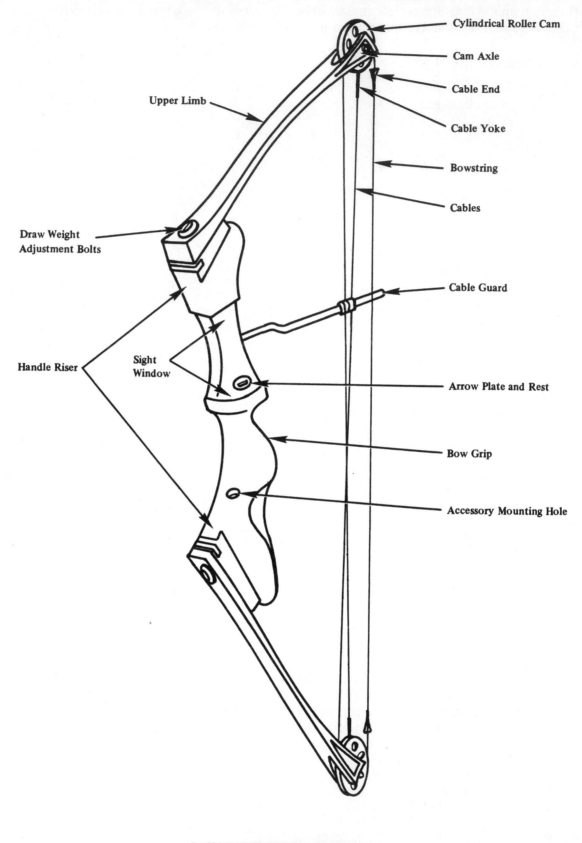

Cylindrical Roller Cam

Cam Axle

Cable End

Cable Yoke

Bowstring

Cables

Cable Guard

Arrow Plate and Rest

Bow Grip

Accessory Mounting Hole

Upper Limb

Draw Weight
Adjustment Bolts

Handle Riser

Sight
Window

**BASIC PARTS OF THE CYLINDRICAL
ROLLER CAM BOW**

The Quadraflex that Bill Hogue shot drew 82 pounds major and 42 minor at 29 inches draw length. Finish was in hunter camo anodized green and black.

Accessories used on this bow:

1. Total Shooting Systems TSS-80 Deluxe hunting cable guard.
2. Killian sight with a Ball of Fire sight pin and a Total Shooting Systems 1100 3-pin bowsight.
3. Action string peep with 1/16" diameter aperture for target and tournament shooting.
4. Nocking point—two conventional clamp-on nock sets at ½" above support finger of the arrow rest.
5. An Adjust-A-Level with adhesive back was mounted on the handle riser at the top of the sight window.
6. The bow was shot with a Total Shooting Systems SY III hunting release, a Stuart Model A Hot-Shot, a Fletch Hunter and a Wilson tab.
7. Arrows used were Easton XX75-2219, 2117, 2114, 2213 shafts at 29 inches fletched with both vanes and feathers. MA-3 125-grain broadheads were used for tournament work. Preferred arrow was an Easton XX75-2213.
8. Arrow rest was an Accra-Springy using a 20- and 25-ounce spring.
9. Arrow fletch was a right-hand helical spiral turned to a "Y" configuration with the nock.

Hogue shot this bow more than 2,500 times over a four-month period. The bowstring was replaced once. The only sign of wear was a slight wear mark on a cable at the upper eccentric. The anodized finish came through in mint condition.

Hogue set the bow up on a Friday, shot the bow on Saturday, and took fourth place in the Arkansas Bowhunter's Spring Tournament on Sunday. It was Hogue's first tournament in two years.

Hogue has owned and shot compounds since 1969. He commented, "The finest hunting bow that I have ever shot. It is very quiet, fast, and very stable. It is an easy bow to hit with and not the least bit sensitive to shoot."

Here is how the bow performed for velocity through the Arrowmeter. The arrows used were 29-inch XX75 Easton shafts with plastic vanes, and a 125-grain MA-3 broadhead. Velocities are averages of three shots.

Shaft Size	Average Velocity
2219	212 fps
2117	222 fps
2114	230 fps
2213	236 fps

Trajectory shots were taken using a 29-inch, XX75-2213 Easton shaft with five-inch plastic

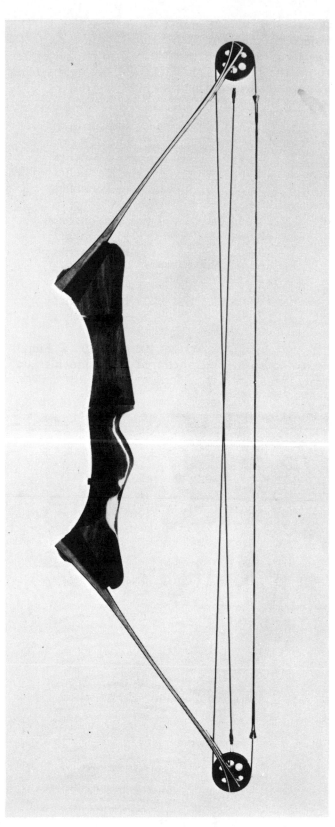

The X-Cellerator cylindrical roller cam bow by Browning.

vanes, and a 125-grain MA-3 broadhead. The trajectory was plotted by zeroing the bow at 45 yards and averaging the distance to impact center above the line of sight. The 45-yard sight setting was not changed during the trajectory test.

Yardage	Impact from line of sight.
5 yds	+ 4 inches
10 yds	+ 9 inches
15 yds	+ 9½ inches
20 yds	+10½ inches
25 yds	+12 inches
30 yds	+11 inches
35 yds	+ 9½ inches
40 yds	+ 7½ inches
45 yds	—0—
50 yds	— 8 inches
55 yds	—16 inches

Hogue used an Action string peep, a Fletch Hunter release, and anchored alongside his jaw.

The long 47½-inch axle-to-axle length and the long sight window makes this bow one of the finest finger-shooting compound bows on the market.

Bear Archery's Brown Bear, Martin's Cougar Magnum, and Jenning's Shooting Star are all top quality two-wheel compounds.

THE GRAHAM DYNABO

I first saw the Dynabo at the 1976 National Field Archery Tournament. Frankly, the appearance of the bow came on pretty strong for a nation of bowhunters that had just recovered from the mechanics of the compound. The Dynabo looked like the top half of a recurve with two strings mounted on a peg leg with two arc-shaped pieces of metal on the lower end of the peg leg. I passed the bow off as just another contraption bow.

That winter *Archery World Bow Report* stated, "The Dynabo design contains more stored energy than any bow tested to date." You can bet that report got my attention.

Bill Hogue shooting the Total Shooting Systems Quadraflex bow in practice. Note how the limbs are mounted for flexing.

The original one-limb Dynabo was invented by Len Subber, a California archer. The first Dynabo was known as the Zip Bow. Two major manufacturers worked with the design but gave it up because of problems.

After further development the bow now known as the Dynabo was placed on the market as the

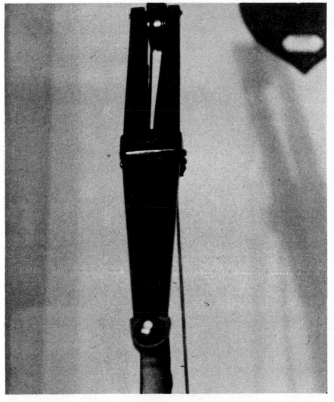

The Quadraflex limbs are slotted and mounted in rubber.

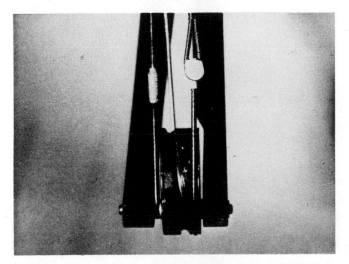

The broad TSS Omega eccentric wheel.

Martin M-10 Cheetah in late 1976, but was ruled ineligible for competition by the National Field Archery Association.

The early Dynabo had several strikes against it. It was noisy, it chewed up strings like mad, and it was never promoted with a strong advertising program. In spite of these shortcomings, the bow's ability to shoot a heavy arrow fast won the bow a loyal following among West Coast archers.

John Graham perfected the present two-limbed version of the Dynabo and was awarded co-inventor status by Len Subber for his work.

The two-limbed Dynabo was ruled to be a legal bow and the string problem was solved. The Dynabo is gaining steadily in popularity.

Late in the summer of 1977 I found myself in the hospital for surgery and I knew that any bow-hunting for that fall was probably out of the question. There was no way that I could draw and hold my heavy hunting recurve.

Bill Hogue called me to his home shortly after my release from the hospital and handed me a 42-pound Dynabo set up with a Killian sight and a Hot-Shot release. He said, "Old man, here is a bow that you can shoot this season." Three weeks later I had worked up to a 55-pound limb and a week later on the opening day of deer season I took a spike buck with the bow. Hogue didn't get his Dynabo back, either.

That fall I made the transition from a heavy recurve and instinctive shooting to a much lighter compound, a bow sight and a mechanical release. I switched to a precision shooting style and I have enjoyed it very much.

Experience with the Dynabos showed a tendency for vertical grouping. We attributed this to the possibility of a nock slipping on the string as the bow was fired. You can detect this unusual motion as the bow reaches the let-off point.

We corrected this problem by using a nock set over the arrow nock and a rubber cushion under the arrow nock thus insuring that the arrow nock remained at the same point on the string during the release.

Instructions with the bow specified an increase of ten pounds in arrow spine above the average compound. Using the Flipper cushion-plunger rest and heavy arrows still left something to be desired. Further experiments proved the vertical and horizontal shock absorbing ability of the Accra-Springy rest to be the answer for the Dynabo.

Use of this rest permitted a wider choice of arrow weight and spine. Field experience has since proved the Accra-Springy rest to be a superior rest for the new eccentric cam high performance bows.

Closeup showing detail of the handle riser of the Martin Jaguar overdraw compound bow.

Closeup of a Martin overdraw conversion kit installed on a conventional compound bow.

Specifications of the Graham Take-Down Dynabo:

Draw Lengths—adjustable from 27½ to 30 inches by moving the draw stop screw in or out.

Draw Weights—40, 45, 50, 55, 60 pounds, non-adjustable.

Let-Off—33 percent at 27½ inches and 40 percent at 30 inches.

Bow Length—49 inches.

Bow Weight—4 pounds, 4 ounces.

Color—black.

Handle Riser—aluminum alloy with Hoyt grip.

Limbs—laminated with Gordon Glass and Old Master Superflex maple laminations.

Other Features—drilled for accessories, positive stop preventing overdraw, can be disassembled and reassembled without loss of bow tune.

Manufacturer—Graham's Custom Bows, P.O. Box 1312, Fontana, California 92335.

Experience with the Dynabos since 1977 has proved to me that the concept makes for a very practical hunting bow. This bow has a good sight window and arrow rest adjustment.

The Graham bow used in this report belonged to my friend Jackie Cochran of Benton, Arkansas. The bow peaked 54 pounds with a 27-pound minor draw weight. This bow shot an 8.4 Bear metric magnum through the Arrowmeter for 196 (average) feet per second.

Trajectory of a Martin M-10 Cheetah drawing 50 pounds at 28 inches and a Bear 308 magnum arrow, 5-inch feather fletch, and a 125-grain MA-3 broadhead is as follows:

Yardage	Impact from line of sight
10 yds	+ 7 inches
20 yds	+12 inches
30 yds	+ 8 inches
35 yds	—0—
40 yds	—10 inches

The noise level is slightly above that of a conventional compound, but is not a disadvantage while hunting.

Field experiments have proved that game jumps at the flash or movement of the bow limbs much quicker than at the sound of arrow release.

The string wear problem around the cam has been corrected by a change in serving material. All in all, the Dynabo concept is one of the most simple compound designs. It is a very stable and easy to shoot bow.

Jim Cox Magnum Dynabos is the only other source of Dynabos. Martin Archery continues to manufacture the bow components for Jim Cox with Cox doing the assembly, finishing, tuning and testing.

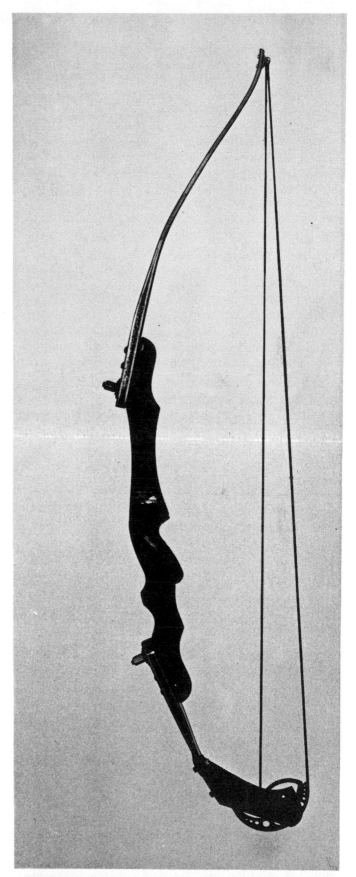

The Graham Dynabo, another of the new concepts in compounds.

THE BEAR DELTA-V

Late in 1981 Bear Archery announced the Delta-V. The claim, "The World's Fastest Bow," coming from the usually reserved Bear Archery people would be comparable to Cadillac's announcing a sport model street hot rod for the high school teenage market.

Field experience, to use the term loosely, has shown Bear Archery able to back up any statement they make. The whole country was itching to see and shoot a Delta-V.

Unfortunately, adverse criticism oftentimes overshadows the facts. I heard stories about breaking cables, breaking bow strings, the bow won't group, it's too heavy, and so on and so forth.

Dwayne Allen and Bill McIntosh assisted in obtaining a Delta-V for testing.

When the bow arrived I told my sons that we would give this bow the "works." A number of friends shot the bow out of curiosity about the speed. The only criticism at this point concerned the heavy weight and the noise level.

My answer to the weight problem is that my guns are heavier, and at this point in development the faster a bow shoots the more noise it will make. This is something that will just have to be accepted for the present.

We shot the bow right out of the box using both feather-fletched 308 Bear magnums and 8.4 metric magnums with vanes and the standard Bear Weatherest. We later used the Delta-V Flipper cushion-plunger. Later we tried an Accra-Springy rest. The shock imparted to an arrow by the new eccentric cam bows makes a shock absorbing rest necessary for best results.

We shot the bow approximately 5,000 times with no problem at all. String wear was very acceptable. There was no sign of cable wear or wear marks on the cams. The bow was lubricated with WD-40 per factory instructions.

Bear advises cable replacement at 5,000 shots or the first sign of fraying or wear.

The appearance of the Delta-V definitely gives the impression of something new. It is the first true center-shot compound. It is the first top quality bow to use solid epoxy matrix fiberglass limbs. The use of the pylon-mounted string stops is a patented first. The multi-ratio cams are glass-filled nylon cams; another technological advance for light weight and strength.

The handle riser is the most unusual in archery. It is a large magnesium casting finished in a pleasing twilight blue color. The two programmed cams are mounted on the string stop pylons giving

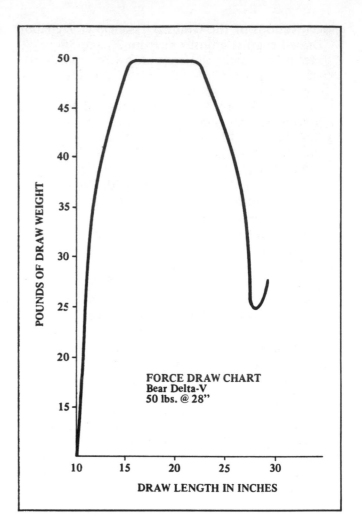

FORCE DRAW CHART
Bear Delta-V
50 lbs. @ 28"

the impression of even greater mass to the handle riser.

The thumbhole grip looks strange at first but is comfortable and adds considerable support to the handle riser. The grip comes with a padded snap-on handle.

The string stops serve several purposes, one of which makes the Delta-V a very recoil-shock free bow. This string stop system, balanced cam movement, bow weight, and a true center-shot string and grip all contribute to the bow's exceptional stability. A word of caution: the string stops cause the bow string to come to a sudden violent stop that sets up a string vibration that will flip clamp-on nock sets off the bowstring with force. Make sure that any string peep is securely lashed in place.

I shot the Delta-V with a Killian sight, a Zero string peep and a Stuart Model A Hot-Shot release. I used 8.4 Bear metric magnum arrows with the Bear Weatherest and the Delva-V Flipper cushion-plunger rest.

The unique handle of the Bear Delta-V bow.

Next, my son Rayburn took over using a Total Shooting Systems SY III hunting release. He used Gilmore #7 supershafts with feather-fletched and plastic-fletched 8.4 metric magnums. He used a Killian Sight, a Zero string peep and the Bear Weatherest.

Travis, my older son, tried the bow using the Delta-V Flipper cushion-plunger rest and a Wilson tab. He used the 8.4 metric magnums, and later changed to an Accra-Springy rest and 308 Bear magnums fletched in a "Y" configuration. The young man has a very clean finger release. He shot the bow both barebow and while using a Total Shooting Systems 1000 3-pin bowsight.

After several months of shooting with several shooting styles we rate this bow to be absolute tops in accuracy, dependability, and performance. It is a smooth, super-stable shooting bow. Accuracy with this bow was like shooting a fine benchrest rifle. It is competitive in accuracy with any compound concept when tuned properly.

This bow should become very popular for broadhead tournament, silhouette and field archery. The weight and noise level may deter some bowhunters but this should be no problem for the tree-stand bowhunter.

The Delta-V is a highly stressed, sophisticated bow. Leave any repairs to an authorized dealer who has the training and equipment for the job. About all that should be attempted by an untrained repairman is to change a bow string, change the draw length, and change the arrow

The Bear Delta-V bow.

The Delta-V handle riser showing the sight window, Accra-Springy rest and the thumbhole grip. Many archers feel this is the "grip of the future." Author's homemade bowsight is also shown.

rest. Have your dealer instruct you on proper lubrication.

The bow tested pulled 51 pounds major and 25 pounds minor at 28 inches. This bow shot an 8.4 Bear metric magnum through the Arrowmeter at 205 (average) feet per second. A friend's 60-pound Delta shot the same 8.4 magnum for 231 (average) feet per second.

Trajectory test for the 50-pound Delta-V using a Bear 308 magnum, and 125-grain MA-3 broadhead is as follows:

Yardage	Impact from line of sight.
10 yds	+ 9 inches
20 yds	+12 inches
30 yds	+ 8½ inches
35 yds	+ 7 inches
40 yds	—0—

Trajectory using a Gilmore #7 Supershaft and a 125-grain broadhead:

Yardage	Impact from line of sight.
10 yds	+ 9 inches
20 yds	+12 inches
30 yds	+ 8½ inches
35 yds	—0—

Specifications of the Bear Delta-V:
Draw Lengths—adjustable from 26 to 33 inches in one-inch increments by changing draw length speed blocks for each inch of desired draw length.
Draw Weights—40, 50, 60, 70 pounds, non-adjustable.
Bow Length—axle to axle, 45 inches.
Bow Weight—5 pounds, 15 ounces.
Color—metallic.
Handle Riser—magnesium casting, thumbhole grip, sight window cut ½" past center.

THE YORK TRACKER

This is another new compound mechanical leverage system available to bowhunters recently. It consists of eccentric cams substituted in place of the conventional simple cylindrical roller cams. The limbs are made of graphite filaments, and are slotted to accommodate the eccentric wheels.

A word of caution: York warns that these cams are not to be used on conventional wood-laminated limbs.

In appearance the bow looks just like any conventional two-wheel compound. It takes a close look to spot the difference. This close similarity to familiar bows may be a reason for the Trackers almost instant acceptance.

Mark Bybee of York Archery loaned us a 50-pound graphite limb Tracker for this report.

My first impression of the bow was that it was definitely a mechanical release-oriented bow. My second impression was that it was one fast little bow. The Tracker shot a feather-fletched 8.4 Bear metric magnum through the Arrowmeter at 199 (average) feet per second.

The bow comes equipped with a finger rest with a provision for a cushion-plunger.

I was never too pleased with my arrow flight while using plastic vanes on this bow. Later I changed to an Accra-Springy rest and feather-fletched arrows before I was satisfied.

Mark Bybee gave me some information about the Tracker. I mentioned that I thought the bow seemed meant for a mechanical release because of the short length and sharp string angle. Mark replied that a great number of bowhunters were shooting the bow with their fingers without any complaints. He said that York designed and built the Tracker to meet the specifications most in demand by bowhunters, and that archer response to the bow has been very encouraging.

My initial setup on the Tracker was as follows:

A Total Shooting Systems SY III mechanical release; a Zero string peep drilled out to 5/32" diameter; a Total Shooting Systems 1000 3-pin bowsight that had to be mounted upside down to obtain pin guard clearance over my arrow; an Accra-Springy 20-ounce arrow rest, and a clamp-on nock set a half-inch above the support finger of the arrow rest. A Neet Eliminator button was slipped on the string as a cushion between the bottom of the arrow nock and the release.

Another nock set was clamped on the string to hold a release in place while in a tree stand.

I used Bear 308 magnums, Bear 8.4 metric magnums, Easton 2114, and Gilmore #7 Supershafts; all feather-fletched in a "Y" configuration. Trajectory with a Bear 308 magnum, and a 125-grain MA-3 broadhead:

Yardage	Impact from line of sight.
10 yds	+ 9 inches
20 yds	+ 12 inches
30 yds	+ 9 inches
35 yds	—0—

My son Travis shot the bow using a Wilson tab. He removed the string peep but continued the use of the bowsight. He preferred the Gilmore #7 Supershaft. Rayburn and I then took turns shooting the bow instinctively. It was an enjoyable experience. The old saying of short bow and long draw makes for sharp release finger pinch is true but we shot the bow with reasonable accuracy.

The York Tracker is the shortest of the new high performance bows. This bow has appeal. Something about it makes you want to pick it up and go to the woods.

After four months of shooting I concluded that the bow was a shade on the sensitive side. It is compact, fast, and will produce if you do your part. It is simply a hard-shooting short to medium range bow. Stay with the heavier arrows for best results. An archer with good shooting form and a little experience will enjoy this bow.

Specifications of the York Tracker:
    Draw Lengths — 27, 28, 29 inches and 29, 30, 31 inches, adjustable by changing the cams.

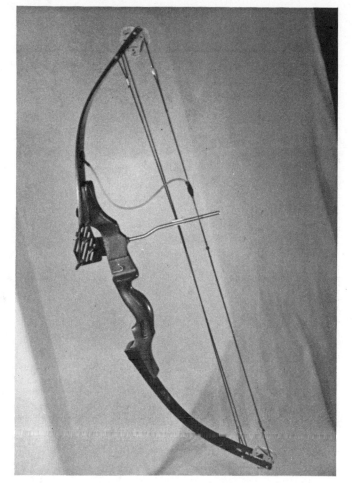

The York Tracker bow.

Draw Weights — 45-60 pounds, 55-70 pounds, 65-80 pounds, adjustable in 15-pound increments.
Let-Off — approximately 50 percent.
Bow Length — axle to axle, 41 inches.
Bow Weight — 3 pounds, 14 ounces.
Color — green and black.
Handle Riser — cast aluminum alloy, sight window 4½ inches long cut ¼" past center, right or left-hand grip.
Manufacturer — York Archery Co., P.O. Box 110, Independence, Missouri 64051.

The Tracker is also available in kit form.

How far has archery progressed since the early 1950s? Consider arrow velocity alone. That early fiberglass recurve that Bill Clements started hunting with pushed an 8.4 metric magnum through the Arrowmaster at 173 feet per second.

And Dr. Smith's old 62-pound Bushmaster shot the same arrow at 178 feet per second. Good for its time, but hardly in a class with a modern

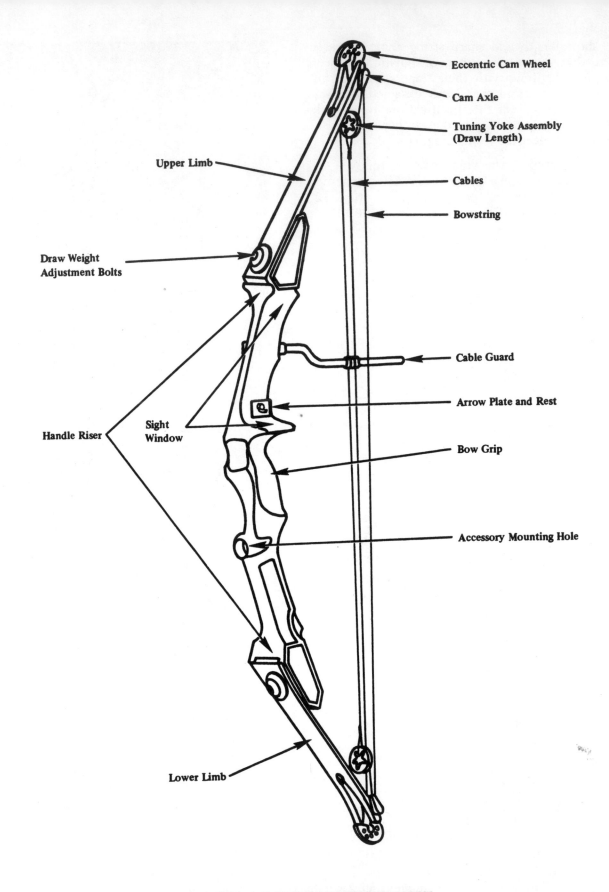

Eccentric Cam Wheel

Cam Axle

Tuning Yoke Assembly
(Draw Length)

Cables

Bowstring

Upper Limb

Draw Weight
Adjustment Bolts

Cable Guard

Arrow Plate and Rest

Bow Grip

Accessory Mounting Hole

Handle Riser

Sight
Window

Lower Limb

BASIC PARTS OF THE ECCENTRIC CAM BOW

Lee Garrett of Custom Archery with the York CNC-1.

The York Alpha Cam eccentric. Notice the double cable ends used to control the draw length.

60-pound Delta V delivering arrow speeds up to 231 feet per second.

Compounds allow us to hold on target and release at a fraction of full draw weight. These two factors, ease of holding and arrow speed, add up to more accurate shooting and deeper penetration into the game, resulting in quicker and cleaner kills and better range scores. Let's not overlook the advantages of bow sights, either.

Then there's the matter of adjustability. The archer can tune his bow to his individual needs, instead of having to adapt to the characteristics of the bow.

Contemporary bow making materials are, for the most part, superior to the old wood and fiberglass laminates, though perhaps lacking their aesthetic appeal.

Today's archer has an array of choices before him. He can use an early recurve design or even a longbow to get the feel of what archery was like decades ago, or he can opt for the latest technologically advanced equipment.

Yes, I would say that archery has come a long way since 1950. Of course, better bows don't automatically make better bowmen. Good shooting still takes knowing your equipment, developing good shooting form, and practice, always practice.

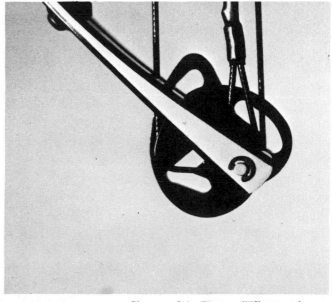

Closeup of the Pearson "Z" eccentric cam.

Arrows are shot through an Arrowmeter to determine velocity.

Chapter 3
Modern Arrows

Aluminum arrow shafts are now the choice of the world's top competitive archers; and foremost in their selection are the shafts made by Easton. In fact, probably 80 percent of American bowhunters shoot Easton shafts — whether they realize it or not. Easton supplies shafts to many arrow manufacturers, and makes Bear Archery's Metric Magnum and Metric Hunter arrows, along with Jim Dougherty's Naturals, to their specifications. Other companies make aluminum arrows, of course, but Easton shafts are considered best by serious archers.

A mediocre aluminum shaft will fail an impact test. Shoot these arrows at a target butt two or three times and then give them a spin test. Very often they will have developed a slight bend from impact with the target. Naturally, accuracy will deteriorate. A good aluminum arrow must be very tough to absorb the shock of impact with a target and remain straight shot after shot.

ARROW MATERIALS

The aluminum arrow eliminated many of the problems of weight variation, spine uniformity and warping so common to the wooden arrow. Man-made materials allow a manufacturer to hold to close tolerances; the closer the better the end product. Exact duplication is the goal.

Think of your arrows as a set. A single unmatched arrow is of little real value. Imagine having a dozen arrows in your quiver that are not matched in spine, weight or length. Just picture the shooting problems involved in shooting several unmatched arrows. Each arrow would fly differently making aiming strictly guesswork.

If you should walk into an archery shop in either California or Florida and order a set of arrows made to your specifications from Easton shafts your new arrows could match those in your quiver so closely that your shooting ability would not reflect the difference. This is just one major contribution among many made by the aluminum arrow to modern archery.

You can look at an Easton hunting shaft selection chart and count the shafts available to match any bow weight or draw length. Some draw weights and lengths can be matched with up to five different shaft diameters and wall thicknesses.

Trying modern arrows with an old fiberglass bow.

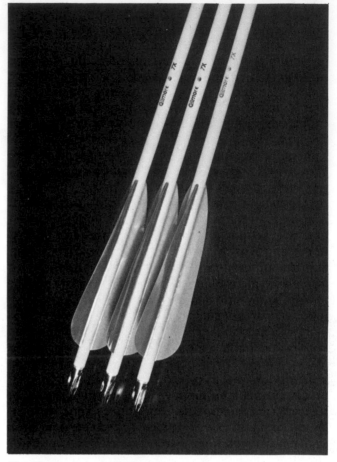

The Gilmore Autumn Gold arrow.

About 20 percent of the bowhunters hunt with arrow shafts made of material other than aluminum. The most popular of these shafts is a carbon-fiberglass combination commonly referred to as a graphite shaft. A few hunters still use fiberglass or wooden arrows.

The fiberglass shaft was introduced in the late fifties and was an immediate success. The recurve bow was at the height of its popularity and the fiberglass arrow was a real improvement over the wooden arrow.

There are still a number of these old Micro Flite fiberglass arrows remaining in the quivers of older bowhunters. These arrows are straight, high quality and shoot well from compounds. Three of these Micro Flite arrows tipped with Zwickey Zudo points for close range rabbit shooting ride in my quiver.

The quality of the Micro Flite shaft made it so popular that the rights and equipment for its manufacture was purchased by an international sporting goods firm.

Almost immediately this firm realized that they could not equal the quality of the original shaft and they sold the equipment to a major archery manufacturer. This manufacturer had the same experience, for some reason, and the Micro Flite arrow shaft is no longer available.

Several companies entered the market vacated by the Micro Flite shaft; however, the compound bow was gaining in popularity and the word was out that aluminum was the arrow for the compound. The fiberglass arrow made a gradual retreat and now survives mainly in school gym archery classes.

The fiberglass arrow does not have the ability to recover from the shaft bend exerted by the modern compound bow as rapidly as a high quality, thin wall aluminum shaft. This somewhat slower recovery rate from finger release and bending around the bow may actually be an advantage in shooting the modern day longbow and hunting recurves.

The combination of carbon and fiberglass was an important improvement to the fiberglass shaft resulting in an arrow suitable for the most modern bows. These carbon-fiberglass shafts are referred to as graphite shafts, and many experienced bowhunters regard the graphite-shafted arrow as the finest hunting arrow ever made.

You can bend an aluminum arrow and many times it can be straightened. There is an old saying originating with the Micro Flite arrow, "If you have a fiberglass arrow in one piece you have a shootable arrow."

The aluminum and the fiberglass arrow shaft manufacturers have presented us with excellent products. But they also marketed products with built-in problems. You should be aware of these problems.

There are several grades of aluminum arrows on the market, apparently made to compete in price with the fiberglass and wooden arrows. This inexpensive grade of arrow is referred to by experienced archers as "throw away arrows" simply because they take a bend or set from the thrust of shooting or impact with a target. There is no way these inexpensive shafts can duplicate the performance or durability of a premium, high quality aluminum shaft. Unfortunately, inexperienced archers buy these inexpensive shafts feeling that because they are aluminum they will give good service. These archers are then disappointed by the constant straightening necessary for accurate shooting. In reality these inexpensive shafts will prove to be the most expensive arrows you can buy in regard to performance and usable life.

The fiberglass and graphite shaft industry has a straightness problem. Some manufacturers handle the problem better than others and these companies will continue to increase their share of the market.

I once ordered some graphite/glass shafts from a well-known manufacturer. When these shafts arrived I rolled them across a table top and listened to the flop-flop-flop sound of crooked shafts. I repacked these shafts and returned them to the

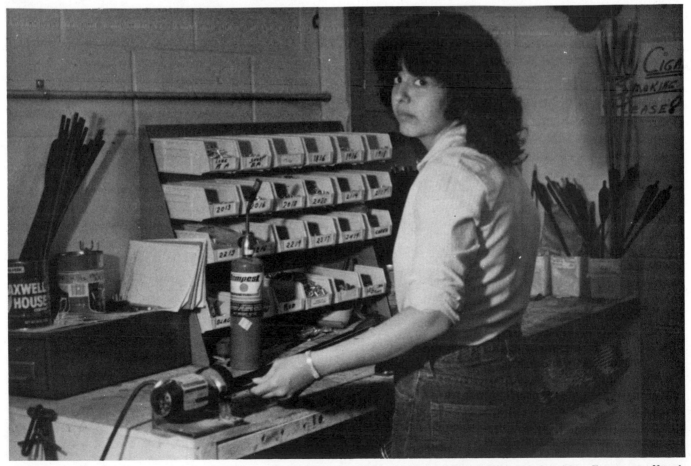

Mona Garrett of Custom Archery trimming aluminum shafts with an Easton cut-off tool.

manufacturer with a letter stating, "Frankly, I expected straighter shafts." Several weeks later and after one long distance telephone call I finally received a set of very acceptable shafts.

We made these shafts into arrows and one of my sons shot them in practice and in three club broadhead shoots. We also shot these arrows with a 45-pound recurve, a 50-pound Delta-V, a Pearson 60-pound Pro Staff and a 70-pound Precision Laser. Performance was excellent with each bow. It is easy to understand why so many bowhunters hold the graphite arrow in such high regard.

I discussed the crooked shaft and inexpensive aluminum arrow problems with a friend who operates an archery shop. He responded, "What do I tell a customer when I sell him a set of arrows and he shows up later in my shop complaining of 'poor arrow flight?' What do I say after I examine his equipment and find his problem is caused by crooked arrow shafts? The customer will ask me very quickly what I intend to do about it — I sold them to him. Now I just don't stock those cheap shafts."

This dealer is correct. You cannot tune a bow properly using crooked arrows. You cannot shoot a crooked arrow with dependable accuracy. This "crooked and bent shaft problem" is a quality problem resting with the companies that make these shafts, and it should be their problem to solve. Your money can buy two kinds of arrow shafts — either crooked or straight.

I have in my collection three broadhead arrows that were given to a friend by Ben Pearson to test the first Deadhead points. These arrows are fletched with natural barred feathers from a mature turkey. These fletchings are much stiffer than the dyed feathers that we use today. When you compare these old fletchings with the present-day plastic hunting fletch the old feather fletch is the stiffer of the two. We considered these stiff natural fletchings to be very high quality and the softer feathers as being suitable only for target arrows shot from light bows. We had a fletch clearance problem years ago but we just didn't realize it.

Really good wing feathers from full grown mature turkeys are very difficult for arrow manufacturers to obtain in large quantities. Arrow makers must also maintain inventories of both right and left wing feathers, not to mention fletching tables each equipped with 24 to 36 jigs set for a specific wing feather.

The plastic vane reduced the need for a big investment in equipment and solved the material inventory problem at the same time. Use of the plastic vane means a significant reduction in production cost for the large manufacturer, and saves the archer money as well. Look at the magazine advertisements concerning arrow sales and read, "Feathers $3.00 extra."

Vanes will make you sharpen up your bow tuning and that's a fact. Walk down the green at the National Target Tournament or spend a vacation attending the National Field and you will find plastic vanes well represented on the arrows of the top tournament archers in this country.

Feathers are still available from several suppliers and from many archery shops. There will be feathers as long as people keep eating turkey. This choice to shoot feathers or vanes is yours to make and your accuracy will not suffer if your bow is tuned properly.

Fletching is placed on an arrow shaft to provide guidance to that arrow in flight. It was not too many years ago that fletching was placed straight up and down the centerline of the shaft or at a

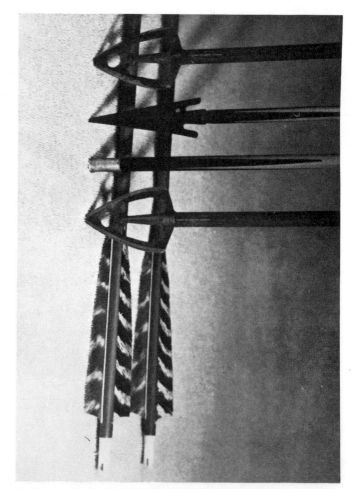

Early broadheads and very stiff, barred feather fletching.

very slight angle to the centerline. Arrows with this straight fletch depended on the natural curve of the feather to produce shaft rotation. Broadhead inaccuracy due to windplaning was a major problem.

Modern broadhead and field arrows are fletched to the Archery Manufacturers Organization standards specifying a minimum of five-inch fletch length and a maximum of 5/8 inch in height for a three-fletch arrow. Field experience has proved that a true helical fletch is the only dependable fletch for a broadhead arrow. It makes little difference whether you use a three- or four-fletch configuration as long as it is dependable in imparting a spin to that shaft.

The alignment of the arrow nock plays a very important part in the grouping of a set of arrows. Should you have an arrow that consistently hits out of the group, without any apparent reason, suspect nock alignment.

The most popular type of bowhunting nocks are snap lock nocks. A design feature of these nocks enables them to simply snap on and retain a grip on the bowstring while the arrow is being drawn. This feature is necessary if the archer uses a "fingers under the arrow" shooting style or a mechanical release device.

String diameter should be matched very carefully to the nock being used. A tight nock can cause poor arrow flight. A loose nock can come

Bjorn, Nirk, Index and Pearson snap locks.

loose from the string unexpectedly and your bow could be damaged by this dry firing.

Proper string nock pressure should be sufficient to support the weight of the arrow yet loose enough to free itself when you give the bowstring a fairly sharp rap with your forefinger.

The Bjorn snap nock is a very popular nock. It is distributed by the Easton Company and is usually available wherever Easton shafts are sold. Nirk Archery and Bohning Products also market a competitive line of nocks in both fluorescent and solid colors. A bright flourescent nock is a real aid in the recovery of your arrows. The Ben Pearson Company markets a unique light green arrow with a nock that will glow in poor light or darkness. Their exclusive glow nock will give off a pale luminescent color that will continue to glow in the dark for several hours after being first exposed to light.

Remove a damaged nock by applying heat carefully then twisting it off with a pair of pliers. Clean off any nock and cement residue with acetone. Scraping a nock insert with a knife can cause a misalignment problem. Always keep a few spare nocks and a small bottle of acetone in your repair kit.

Install a nock with a minimum of fletching cement. Use just enough cement to coat the nock swage then seat the nock by rotating the nock as you press it in place. Wipe off any excess cement and inspect for alignment. Excessive cement can damage a nock by chemical reaction and weaken the string seat.

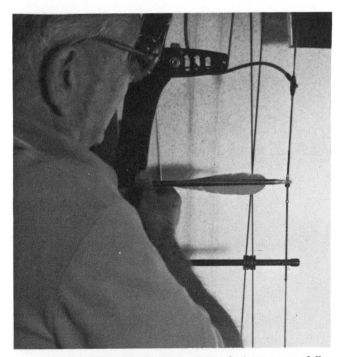

Check the string diameter and snap lock groove carefully. The bowstring should not follow the arrow more than ¾ inch.

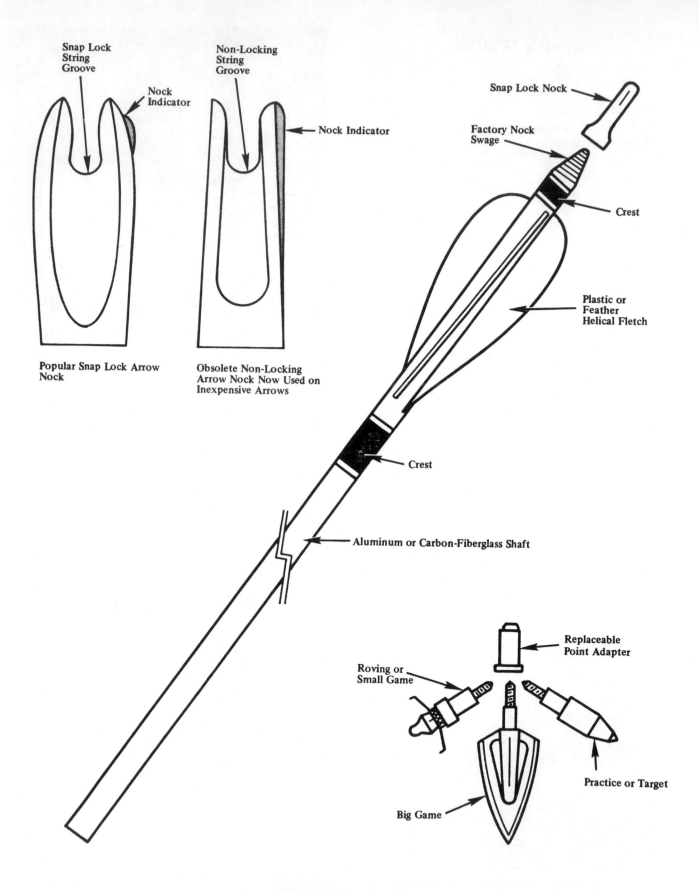

Snap Lock String Groove

Nock Indicator

Non-Locking String Groove

Nock Indicator

Popular Snap Lock Arrow Nock

Obsolete Non-Locking Arrow Nock Now Used on Inexpensive Arrows

Snap Lock Nock

Factory Nock Swage

Crest

Plastic or Feather Helical Fletch

Crest

Aluminum or Carbon-Fiberglass Shaft

Replaceable Point Adapter

Roving or Small Game

Practice or Target

Big Game

THE BOWHUNTER'S ARROW

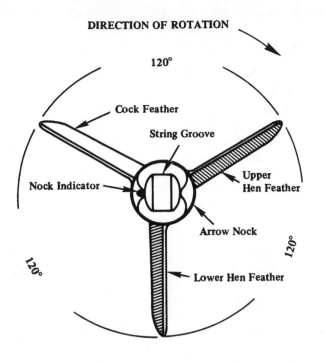

DIRECTION OF ROTATION

120°

Cock Feather

String Groove

Upper
Hen Feather

Nock Indicator

Arrow Nock

120°

120°

Lower Hen Feather

Standard three, 120° feather helical fletched arrow rotated to "Y" configuration with the arrow nock. Drawing shows the use of right wing fletch for a right handed archer.

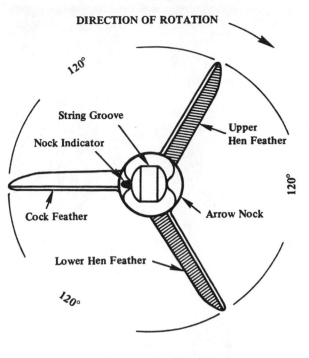

DIRECTION OF ROTATION

120°

String Groove

Nock Indicator

Upper
Hen Feather

120°

Cock Feather

Arrow Nock

Lower Hen Feather

120°

Rear view of standard three 120° feather helical fletched arrow using right wing feathers.

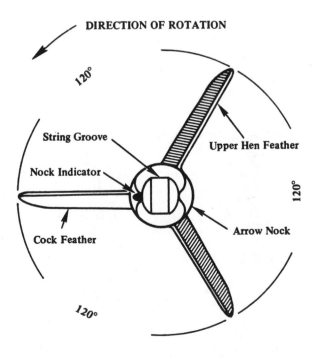

DIRECTION OF ROTATION

120°

String Groove

Upper Hen Feather

Nock Indicator

120°

Arrow Nock

Cock Feather

120°

Rear view of standard three, 120° feather helical fletched arrow using left wing feathers.

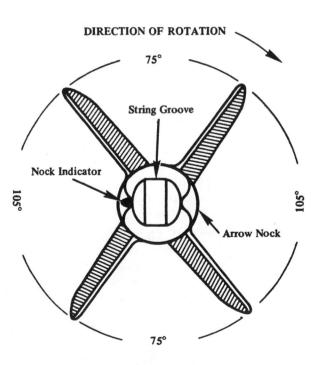

DIRECTION OF ROTATION

75°

String Groove

Nock Indicator

105°

105°

Arrow Nock

75°

Rear view of four, 75°-105° feather helical fletched arrow using right wing feathers.

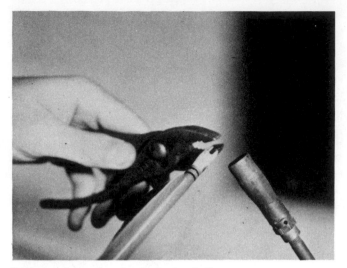

Remove a damaged nock using heat and pliers.

The convenience of the replaceable screw-in point system makes it very desirable for the bowhunter. This system should be installed on all your arrows either aluminum, graphite or fiberglass.

Many broadhead manufacturers are changing over to the new system. It seems that the day of the permanently mounted broadhead point is past.

SELECTING ARROWS

A beginning archer's first arrows should be considered as training arrows to teach him the basics of shooting. However, be sure they are of good quality. "Good enough to learn with" is a compromising and misleading statement.

Start with half a dozen quality shafts such as the Game Getter, 24SRT or XX75 arrows from Easton. This may seem a bit high priced for starters but accuracy and confidence will come much quicker with good equipment. There's nothing like crooked arrows for confusing and discouraging a beginner.

Experience is the only way to determine an archer's final correct draw length. Here are some suggestions to get you started:

• Determine the archer's draw length by using a measured draw length arrow and having the new archer draw and anchor several times. Observe the archer for under or overextension of his muscles while holding at full draw and measure the distance from the anchor point to the back of the bow. Add 3/4 inch to provide clearance for a broadhead point. The reason for this clearance originated centuries ago to keep the broadhead from contacting or cutting the archer's hand when shooting an arrow "off the fist" or from a low arrow rest. Selecting a

draw length that completely stretches or overextends one's drawing ability is a common cause of inaccurate shooting. The first draw length may be too long, and there is also a possibility that it may be a little short. Observation and shooting experience will indicate the proper length. A new archer will underdraw a heavy bow and overextend with a light bow.

When ordering arrows the bowhunter should get hunting shafts adapted for screw-in replaceable points. By switching from field points to broadheads he has, in effect, two sets of arrows. Order to draw length. Hunting shafts will be slightly longer in overall length to provide broadhead clearance.

Another factor to consider is that the "learning" arrows may not suit the archer's eventual shooting style. If he decides later to shoot with a tab or glove he will need heavier, stiffer-spined arrows than those used with a mechanical release.

• If you shoot a recurve, check your draw weight at your newly determined draw length.

• If you shoot a compound check your bow for your newly determined draw length. Some bows can be set very precisely. Ideally you should be at the let-off low point at full draw. Consult your archery dealer about this draw length setting for your bow. Changing compound bow draw length can effect your peak and let-off weights. Weigh your bow for this peak weight and holding weight. Now determine your percent of let-off.

• Consult an Easton shaft selection chart for your bow weight and draw length. The shaft size highlighted in bold type is the most popular size selected for this draw length and draw weight by experienced archers. Usually a beginning archer will have fewer problems by choosing a shaft slightly

Measure draw length several times using a marked arrow.

EASTON ALUMINUM HUNTING SHAFT
SELECTION CHART SAMPLE
(This is only an abbreviated portion of the entire chart)
(Most popular size selection is shown in bold type)

Actual Bow Weight (At Your Draw Length)	CORRECT HUNTING ARROW LENGTH (Your Draw Length Plus ½ to ¾ Inch Clearance)						Compound Bow Peak Weight
	(26½ – 27½)		(27½ – 28½)		(28½ – 29½)		
	27"		28"		29"		50% Let-off
	Shaft Size	Arrow Weight	Shaft Size	Arrow Weight	Shaft Size	Arrow Weight	
45-49	2013	433	2114	466	2114	476	54-59
	1916	461	**2016**	486	**2016**	496	
	1917	479	8.4	487	8.4	497	
	1820	517	1917	490	2115	502	
			1918	514	1920	559	
50-54	2114	456	2114	466	2213	475	60-65
	2016	475	**2016**	486	2115	497	
	8.4	477	8.4	487	8.5	541	
	1917	479	2115	487	**2018**	546	
	1918	503	1920	546	1920	559	
55-59	2114	456	2213	465	2213	475	66-71
	2016	475	2115	487	**2117**	539	
	8.4	477	8.5	529	8.5	541	
	2115	477	**2018**	534	2018	546	
	1920	531	1920	546	2020	582	

NOTE: *The arrow weight in grains (437.5 grains per ounce) includes a 125-grain broadhead, 30-grain insert and 35 grains (average between plastic vanes and feathers) for nock and fletching. 8.4 and 8.5 are Bear Archery shaft sizes.*

heavier and stiffer in spine if he does not use a mechanical release.

• Use your experiences and increased skill in choosing your next arrows. It would be a good idea to consult a more experienced archer about your new choice.

• If possible, shoot some arrows of the shaft size that you are considering. Many indoor ranges have arrows of the most common sizes for use as try-out arrows to assist you in making a new shaft selection.

Aluminum shafts are available in a wide range of spine and weight combinations. Look at the abbreviated sample section of the Easton hunting shaft selection chart. As an example, for a compound bow with a peak weight of 67-72 pounds and 50 percent let-off at 28 inches you could choose a 2114 shaft with a finished arrow weight of 465 grains as a minimum, or a 1920 shaft with a finished arrow weight of 546 grains as a possible maximum. That's a weight range of 81 grains.

The lighter 2114 arrow will shoot faster with a flatter trajectory than the heavier 1920. If your hunting is for deer and antelope the lighter 2114 shaft will give plenty of penetration on the thin-skinned animals with a sharp broadhead.

Remember the old bowhunter's saying, "Shooting a really sharp broadhead is like increasing your draw weight an additional 10 pounds in penetrating ability."

Deep arrow penetration is more difficult on large thick-skinned animals like moose, elk and bear. Heavier aluminum or graphite shafts are needed, along with big broadheads. The Black Diamond Delta, Rothhaar Snuffer and the Rocky Mountain Razor broadheads are all popular choices for use on these heavier arrows for really big game.

The graphite shaft is a very versatile shaft where spine is concerned. Several manufacturers offer one shaft size for every ten-pound increment of bow draw weight. They do not offer as flexible a choice in shaft weight of finished arrow weight, however, compared to aluminum arrows.

The graphite shaft has an extremely fast recovery rate from the sudden thrust of the bow and arrow paradox. This fast recovery rate permits a knowledgeable bow tuner to under-spine the manufacturer's recommended graphite shaft selection, and compete with the aluminum for a fast, flat trajectory hunting arrow.

For hunting, avoid bright reflective arrow shafts. Both aluminum and graphite shafts can be had with a dull, non-reflective finish especially made for bowhunters, including camouflage.

Select the oranges, light greens and light red-pink colors for your fletching. This is a help in following the arrow's flight and determining whether or not a hit has been made. Personally, I stay away from white or yellow fletching, even though Hill, Pearson and Bear used white arrows for photographic purposes while making their films about bowhunting. The audience could see the flight of the arrow from the bow to the game. The visual effect is dramatic and makes the difference between a great bowhunting film and a nice picture story about hunting with a bow and arrow. I think the animals notice the contrast of white and yellow against the natural background much faster than they do the other colors mentioned. And, when I'm deer hunting I don't want anything white flashing near my body.

Get into the habit of checking your arrows for straightness after each shot at game. Rest an arrow on the fingernails of your thumb and forefinger with the arrow point in the palm of the opposite hand. Blow gently on the fletch causing the arrow to spin. A right-fletch arrow spins easiest in a clockwise direction.

Always check shafts when you buy them directly from your dealer. Roll a shaft across a flat surface and listen to the sound as the shaft rolls along. A crooked shaft makes a flop-flop sound.

Check frequently for any nock damage. Carefully examine the string seat of any nock that snaps on the bow string in other than its usual manner. A cracked nock can split as you shoot, producing the same effect as dry firing your bow. Retire those arrows until the nocks have been replaced.

Examine its feather fletching as you recover each arrow on the target range or in the field. A fletch starting to come loose can cut or stick into your hand. Fletching falling off or coming loose in flight can cause dangerous or erratic arrow flight. Replace a damaged fletch before shooting the arrow again.

The same applies to a damaged plastic fletch. I do not know of anyone being injured by a cracked or damaged plastic vane, although the potential is there. I do know of an arrow rest being jerked off a bow by a damaged vane. It only takes a few seconds to check arrows for soundness.

The oldtime bowhunters liked to shoot at stumps and anything that presented a suitable target while just walking through the woods. We

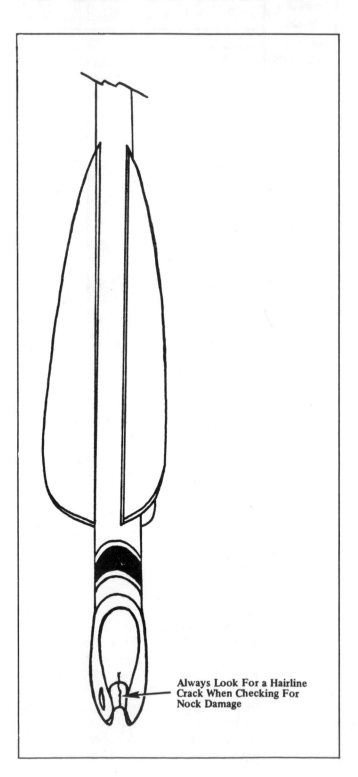

Always Look For a Hairline Crack When Checking For Nock Damage

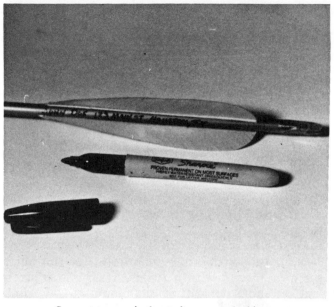

Some states require hunter's name and address on arrows.

called it "roving." We shot blunts or field points on heavy wooden arrows. Each time that we recovered an arrow it was flexed very lightly or tapped against something solid to check the shaft for cracks. A cracked shaft could splinter and penetrate your arm or hand causing a serious injury the next time that the arrow was shot.

New Hampshire, Rhode Island and Texas require that your arrows have your name and address printed on them with a non-water soluble ink or paint. There are several different types of felt tip pens containing water resistant inks available at office supply stores that are satisfactory for this purpose. It is a good idea to number your arrows and keep track of any arrow that consistently hits outside of a group.

A surprising number of older bowhunters make their own arrows. We save a few bucks and keep our arrows in first class repair. We also maintain a continuity from old arrows to a new set.

A fletching jig is necessary to replace damaged fletch. Actually this is the only special tool that you will need. The Bitzenburger jig is the standard of the industry. You can purchase jigs that will fletch six shafts at a time, or one. Whatever your choice make sure that the jig is equipped with a helical spiral clamp.

Most archery shops will rent you a straightening tool, or straighten a bent shaft for a small fee.

It seems that arrow cresting is rapidly disappearing from all but factory made arrows. Most archery shops discontinued this form of arrow decoration as the aluminum arrow gained in popularity. Cresting was a hand labor job that just added weight to a hunting arrow. Most bowhunters prefer the less expensive cost of arrows without cresting.

MAKING ARROWS

Die cut feathers, plastic vanes, and aluminum and graphite shafts have all greatly simplified arrow making. One 25-year-old Bitzenburger jig keeps myself and two sons in arrows. Of course, we don't wait until the night before hunting season to fletch a new set of arrows. The jig stays in the utility room and I rotate the shaft and glue on a new fletch whenever I pass through over the course of several weeks.

Making a new set of arrows starts with the purchase of the components (shafts, fletching, nocks and inserts) at a local archery shop. Have your shafts cut to length at the time of purchase. Usually the cost of trimming to length is included in the cost of the shafts. Your dealer has a special tool to cut aluminum shafts and there is a very good reason to use this tool, and a specific procedure to follow to install the inserts.

Here, with Easton's permission, are their instructions:

Author's 25-year-old Bitzenburger fletching jig.

Little space is needed to make your own arrows at home.

3. Apply enough heat with a small gas or alcohol flame on the end of the shaft to readily melt a ring of ferrule cement (Bohning Ferr-L-Tite or equivalent) on the inside of the shaft. Caution: do not overheat.

4. While the cement is fluid, put the insert about 1/4 inch into the shaft.

5. Heat the insert enough to melt a thin layer of ferrule cement on the entire insert shank.

6. Lightly heat and re-melt the cement on the insert, and also very lightly heat the shaft about one inch up from the end.

7. Quickly, while the cement is fluid, push the insert into the shaft until it seats on the end of the shaft.

8. Wipe off excess cement.

You can make a simple tool for installing screw-in inserts with a two-inch 8/32 inch screw and a short length of aluminum arrow shaft equipped with a screw-in insert.

Cut the head from the 8/32 inch screw and thread it into the insert in the short length of arrow shaft until it bottoms out. Cement the 8/32 inch screw into the insert with a fast setting epoxy.

Use this simple tool to hold a new screw-in insert as you apply Ferr-L-Tite cement and to gently heat and press this new insert into an aluminum shaft.

This tool prevents mashing or damage to an insert, which could happen if pliers were used to hold an insert as it is being installed.

If you buy your Easton shafts full length, be sure the shaft cutting and insert installation instructions listed below are followed carefully.

To produce the most bend-resistant shaft possible, extremely high yield strength and internal stresses are built into each shaft. Therefore, care must be taken when installing the adapter or insert to prevent splitting the end of the shaft due to over-stressing or softening the shaft from overheating.

1. Cut shaft to length on a high-speed abrasive wheel cut-off tool. A high speed steel blade cut-off saw or lathe can be used but the anodize finish will dull the tool quickly.

Do not use rotary tube cutters, hacksaws, or other methods that can stress the tube and leave a rough cut.

2. Very lightly, chamfer the inside diameter of the tube just enough to remove the burr — but not so much as to remove more than a quarter of the wall thickness.

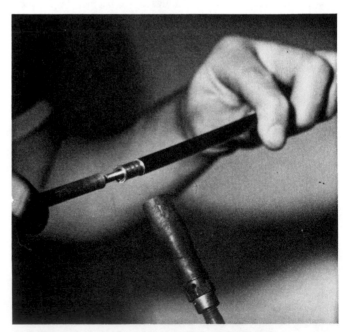

Installing screw-in inserts with a simple homemade tool.

Graphite and fiberglass can be cut to length with a hacksaw by scoring the shaft and then snapping off the trim end. Dress the trim end with a smooth-cut file or sandpaper. You will have a better job if you have your dealer trim these shafts at the time of purchase. A square trim distributes the shock of impact evenly around the end of the shaft, and reduces the possibility of splitting.

Roughen up the inside of both ends of the shaft with fine sandpaper. Now clean the inside of the shaft with a cotton swab dipped in acetone. Cement the nock insert and screw-in adaptor insert in place with a slow curing epoxy cement and let cure for 24 hours.

Next, clean your shafts. Give aluminum shafts a good scrubbing with an ajax-type cleanser or acetone. Acetone or lacquer thinner should be used on graphite or fiberglass.

Use a minimum of fletching cement to install your nocks. Place two drops on the end of the nock insert and rotate the nock several times to spread the cement evenly and align the nock. Examine the seated nock for alignment.

Use Bohning Fletch-Tite cement to attach nocks and fletchings. It works equally well on aluminum, graphite, feathers or vanes. Fletch-Tite has been used for years by the arrow industry.

Apply a light film of vaseline or bowstring wax to the edges of your fletching clamp. This coat of vaseline or wax keeps fletching cement from gluing the clamp to the fletch or shaft.

Examine your fletchings to see that they are all from the right or left wing of the turkey. Some dealers stock only die cut fletch from one side (wing) of the turkey. This prevents an accidental mixup in their stock.

You cannot mix right and left wing feathers on the same arrow. Mixed fletch will prevent the arrow shaft from spinning and cause erratic arrow flight. The fletching jig must be adjusted for the wing feather that you are using. Your helical fletching clamp must be for either a right or left feather and it will be marked accordingly.

You can identify a right or left wing feather by holding the feather horizontally with the top of the feather facing up and the trailing edge of the feather pointing towards you. The tip of the feather will be on the right for a right wing feather; and on the left for a left wing feather.

Sometimes it helps to visualize yourself standing behind a turkey with its wings spread out. Feather identification can be simple when you can visualize the feather in place on the bird.

Most experienced bowhunters prefer a lot of spiral to their fletch. Considerable spin will slow arrow velocity but it stabilizes a broadhead better in crosswinds and helps prevent windplaning. Too much spiral acts as a parachute, causes nosediving and creates excessive arrow noise.

Look at commercially fletched arrows and the good shooting arrows of your friends and duplicate this setting with your jig. Later you may reduce the angle of spiral and even reduce fletch length and area for small broadheads often used in tournament shooting.

Set your fletch in the clamp with about 1/16 inch between the quill and the clamp jaws. This

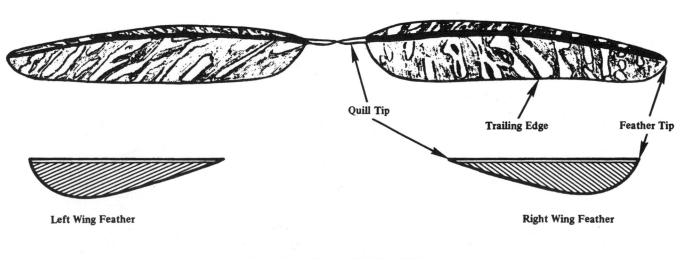

Left Wing Feather

Quill Tip

Trailing Edge

Feather Tip

Right Wing Feather

WING FEATHER IDENTIFICATION

allows for the arc created when you set your spiral. This first fletch should be the odd or cock feather. Make a mark on the jig index knob to indicate this position.

Run a bead of cement, just enough to cover the quill the full length of the fletch, and seat the clamp in the jig.

Wipe the base of plastic vanes with acetone or lacquer thinner to remove any trace of a mold release agent and to insure good adhesion.

Let the cement cure for 20 to 25 minutes then remove the clamp and rotate the shaft to install the next fletching. When the fletching is complete apply a small drop of cement to each end of the

Use a five-inch fletch for a three-fletch arrow and a four-inch fletch length for a four-fletch arrow.

• A broadhead mounted out of alignment with the arrow shaft is another cause of windplaning. The use of the replaceable screw-in system solved most of the problems arising from poor point alignment. Use the long adapters that completely fill the point ferrule for increased point strength and better alignment if your points are purchased separate from the screw-in ferrule. Sometimes poor quality point construction will prevent alignment with the shaft. Examine your points for symmetry. If you're dissatisfied with one manufacturer's points try other brands.

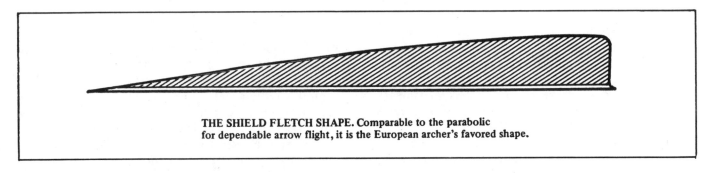

THE SHIELD FLETCH SHAPE. Comparable to the parabolic
for dependable arrow flight, it is the European archer's favored shape.

fletch to seal the fletch from moisture and to improve fletch adhesion to the shaft.

ARROW PROBLEMS

The accurate shooting of a broadhead arrow was a major problem until the helical spiral fletch was adopted. Windplaning occurs whenever the broadhead point overcomes the directional force exerted by the fletching. Here are some of the common causes of windplaning:

• Use of the obsolete straight fletching. This was common practice during the early years of bowhunting. The helical fletch is the only fletch that should be used with broadheads. This spiraling fletch using either three or four fletchings will eliminate most windplaning problems.

• Crooked, bent or weak-spined arrows can cause all sorts of weird arrow flight. I've mentioned this before but it bears repeating. Spin test your arrows often and check for alignment and bent shafts. Make it a habit to check your nocks for alignment. Examine the string seat area of your nocks for cracks.

• Using the larger and heavier points normally requires an increase in shaft spine. A slightly weak-spined arrow generally fails to group well and causes a change in location of the group center. Suspect under-spined shafts if you have an unusual change in grouping when trying different broadheads of the same weight. Erratic broadhead flight caused by weak-spined shafts is considered windplaning.

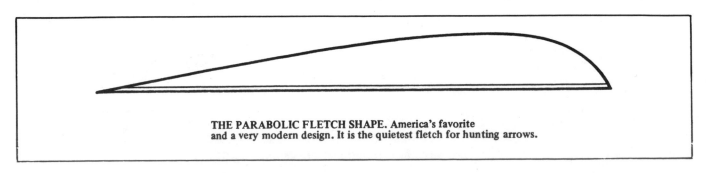

THE PARABOLIC FLETCH SHAPE. America's favorite
and a very modern design. It is the quietest fletch for hunting arrows.

Sometimes you can save yourself a lot of time and aggravation with arrow problems by visiting a good archery pro shop. Whatever the sport, a professional can help. Golfers do it all the time. Why not archers? No bowhunter should feel embarassed to ask for advice and opinions from others with more experience. Chances are the pro has seen it all before. Few archery problems are unique.

Allow 3/4 inch extra draw length for broadhead clearance.

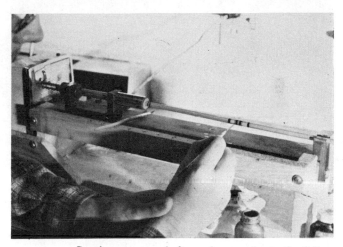

Cresting an arrow shaft on a homemade cresting lathe.

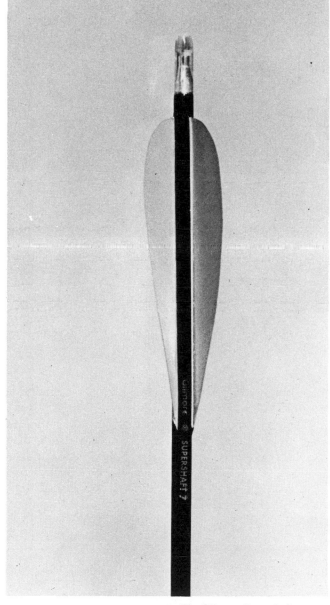

The Gilmore Supershaft arrow.

One thing that hasn't been mentioned so far is the care and storage of arrows. In the early days, wooden shafts tended to warp unless stored care-fully. Modern shaft materials are virtually maintenance free. Keep the shafts clean and stored in a safe place so they won't be damaged accidentally. Then about the only thing that can hurt them is moths chewing up the feather fletching. Plastic vanes, of course, are immune.

I like to store my broadheads separately where there's no chance of kids getting at them. Some archers, who also hunt with a gun, keep their broadheads locked up along with their ammunition. Whatever facilities you choose, make sure the storage area is dry. It's also a good idea to coat the broadheads with a light film of oil to prevent rusting.

Here is an interesting bit of arrow trivia. Acie Johnson, the president of the Ben Pearson Company, once told me, "If all the arrows made by the Pearson Company since the company was founded in 1930 were placed end to end they would reach around the world four and one half times at the equator."

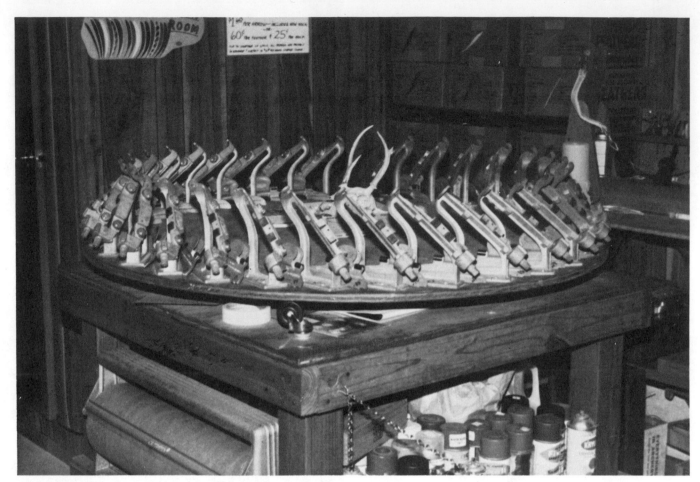

A commercial fletching jig setup at The Archery Center.

Chapter 4
The Bowstring

The modern bowstring is taken for granted. Read the advertisements and see how many manufacturers mention the strings that are supplied with their bows. While fiberglass and epoxy adhesives have made modern bow designs possible, it is the dacron bowstring that makes those bows perform.

Good bowstring material must possess several vital properties; first and most important is the ability to resist stretching. A high tensile strength to diameter ratio is another requirement. The material must be light in weight and have a long life under flexing. Only one material, dacron, a modern synthetic produced by Du Pont, excels in all these properties.

Let's discuss these properties and their effect on bow performance. Any material under consideration for use as a bowstring is first examined for its stretch resistance. A good material completes its stretching as a bow is strung. It should not stretch as the bow is drawn. A spongy string will reduce arrow velocity. A minute amount of elasticity at the instant a bow returns to brace position serves as a shock absorber to cushion the shock of firing.

A bowstring with no stretch at all, like wire, would soon cause your bow to delaminate (come apart) from the shock of firing. Too much stretch reduces arrow cast. Too little stretch can destroy your bow.

Both Type B and B-50 dacron have excellent stretch characteristics. Type B makes an excellent string for the heavier recurves and longbows. B-50 will produce a slightly faster string and is the preferred string material of the compound bow and many recurve archers.

Kevlar, another Du Pont-produced synthetic, has less stretch than dacron. This is the preferred string material of the recurve shooting tournament archer. Kevlar should never be used as a bowstring on a bow that is not built to stand the shock. You should seek the bow manufacturer's approval before using a kevlar bowstring on his product.

The greater the tensile strength of a material the fewer strands necessary to contain the energy of the bow. The smaller the diameter of these strands the better the string can be tailored to fit the string seat of your arrow nock. Good string fit pays off in better arrow flight and easier bow tuning.

A light bowstring weight increases arrow velocity. The lighter the load that is placed on the bow limbs by the physical weight of the bowstring, and arrow weight, the faster the bow will shoot. However, bowstrings must also meet other qualifications for practical shooting.

Flex ability determines the life of a bowstring. The use of a mechanical release creates a double stress point on a bowstring; once as the bow is drawn, then at the string seat of the nock as the arrow is released.

The use of a tab or glove spreads out string flex stress as the bow is drawn. As the bow is fired the nock point is stressed by the weight of the arrow.

A normal string failure would be a break that occurs at the nock point. If you use a mechanical release be sure to take into consideration the resulting shorter string life. A good string material must have the ability to withstand this concentration of both tension and flexing.

Flexing is the one property that keeps kevlar from being the supreme bowstring material.

Some materials used in making and repairing bowstrings.

Kevlar exceeds dacron in all desired bowstring properties but one — it has a much shorter string life due to poor flexibility.

The tournament archer usually keeps better records of his shooting than the bowhunter or casual archer. This record enables the tournament archer to predict kevlar string failure and replace the string before a failure occurs.

The compound bow changed the bowstring habits of many bowhunters. The old bowhunter made his bowstrings. Making his own strings was just about the only way to get what he wanted.

Today you can buy a high quality string and you can count on this string being duplicated as long as you stay with the same manufacturer. You will have to install the string, nocking point, and fit the string to the string seat of your arrow nocks.

If the string serving at the nock point is unsuitable either in material or diameter then replace or correct it in the following manner:
• If the factory serving is too small a simple solution is to build up the nocking point with waxed dental floss until the arrow nock will just snap on the string and support the free swinging weight of the arrow. A sharp rap on the bowstring with a finger should cause the arrow to fall free.
• The release shooter should replace the soft nylon serving with monofilament. Before you remove the factory serving measure the diameter of the bowstring with a micrometer.

Remove the old serving and measure the diameter of the serving material. Knowing these two diameters makes it easy to determine the proper diameter of the new serving.
• Make a trip to the local sporting goods store and measure the diameters of several different pound tests of monofilament fishing line. You can pro-

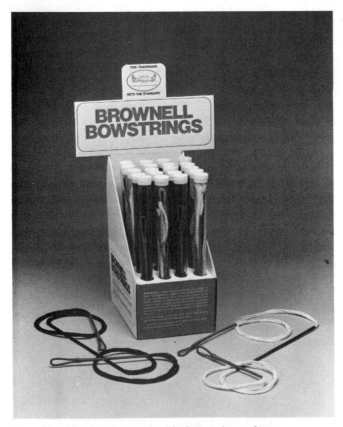

Type B and B-50 dacron are used in factory bowstrings.

duce a custom-fitting string serving by selecting an exact monofilament size. Incidentally, monofilament is sold on small spools (less than 100 yds) as leader material.

• Having and using a micrometer makes custom fitting a string serving easy. If you don't have access to a "mike" may I suggest stocking three different pound test ratings of monofilament. Usually 12-14-16 pounds will fit several string and nock sizes.

As an example, I was once required to equip a Delta-V bow with a yellow or white bowstring for a special photographic project. Yellow bowstring material was unobtainable on short notice so I used 18 strands of white B-50 dacron. The string loops were served with a bright yellow nylon upholstery thread purchased at a wholesale upholstery supply house. The fluorescent yellow string serving was 12-pound-test Stren monofilament fishing line. This combination made an excellent fit for a 5/16 inch Bjorn nock on my 308 Bear Magnum shafts. I had to build up the nocking point serving with a short length of dental floss to fit the 11/32 inch Bjornock on the 8.4 Bear Metric Magnum shaft used later.

• Serve in the new monofilament serving using a medium pressure. A too tight serving can cause an early string failure. If it's too loose the results will be obvious. Finish the serving by using a short separate loop to pull the end of the monofilament back under the serving, just like wrapping a guide

on a fishing rod. Clip the monofilament close and very carefully heat the end with a match to melt the mono into a knob. This will prevent the end from slipping out from under the serving wraps.

You need a bowstring server in your repair kit along with a container of waxed dental floss and a tube of bowstring wax to repair and maintain your bowstring. A small piece of scrap leather makes an excellent pad to burnish string wax into a bowstring.

A new bowstring needs a good break in. Place the new string on the bow and draw the bow several times. If you plan to replace the nock serving then give the string a good waxing. Burnish the newly waxed string with the small piece of leather until the leather is warm and the wax flows into the string. Replace the serving with a material of your choice. A good application of wax before you replace the serving lubricates the string and improves flex life at the nocking point.

Install your nocking point, string peep and silencers then shoot the string to check the positioning of the accessories. If everything is correct shoot the string 50-100 times.

Your new string is now broken in. Replace with the original string and store the new string in your quiver. It is ready for service if the original string becomes damaged.

Factory made strings are of continuous loop construction. This type of string is produced by mechanical equipment which keeps the cost down to a reasonable amount.

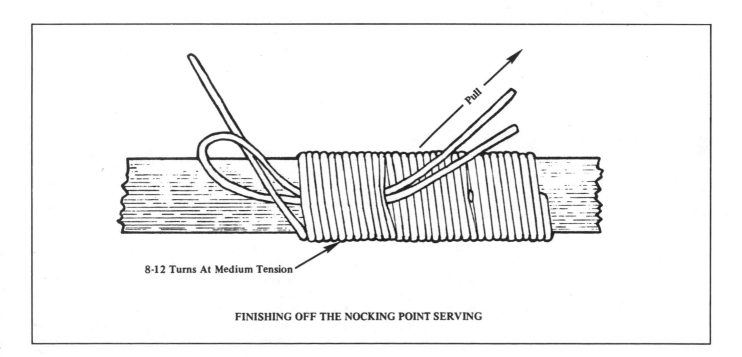

8-12 Turns At Medium Tension

FINISHING OFF THE NOCKING POINT SERVING

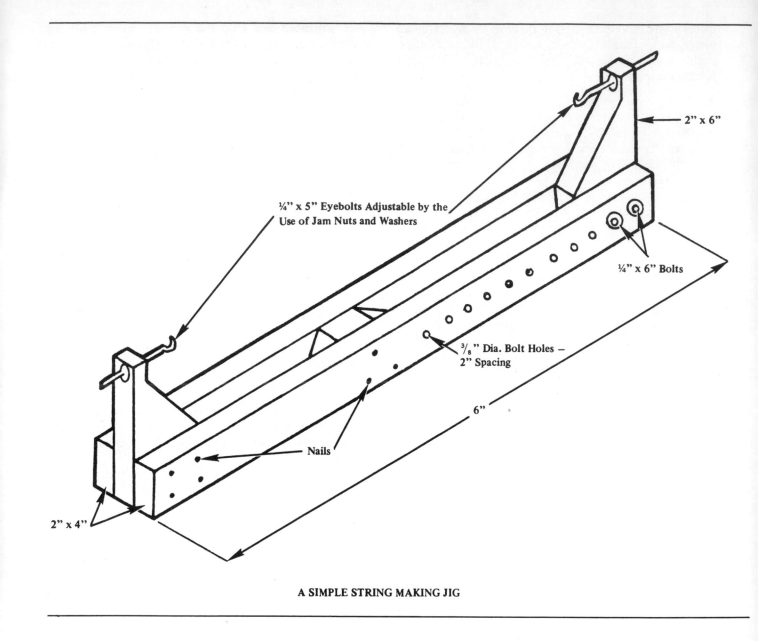

A SIMPLE STRING MAKING JIG

We watched a custom string maker at the 1972 National Field. He had a mechanized string-making table in operation and could produce a new recurve string in about four minutes.

The continuous loop string is an economical, high quality string and usually gives excellent service. A common failure is having one strand break under the serving. When this happens the string begins a slow and almost undetectable letdown. Your first indication of such a failure would be some unexplained low arrows at the longer distances.

The old Flemish Twist bowstring is the ultimate in bowstrings for the recurve or longbow archer. This string is a handmade operation and

cost prohibitive for general sales and use by bowstring and bow manufacturers. A handmade twisted string is, however, supplied with the Fred Bear Signature Collector's bow.

A Flemish Twist string is made of a number of individual strands twisted together. The independent strands prevent a letdown should one strand break under use. The twisted loop ends wear well and it makes a quiet-shooting string on a recurve bow.

I made my son a twist string as an experiment for a Carroll four-wheel compound. We found that we could regulate the string length very precisely after the string was broken in by twisting the string a few additional turns to make up for the stretch.

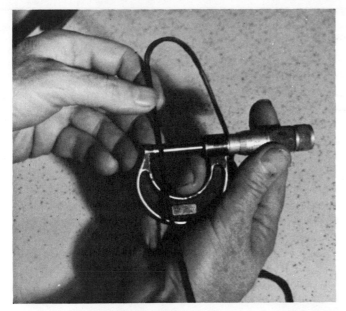

Use a micrometer to measure the diameter of an old favorite bowstring, so the same dimension can be duplicated.

For Compound or Recurve Bows

Draw Weight	No. of Strands
40 lbs.	12 (6 on each side)
50 lbs.	14
60 lbs.	16
Over 60 lbs.	18 and up

For Eccentric Cam Bows

Draw Weight	No. of Strands
Up to 50 lbs.	16
50 lbs. and over	18

Now let's make a bowstring.

1. Set your string jig for the required string length.

2. Lay out the selected number of strands between the eyebolt string supports. Hold the two loose ends together and make a common mark with a felt tip pen, or a chalk mark if you are making a black string. Join the two loose strands together at the mark by use of a fisherman's knot.

3. Start sliding the continuous loop of strands around the eyebolt hooks. Sliding the loop allows each strand to equalize itself in length.

We did not have to make a single adjustment on this bow.

I have never seen instructions for the making of a Flemish Twist string. A search of some books on knot tying and braiding failed to turn up any useful illustrated information. It's the sort of thing that's been handed down by demonstration from one archer to another.

Jodie Parker taught me the process and it's really quite simple, though almost impossible to describe in words and diagrams. Seek out an old time target archer and ask him to teach you how to make a twist string. Or, consider making a loop bowstring.

If you should desire to make a continuous loop string you will first have to buy or construct a simple jig to hold the strands. Construction of this jig requires only common hand tools, some 2x4s and a little time. Notice that part of the eyebolt is cut away to open it.

Brownell and Company, Moodus, Connecticut 06469, has supplied archers with string making materials for years. Your local dealer may stock these materials or can get them for you.

Depending on the string material used, and the bow weight, the number of strands in a continuous loop bowstring will vary. Follow the instructions of the material manufacturer. In general, most strings are made up as follows:

Step one in making a bowstring is to set up the string jig. Slip on the old bowstring or measure it with a tape and adjust the jig accordingly. Make sure the inside surfaces of the eyebolts are smooth so as not to abrade the bowstring strands.

4. Give this continuous loop a good application of bowstring wax. Burnish the wax into the string by a brisk rubbing with a piece of leather. Rub until the leather becomes warm from friction. This lubricates the bowstring.

5. Separate the continuous loop into two equal parts and center the loop in your jig according to the marks you made earlier. Insert the two string spreaders to hold the strands apart. Serve (wrap) with nylon serving material equally on each side of the string center marks, just long enough to form

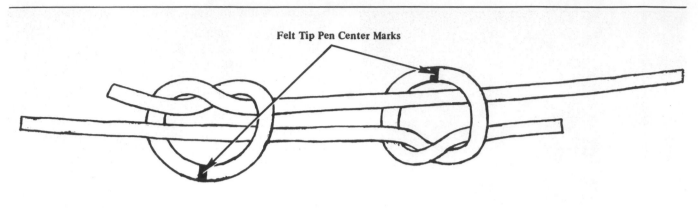

Felt Tip Pen Center Marks

Detail of the Fisherman's Knot used in joining the loop strand of a bowstring.

the loop ends. Determine the loop end size by comparing your new string with an old string. Then take off the spreaders.

6. Slide the string so the served sections are looped around the eye bolts. Lash the ends together to form the string loops. Do not use monofilament for string loop servings. Monofilament can wear into the bow tips by abrasive action.

7. Select the type and diameter of the string nock serving. Use a medium pressure on this serving. A tight serving can cause an early string failure.

Just as an experiment we shot a Lewis Model Carroll recurve equipped with a B-50 dacron string and a X7-1714 arrow through the Arrowmeter for a velocity of 176 feet per second. After switching to an identical kevlar string the 40-pound bow produced 184 feet per second for a gain of eight fps.

Slide the strands around the eyebolts to equalize.

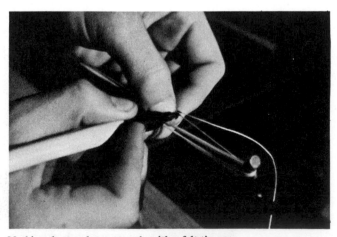

Marking the two loose strands with a felt tip pen.

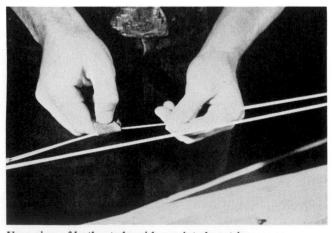

Use a piece of leather to burnish wax into bowstring.

Insert the two string spreaders to separate strands.

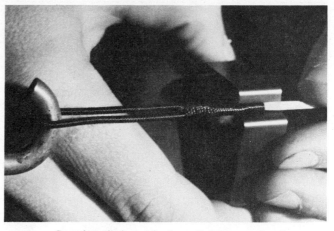

Complete the bowstring loop. Pull loose end under wraps.

Starting the serving on string loop area. A serving tool holds spool, maintains tension and helps make a neat job.

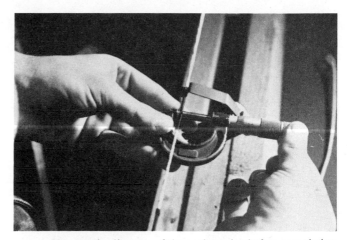

Measure the diameter of the nock serving before completing the wrap. Use only medium pressure on this serving.

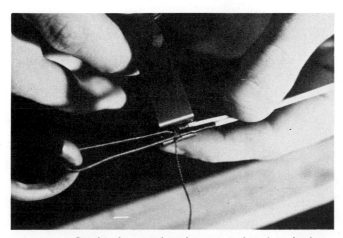

Starting the second serving to complete the string loop.

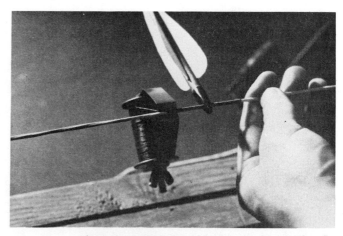

Check the nock serving with an arrow for a perfect fit.

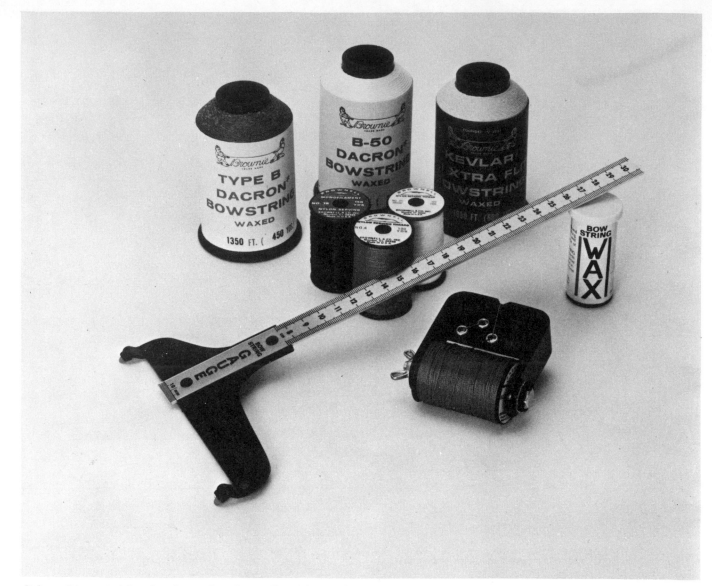

String making materials and equipment from Brownell, a major supplier.

Chapter 5
Arrow Points

Modern bowhunting arrows should be equipped with the screw-in replaceable point system, which allows you to change points at will. The same arrow can be used for indoor practice on Friday night, then for deer hunting on Saturday morning tipped with a broadhead.

In the old days it wasn't unusual for an archer to own several dozen arrows, each dozen meant for a different kind of shooting: big game hunting, small game and target shooting. Of course, these old shafts had permanently attached heads. At today's prices this would mean a considerable, and unnecessary, investment. Now all you need is a set of good quality shafts and a variety of points to suit your needs.

While hunting, my quiver generally contains six to nine arrows. Usually three of them are heavy glass shafts meant for close range shooting of squirrels and rabbits. The compartment in my quiver always carries six additional sharp and ready-to-hunt broadheads. If needed, I simply exchange the dull point for a sharp point, or a small game point for a big game head. I don't believe that I have used a fixed point hunting arrow since 1974.

You should have a set of different type heads. A practical minimum would be a set of 125- to 145-grain screw-in field type points and twelve replaceable broadheads. The field points can be the long type field point or the semi-blunt low penetration point by Bear Archery. I like the Bear point for the simple reason that it pulls out of the target butt easier. This weight field point can also be used in field archery competition in the bowhunter division.

By owning twelve broadheads you have six for broadhead practice and small game. This leaves six well-sharpened heads for your hunting arrows. Your hunting practice should be with broadheads identical to your hunting heads.

Most indoor ranges prohibit the use of broadheads, requiring target or field points which are much easier on the targets. If you are fortunate enough to have a backyard range, using target or field points will keep target butt damage to a minimum.

Always use screw-in inserts and screw-in target or field points to match inside and outside shaft diameters. Mismatched inserts and undersized points will cause shaft splitting. This is especially

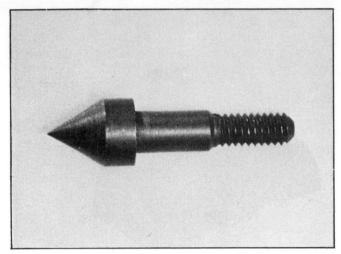

A screw-in target point.

true with the large diameter thinner wall aluminum shafts.

Target and field points are penetrators. They transmit little if any shock and cause almost no hemorrhaging. They kill only with a direct hit on a vital organ. Any other hit causes a slow, lingering death. All hunting of game animals should be with a suitable cutting point.

The metal or rubber-tipped blunt point is another hangover from the old days. Their principal use was for stump shooting when roaming the woods. They are poor performers on the smallest of game. They will penetrate rabbits and squirrels without stopping the animal. These points will slide and hide under grass and keep you looking more than shooting. If you like this type of shooting then use the Zwickey Zudo point.

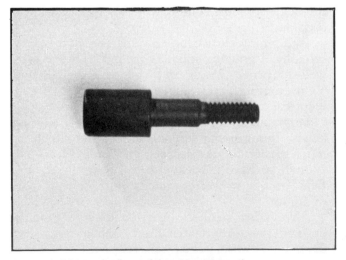

A screw-in blunt point for roving and casual practice.

The only use we have for a blunt arrow is in flu-flu shooting at hand-thrown aerial targets. If you hunt small game use the Zudo or the MA-3 broadhead. Bear Archery markets an adapter to increase shock when using conventional broadheads on small game.

The Zwickey Zudo point is a unique product that does a superb job. It is a blunt type point equipped with four spring-loaded wire arms.

This point looks as if it is equipped for space travel. In reality the extensions prevent an arrow from sliding under grass. Instead, the arrow flips over on top of the grass in plain sight. Zwickey Archery advertises them as the "unlosable point."

The spring arms also act as cutting edges on small game. It is the only non-broadhead type point that I will use on squirrels and rabbits. Combining the Zudo with heavy glass arrow shafts has proved very satisfactory in heavy cover.

There is no magical shape for a broadhead arrow point. Nothing succeeds like a point of good aerodynamic shape, designed from field experience and constructed from tough alloys and hard, well-sharpened steel cutting edges.

There are three broadhead concepts worth consideration:

● The two-bladed heads as represented by the Zwickey Black Diamond point and the Bear Super Razorhead are old favorites.

Here is an excerpt from a letter sent to me by John Zwickey and reproduced here with his permission.

My father, Clifford Zwickey, began producing Black Diamonds in 1939 and the design has changed very little since. They are now the oldest broadhead on the market in continuous production by the same owner. The four-blade broadhead invented in 1940 was the first to popularize the multiple blade concept and was termed the "Eskimo" because they inserted a bone in their hunting heads to make a crosscut. Black Diamonds originated the five-degree taper which became the standard for the industry.

The Black Diamonds were here when bowhunting started its post World War II growth in popularity. Looking back, very few of us recognized just what superb points they were. Frankly, we were inundated in those days by the high powered advertising of many junk points. Today the Black Diamonds are still here and appreciated by the bowhunting fraternity.

The Bear Razorhead was placed on the market in the late 1950s. It found a ready market. The

THE ZWICKEY BLACK DIAMOND DELTA
1⅜" X 2⅞" — 177.3 Grs.
2-Blade

Razorhead and its large replaceable insert had that certain deadly look appeal. Its performance on game was equal to its looks. There are many bowhunters who swear by them and would not shoot any other broadhead. Bear Archery claims that there have been more Razorheads sold, and more game killed with Razorheads, than any other point.

The Super Razorhead is a very good update in design and blade steel. Point alignment is no longer a problem with the screw-in shank. The stainless steel blade is harder and will take and hold a better cutting edge than its predecessors.

The Black Diamond Eskimo and the Super Razorhead are very versatile points. Well sharpened, they will do their part—you would not be overpointed hunting deer with a 45-pound recurve nor underpointed hunting moose with an 80-pound compound.

Some hunters have rejected Black Diamonds because they found them to be difficult to sharpen, or at least beyond their sharpening skills. That's a pity and no fault of the point. We'll deal with sharpening broadheads later on.

The Super Razorhead, with its shiny stainless steel blade and blue alloy shank, is too doggone pretty and I put new Super Bears in a glass beading machine for a few minutes to dull the finish. I don't like shiny heads or arrow shafts in the deer woods.

● The fixed, three-blade arrow point dates back to early civilizations at the beginning of the Bronze Age. Multi-blade points developed along with man's ability to work with metals.

Today, three-bladed points are well represented by the MA-3 and Roger Rothhaar's giant-sized Snuffer. The latter will slice a 1½-inch wound channel and has an awesome potential. Its use to date has been in the hands of skilled bowhunters who are capable of handling heavy bows shooting heavy-shafted arrows. A friend of mine took a buck using a Snuffer point one year and he reported a massive wound channel. The deer ran less than 30 yards and was dead within seconds. My friend was shooting from a tree stand and used a 75-pound PSE compound with 2117 shafts. Don't try to shoot the Snuffer with light, out of balance shafts.

The MA-3 point is a very sturdy point. It is a fine hunting head when sharpened properly. Its flying ability and ease of tuning coupled with rugged construction and economical cost have made it one of the most popular tournament broadheads. This point with the tip filed off 1/4 inch to prevent penetration in trees or roots has no equal for small game.

The design of the fixed, three-blade head creates extremely sturdy cutting edges. They are not easy points to sharpen. Their ability to retain their sharpness completely through an animal and their fine flight characteristics make the time spent in sharpening well worthwhile in the hunting field. Many bowhunters are too impatient to sharpen

THE STAINLESS STEEL BEAR
SUPER RAZORHEAD
1⅛" X 2¼" — 140.5 Grs.
WITH INSERT.

ROGER ROTHHAAR's SNUFFER
1½" X 2½" — 194.6 Grs
3-BLADE

THE RUGGED MA-3 FOR LARGE AND SMALL GAME. A VERY OUTSTANDING BROADHEAD TOURNAMENT POINT

these points properly. It takes time on the sharpening stones to get the right edge.

● The factory sharpened, replaceable-blade points have done much for bowhunting.

These heads are all equipped with the screw-in adapter incorporated in the construction of the point. This has eliminated the old point alignment problem. Having good, sharp, replaceable blades is a real convenience. The Satellite, Savora, Wasp and Rocky Mountain Razor have all been extensively field tested and have proved to be dependable performers.

These heads are available in both tool steel and stainless steel blades. There are three, four and sometimes five-bladed versions. Weights range from 110 grains to 145 grains. You can match any bow or balance any arrow from the replaceable-blade group of points. The Rocky Mountain Razor is a very popular replaceable-blade head. It comes as a super-sized four-blade, or a tree-blade medium point.

BOB BARRIE'S ROCKY MOUNTAIN RAZOR 1¼" X 2" – 138.0 GRS. REPLACEABLE INSERT 4-BLADE

Safety and reliable usage require that these heads be tightened in place or removed with a broadhead wrench. Left-hand rotating arrows tend to loosen up on impact and a finger tight only head may come loose as it penetrates letting the blades come apart inside game. Always use a broadhead wrench for snug seating.

New Archery Products has approached the broadhead market with a new concept called the Razorbak System. The replaceable blades are contained in a blade cartridge, and are available in either four or five-blade versions. This company has some interesting ideas about filling broadhead needs.

The points come packaged in a well constructed plastic storage box. The replaceable blade cart-

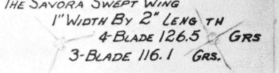

THE SAVORA SWEPT WING 1" WIDTH BY 2" LENGTH 4-BLADE 126.5 GRS 3-BLADE 116.1 GRS.

ridges and the broadheads are protected with good, reusable plastic shields.

Part of the Razorbak System is a set of replica high impact plastic practice heads duplicating in every way the real hunting heads. These replica heads shoot just like the real thing. This is the first time that a complete broadhead system has been available. Expensive? Yes, but considering quality, performance and convenience, not really. These points are very popular, and deservedly so.

The Rothhaar Snuffer, the large Zwickey Delta and the replaceable-blade Rocky Mountain Razor are popular extra large heads. Field performance has given these "magnum" points the reputation of being super killers when shot from heavy bows in the hands of experienced bowhunters. Don't

The Razorbak 4 and 5 broadhead combinations in storage boxes and with protective shields. System provides various heads.

get "large point fever" without having the equipment and experience to shoot them.

There is no way that these big points will perform when shot with light equipment. You will need a minimum of 50 pounds draw weight and heavy-shafted arrows when shooting down on deer from a tree stand. Sixty to 70-pound bows make these points begin to fly. With 70 or more pounds you can chop a railroad tunnel through a bull moose with any one of them. Keep your tackle in balance. You cannot drive a railroad spike with a tack hammer.

I keep referring to the Black Diamonds and Razorheads as two-blade heads. The reason is the long cutting edges of the main point. The small fixed blades on a Black Diamond do provide an "X" cut; however, I feel that their main advantage

is in providing arrow shaft relief as an aid to penetration.

I have heard some good arguments as to the purposes of the Razorhead insert. Some say that it is a hide splitter. Others say that it is there for shaft relief and a killing blade to compliment the main blade. On thin-skinned game, field experience has proved it to be a good killing blade.

On heavy thick-skinned game the insert is of more value as shaft relief to aid in complete penetration. Again may I say that this insert should always be shaving razor sharp.

All of the heads mentioned have one design feature in common besides steel cutting edges. All, regardless of the concept, have an absolutely rigid center section. Avoid any head with flexible blades. A point that bends on bone will deflect,

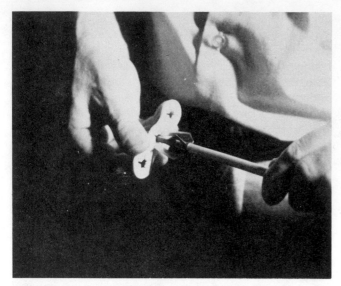
Using a Tetra wrench to tighten a replaceable screw-in head.

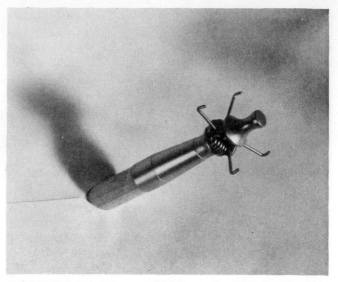
Zwickey Zudo point. Very practical for small game hunting.

give poor penetration, and unpredictable performance.

There is a trend toward harder steel for blades and this is good. I tested a Snuffer at 46 Rockwell, a Black Diamond Eskimo at 50 Rockwell, blades from a Rocky Mountain Razor at 51 Rockwell, a new stainless steel Super Razorhead at 46 Rockwell and an old Razorhead at 43 Rockwell hardness.

Don't fall victim to the old misconception that you can sight in and practice with compatible weight field points and then switch to broadheads. Precision shooting skills have proved this common belief to be wrong. Practice and sight in with the same type head and then go hunting. Broadheads and field points do not fly alike. Neither do the same weight heads from different manufacturers, nor the same weight heads of different configurations fly the same way.

SHARPENING BROADHEADS

The broadhead point is designed to inflict a deep, penetrating wound in a game animal. A hunting head should be scalpel sharp before being used, and honed in such a manner that the edge will remain sharp as it penetrates the animal.

One wildlife agency controlling bowhunting on an island off the East Coast requires that applicants demonstrate proficiency with the bow before being allowed to hunt. This is a good idea but they should go further and also make the archer show his skill in sharpening broadheads. After all, a good archer can hit with a dull or poorly sharpened blade. Shooting a dull broadhead is inexcusable; shooting an improperly sharpened arrow is a matter of a lack of knowledge.

There are very few junk arrowheads around any more. Modern, knowledgeable archers quickly see through exaggerated and misleading claims. Some oddball heads are still sold, mostly to arrowhead collectors.

There are some super good heads available today. They are well designed and built of tough alloys and hardened steel cutting edges. These points, when correctly sharpened and mounted on good heavy shafts and shot from the proper weight bows, are capable of taking any game on earth in a humane manner.

The manufacturers have recognized a market for factory sharpened heads and they have given us the replaceable blade head. It is possible to bowhunt with sharp heads and never have to sharpen a broadhead. Just flip out the dull blades and replace them with new factory sharpened blades. However, many of the more popular heads are not factory sharpened, but if they were they would stay sharp only until shot. Some of these heads have the edges beveled and the purchaser has to finish out the edge to shaving sharp. Every bowhunter should master the skill of sharpening his hunting arrows and knives.

A sharpening kit should include three sharpening stones, a supply of honing oil, an eight-inch flat file with handle, a sharpening handle for broadheads and a sharpening jig to resharpen replaceable blades. Naturally, you can buy sharp replaceable blades but you can also resharpen the originals and save money.

Let's look at the various sharpening stones and understand their uses. Your first stone should be a combination (medium/fine grit) stone. Make it a fairly large stone about 8" x 2" x 1" in size. A Norton Crystolon/India stone would be an excellent choice. India grade stones are used by many journeymen machinists for general hard steel work. This is a very reasonably priced stone.

The medium grit is fast cutting and should be the first side to be used. Use it to remove nicks, reestablish bevels and as the first step in resharpening a really dull blade.

The fine grit side of an India stone will put a good edge on hard steel. This side smooths off the rough edge left from the medium grit side. Use this side until the little light reflections which highlight the dull spots disappear from your cutting edge.

Learn the "light reflection" check for a dull edge. It's simple. Hold a knife by the handle with the point away from you and the cutting edge up. Position the blade several inches below a lamp shade with the blade tip pointed at the glowing light bulb. Look at the cutting edge. The little bright spot that you see is light reflecting from the dull spot on the cutting edge. When the edge is sharp the light reflections will disappear.

The second stone should be a soft Arkansas. This is a natural abrasive and is known the world over for its sharpening ability. Arkansas stones are the choice of the custom knifemaker. This stone can be used to rework a dull blade or to finish out a fine edge. This stone is fast cutting yet

gentle to steel. These stones are not cheap. Shop around and watch the advertisements from hardware and sporting goods stores. Buy as large a stone as you can comfortably afford. Your basic use of this stone on broadheads will be as a finishing stone. Use this stone until your point edge begins to look like polished glass, then go to the hard Arkansas.

The third stone should be a hard Arkansas. This stone is not a sharpening stone but a 100 percent finishing stone. A 6" x 2" x 1" dimension is a good size to work with. Its purpose is to polish out the microscopic wire edge left by your soft Arkansas. Finishing an edge on this stone can produce the super sharp, hide-popping edge that causes massive hemorrhaging and a heavy, lasting blood trail.

Hard Arkansas stones are expensive. They are necessary if you shoot the fixed, three-bladed points like the Snuffer, the MA-3 or the Bodkin. It takes patience, equipment and know-how to do the edge on these points right. The blunt 60-degree cutting edge is the reason why these points remain so sharp as they penetrate an animal.

These stones are considered as bench stones. Use them at home or in an established camp. They are too big and heavy to carry while hunting. Carry a knife steel by Schrade or Gerber in your field kit. Use these steels to touch up a knife edge or broadhead. Another use for these sharpening steels is to split a pelvic bone while dressing out big game.

Honing oil is required with your sharpening stones. A good oil keeps the stone pores from filling with metal particles. It floats the metal particles out and away, keeps the stone clean and cutting and assists in polishing the edge.

Buck Cutlery and Smith Washita market good honing oils through sporting goods stores. If you can't find these oils try light white mineral oil from your druggist.

If you shoot two-bladed heads like the Black Diamond or the Super Razorhead you will need an eight-inch flat file. Make sure that the file has a secure handle.

Use a file to establish cutting bevels, remove nicks and to slightly round off the point of the head. Never use a file to sharpen a knife or you will dull your file and tear the metal in your knife blade. Most good knife blades will test out to Rockwell 56-58 in hardness. Broadheads run Rockwell 40-51. A new file will check out to Rockwell 63.

Make yourself a customized handle to hold a broadhead while sharpening. These handles are very simple to make and cost practically nothing.

Sharpening kit includes two Arkansas and an India stone.

Sharpening permanently mounted point using homemade device.

You cannot hold a broadhead in your hand securely enough to prevent "rolling the edge" as you use a file or a stone. Try one of these handles. You will notice an immediate improvement in your cutting edges and a reduction in sharpening time.

The next item is a sharpening jig for replaceable blades. I just don't like to throw anything away, especially a perfectly good insert that just needs resharpening. The small blades are very hard to hold and this makes them difficult to sharpen without a jig.

It takes a special tool to do it properly. If you have access to a drill press, a bench grinder and some shop skills go ahead and make one. Or buy one. Every bowhunter who sees one wants one. You can sharpen any insert blade, including the insert for the Super Razorhead.

There is a lot more to sharpening a blade than just moving it back and forth on a stone. Given a good quality knife you have complete control over how well that blade cuts and how long it will hold an edge. You also have complete control over the type of edge on your blade. How the knife will be used dictates the type of edge needed to obtain maximum cutting efficiency.

Many people think that if a recently sharpened knife stays sharp with repeated use it is considered to be a good knife made from good metal. If it dulls quickly it is commonly said that they "don't put good metal in knives anymore."

Nothing could be further from the truth. The finest steels ever made and the most advanced tempering technology are available and being used today. The problem lies in the ability and knowledge of the knife owner to sharpen the blade with an edge of the proper included cutting angle for his common uses. The included angle of the cutting edge of a good quality blade is a major factor in how long that edge will last. Your skill with the sharpening stone determines how sharp it will be. Look at the illustrations to better understand the term "included angle."

Most over the counter knives will have an included angle of 38 to 42 degrees if it is a tool steel blade. A good quality stainless blade will run 42 to 46 degrees for light general uses.

Two good examples of how included cutting angle should be modified for special uses would be my small caping knife and my heavy-duty sheath knife.

Both of these blades test to Rockwell 60-61 in hardness. The included cutting angle of the small caper is 30 degrees. It's used on hide and flesh only and never on bone or wood. Using this thin edge on a pelvic bone or tree limb would destroy the edge in a hurry.

My heavy sheath knife has a cutting angle of 45 degrees. It is designed for general cutting. This knife has dressed out a lot of game and cut many branches to clear arrow paths.

This heavy blade will never be capable of the fine edge of the small caper but it is easy to sharpen and holds that shaving edge after hard use. The same ability to hold an edge is vital to the performance of a broadhead arrow point.

The cutting thrust of a broadhead point can be compared to an ax chopping wood. The edges of both the ax and the arrow encounter great resistance. What would happen to an ax head with a very slight included cutting angle? One chop and the ax would be dull.

Picture what happens when a broadhead hits the rib cage of a deer. First, there is hide to be cut, then fat and muscle tissue, and then there are the tough elastic rib bones to be severed—all protective structures surrounding the heart/lung area. The thin-edged point is dulled on the rib bones before the arrow has even penetrated the chest cavity to reach the large arteries, veins and lungs. A dull broadhead will push an artery aside. A sharp broadhead will sever that artery. This makes a big difference in blood trails and shortens the distance that animal runs before expiring.

There are three basic types of broadheads in general use today: the two-edged blade with a small insert like the Bear Razorhead; the fixed, three-bladed head like the Snuffer; and the factory presharpened, replaceable-blade head like the Razorbak.

Sharpening these heads is no big problem with the right equipment and a little instruction. Let's start with the popular Super Razorhead. This point comes factory presharpened with well established bevels. This is a good point with which to start your sharpening experience.

Mount a Razorhead in a holding handle and clamp it in a vise with the blade in a flat position. A word of caution: be sure that you or someone else cannot walk into the head accidentally in its fixed position. Now take your file and reestablish the bevels by resting the file on the edge of the blade and using the ferrule as a bevel guide. Remove the nicks and dress up the bevels and tip. Try to avoid filing into the ferrule. When complete, the cutting edges should look like the illustration when viewed from the ferrule end. Be sure that you round off the sharp tip slightly. A sharp tip is a weak tip and it will dig into bone and bend too easily. Rounding off the tip of a flat-bladed point adds considerable stiffness. A bent or flexing blade reduces the penetrating ability of a broadhead arrow. Rounding off the tip is not necessary for a three-bladed or a replaceable-blade head because of their structural design. Take the holding handle out of the vise.

Place enough honing oil on the medium India to coat the stone. Lay the broadhead flat on the

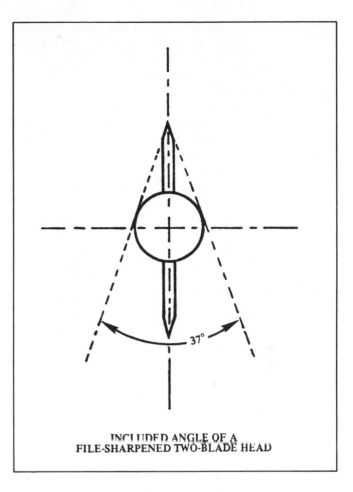

INCLUDED ANGLE OF A FILE-SHARPENED TWO-BLADE HEAD

stone. Next, raise the trailing cutting edge until the back corner of the head is ½-inch up off the stone. Refer to the sketches. Now, maintaining that angle, give the blade some motion left to right. When you raised the trailing edge you stopped using the ferrule as a guide or rest. You are now increasing the included angle of the cutting edge.

After you have completed your first stroke rotate the head 180 degrees clockwise and pull the blade to you (right to left) duplicating your first motion in reverse. You are sharpening first one side and then the other of a single cutting edge. Keep going back and forth using firm pressure, just as if you were slicing very thin slices off the surface of the stone. Try to maintain as near as possible the same bevel angle stroke after stroke.

If you become careless in maintaining a constant bevel angle then you begin to roll the edge of that blade. This is the reason some people spend a lot of time trying to sharpen a knife without success.

When you have established your new bevel turn the point over and do the other edge of the broadhead duplicating the motions just described.

Screw-in broadheads fit into homemade handle for sharpening.

Next, use the fine grit side of the India stone. If you have done your work well on the medium surface just a few strokes over the fine grit will produce a shaving-sharp edge. The color will be a dull steel gray. Move on to the soft Arkansas stone.

Lay on about 25 to 30 strokes per bevel and you'll see a big difference. The color of the edge will now have a reflected polished appearance, and if you touch it with your thumb, carefully, you'll feel it has a grabbing bite to it.

After the soft Arkansas finish off with the hard Arkansas. Again, give each bevel 25 or 30 strokes. Now those edges are really sharp. They'll look like polished glass, and will cut and keep cutting.

The replaceable insert blades are fairly easy to sharpen when using a holding jig. I like my home-made jig but you can buy one if you'd rather. Robert Barrie of Rocky Mountain products markets a blade holder.

Working with one of these little jigs is a lesson in blade sharpening. They quickly show the importance of holding a constant included angle stroke after stroke. If you work with the jig and let it guide you there's no chance for edge roll over. You'll be surprised at how few strokes are needed to get a good edge.

Start with the fine grit India stone surface and plenty of oil. Put the insert blade firmly in the jig. Place the blade edge on the stone with the jig bevel determining the included angle. Proceed with the normal knife sharpening strokes, always pushing or pulling the edge into the stone and rotating the blade between strokes.

Move on to the soft Arkansas and then to the hard Arkansas. These small blade inserts sharpen fast.

The fixed, three-bladed heads are very difficult to sharpen unless a person understands the blunt included cutting angle. Follow each step with care and all of a sudden you have a sharp broadhead. To the experienced person obtaining an edge is just a matter of time and elbow grease. To the inexperienced it seems as if the edge will never appear.

Each cutting edge forms a corner of an equilateral triangle and as such is definitely considered to be maximum for a really sharp edge. This heavy included angle gives these points an amazing resistance to dulling.

Place the head in your sharpening handle. Then support the handle at an angle on a table edge. Next, lay a file flat on the upper two edges of the point. Maintain this angle and file out any nicks and burrs. Rotate 120 degrees and repeat until you have completed all three edges.

Skip the medium side of the India stone and go to the fine grit side. Lay the head flat on the stone and push the head away from you. Maintain a 30-degree angle with the stone and the centerline of the head. Rotate the head 120 degrees each stroke. Use plenty of oil and continue until the light reflections disappear from each edge. The blunt included angle will keep you working longer on this point but be patient. The edges will finally appear.

The soft Arkansas will put the bite on each edge. This stone is gentle to steel and a soft cut is necessary to complete a proper edge with these heads. You are working on two edges at the same time, pushing one edge into the stone and dragging the other. Making 25 to 30 strokes on this stone should do the trick. Lay your thumb on the edge

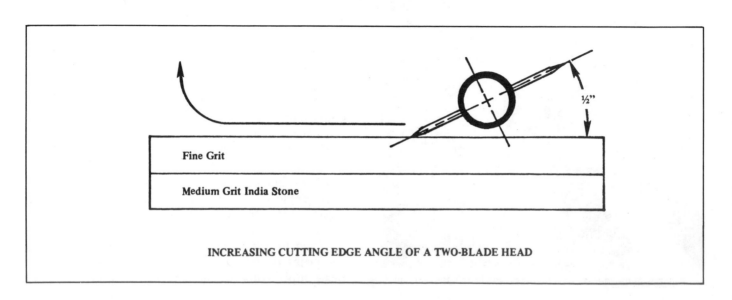

INCREASING CUTTING EDGE ANGLE OF A TWO-BLADE HEAD

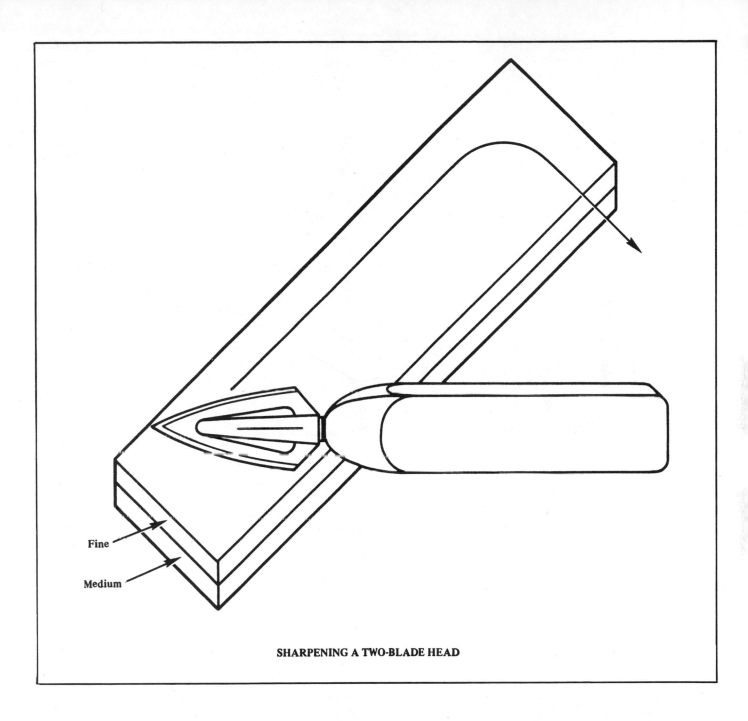

Fine

Medium

SHARPENING A TWO-BLADE HEAD

and feel the bite. It has a slightly different feel than a thin edge but the "shave" is there and it will remain there completely through the animal.

Finish out the point on the hard Arkansas using plenty of honing oil. Keep using the same pushing motion until the edge has that highly polished look.

I have not discussed ceramic stick sharpeners or any other new sharpeners. I have stayed with the old tried and true methods and stones because I feel that they are the best for broadheads.

There are some synthetic dry stones that do not require honing oil. Some of these stones may be too harsh for the 40-50 Rockwell hardness range of the steels used in broadhead construction, yet work fine on the much harder steels used in knife making. If you find a good synthetic stone that will fill one of your requirements at a reasonable price then buy it.

Equally important as sharpening is your treatment of these sharp heads until they are shot. There is no sense in spending your time sharpening and then letting these heads become dull or nicked in storage or in your quiver. Give this problem some thought. Keep a supply of point

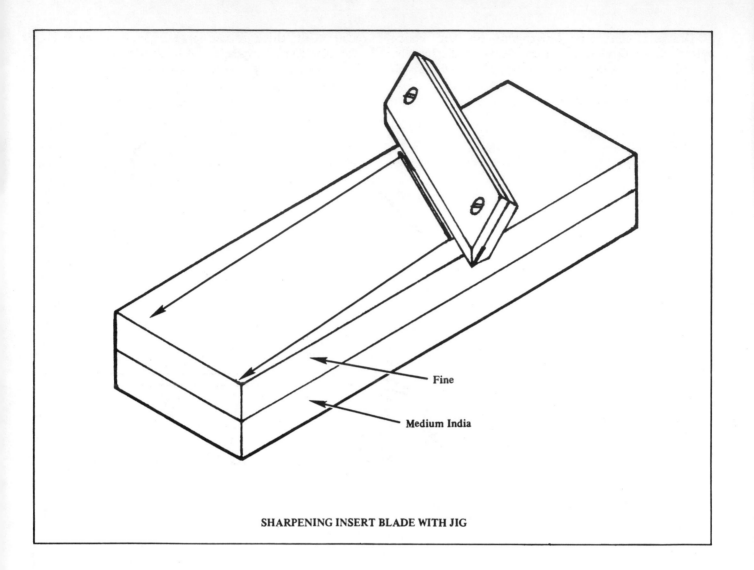

SHARPENING INSERT BLADE WITH JIG

Fine

Medium India

protectors on hand. Most archery shops keep them in stock. Specially designed boxes to hold broadheads are also available. I've used simple boxes meant to hold plastic fishing worms. It doesn't make much difference. Just make sure the heads don't rattle around and bang together.

Many bowhunters give each sharpened head a light coat of mineral oil and then wrap them individually in a piece of paper towel until ready for use.

Your bow or shoulder quiver should have a foam rubber spacer to keep sharp broadheads apart, and quiet. You can make a spacer out of a piece of scrap foam rubber three to four inches thick.

Trace the size and shape you'll need and cut it out with a sabre saw. Make an "X" slit in the rubber to hold each broadhead. Glue the spacer in place with rubber/leather adhesive.

Whichever type of bow quiver you choose, be sure it has a protective hood that a broadhead

can't penetrate. Exposed arrow points are a deadly hazard.

Making a holding handle for broadheads with screw-in adapters.

1. Study the drawing. Notice that the width and thickness are those of a finished 1'' x 2'' available at your local lumber supply.

2. Notice that the sides are flat. These flat sides aid in holding, clamping in a vise or clamping to a table top.

3. Drill a hole large enough to accommodate a screw-in insert.

4. Round off the end of the handle to allow good access to the point that is being sharpened.

5. Use a fast-setting epoxy to cement the insert in the handle.

Holding handle for permanently mounted broadheads.

1. Cut two six-inch pieces of finished 1'' x 2''.

2. Draw a centerline lengthwise on the inside matching surfaces of the two pieces of the handle. Decide which end will be rounded and which will be the top and bottom pieces of the handle.

3. Round both pieces at one end to the centerline as shown.

4. Match both pieces together and clamp in a vise. Drill two clearance holes for No. 10-32 screws with a No. 7 drill. Drill through both pieces equidistant from the centerline.

5. Come up through the bottom piece with the 10-32 screws and pull the hex nuts into the bottom handle piece. Use just enough pressure to mark the location of the nuts. Embed them flush using a carving chisel or hand grinder. Cement the hex nuts in place with a fast-setting epoxy.

6. When the hex nuts are secure join the handle pieces together and embed and epoxy the two washers to the handle top.

7. Disassemble and rough cut the holding vees with a pocket knife or grinder. Finish with a 3-corner file. Cut this groove large enough to clamp an arrow shaft securely without damage.

Sharpening jig for insert blades.

1. Secure two pieces of steel flat stock 2½" x 1" x 1/8". Use steel because brass or aluminum will clog up your stone.

2. Locate the screw holes on centerline and drill both pieces at the same time with a No. 42 drill. Tap the bottom piece with a No. 4-40 tap. Clearance drill the top piece with a No. 32 drill and chamfer for a ¼-inch 4/40 flathead screw.

3. Clamp both pieces together with the screws and grind or file the ¼-inch bevel as indicated. This angle will give an included angle of 40 to 46 degrees.

4. Make the locating guide from a piece of .005-inch shim stock. Trace the outline of your blade insert on the shim stock leaving a minimum of 1/16 inch of the cutting edge projecting out from the jig bevel to contact the sharpening stone. This will give an approximately 46-degree cutting edge. Cut this guide out with small tin snips or shop

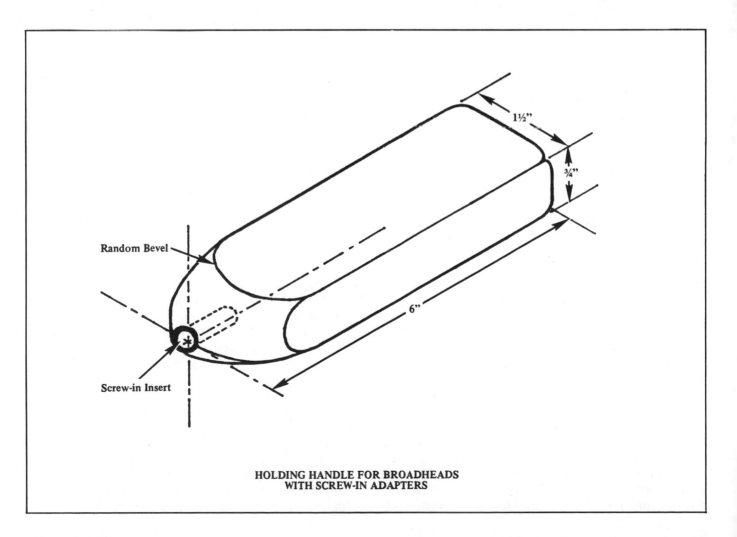

**HOLDING HANDLE FOR BROADHEADS
WITH SCREW-IN ADAPTERS**

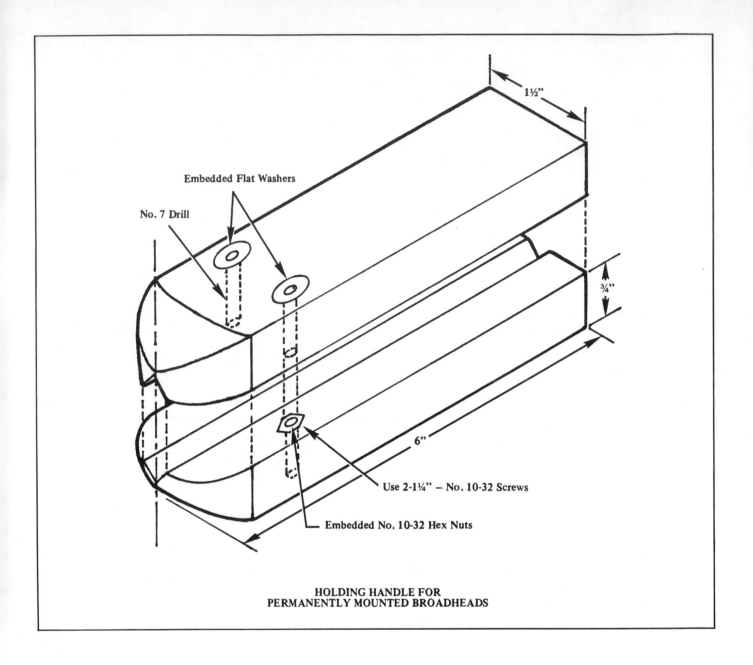

Embedded Flat Washers

No. 7 Drill

1½"

¾"

6"

Use 2-1¼" – No. 10-32 Screws

Embedded No. 10-32 Hex Nuts

**HOLDING HANDLE FOR
PERMANENTLY MOUNTED BROADHEADS**

scissors and solder or epoxy in place. This guide is a locating aid used to position your blades and insure uniformity in sharpening from blade to blade.

5. The opposite edge of the jig can be treated the same way to accommodate another type of insert, if desired.

After examining the various modern broadheads it is interesting to compare them with the points used by prehistoric hunters and realize how much things have changed, and how much they stay the same.

We know that primitive hunters chipped spear points out of a flint. One of these, the famous Clovis point, found in Colorado, may have been used to kill mammoths. When we compare the Clovis point to a modern two-blade broadhead side by side the similarities of form are remarkable.

Ancient man came up with a functional, efficient shape for a penetrating point and the design has persisted for countless thousands of years. Considering the circumstances, theirs was a magnificent achievement.

Basically, what we've done since then is change the materials and refine the design somewhat. The principle remains the same.

Stone Age man hunted to survive; we hunt for sport and in doing so accept the responsibility for quick, humane kills when we send that broadhead on its way.

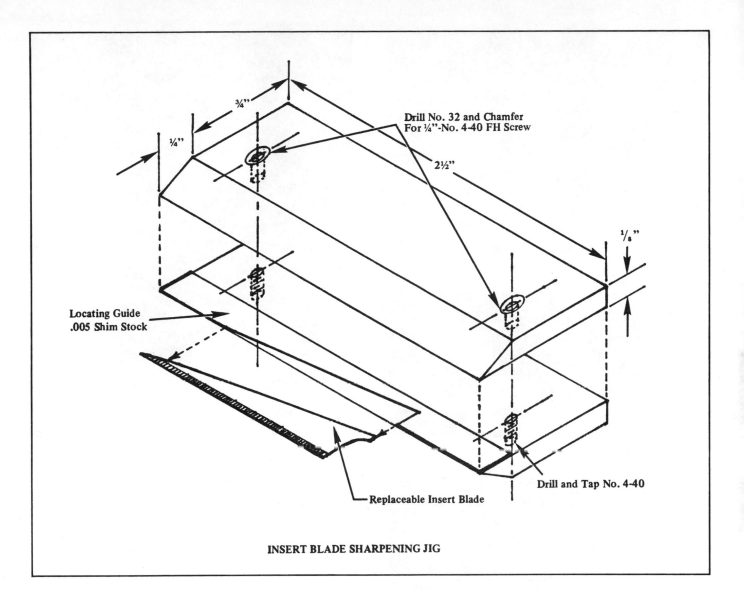

Drill No. 32 and Chamfer
For ¼"-No. 4-40 FH Screw

¾"

¼"

2½"

⅛"

Locating Guide
.005 Shim Stock

Drill and Tap No. 4-40

Replaceable Insert Blade

INSERT BLADE SHARPENING JIG

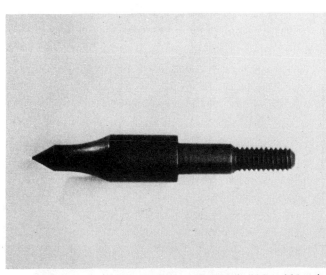

A screw-in field point, usually 125 to 145 grains.

The insert blade sharpening jig in action.

Powder scale weighs broadheads and is an aid to accuracy.

Sharpened broadheads should be kept in boxes or covered.

A Gerber knife steel used to touch up edges in the field.

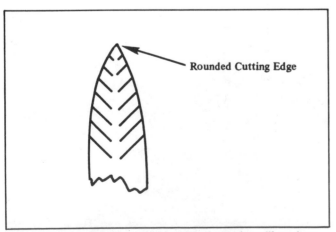
Failure to maintain a constant angle while sharpening will produce a rounded and dull cutting edge.

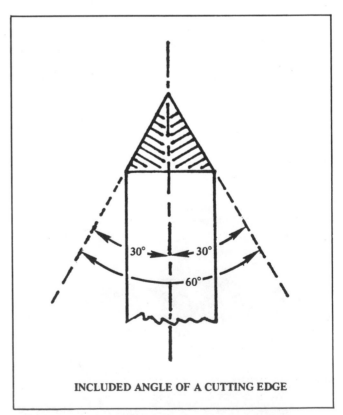
INCLUDED ANGLE OF A CUTTING EDGE

A fixed, three-blade broadhead edge hones to a heavy angle.

Chapter 6
Bow Accessories

Before the advent of the crossbow, gunpowder and firearms, the bow was a principal military weapon. Clouds of arrows were fired against advancing foes. This called for rapid shooting. English bowmen shot their heavy longbows barehanded through necessity, and they were very effective. Both the tab and shooting glove were known to European archers, but where massive firepower was required, barehanded shooting was standard. These military bowmen must have been hearty men with great arm and back muscles, and leather-like calluses on their shooting fingers.

MECHANICAL RELEASES

The mounted Mongol and Chinese archers shot their short and powerful recurve bows with a ring-type slip release. The sharp string angle of the short bow made the release a necessity to obtain reasonable accuracy. The modern rope-spike and slip releases returned to use with the gain in popularity of the bowsight for tournament field archery.

Bowhunters found the slip release and the rope-spike difficult to use for hunting. The deliberate squeeze necessary for accurate shooting sometimes made it impossible to get off a shot at the right time on game. Laugh if you will but I have heard of deer walking away from a hunter before he could complete his squeeze.

The bowhunter quickly switched to a trigger release, and in the mid-1970s the trigger release was legalized for competition by the National Field Archery Association. This action prompted many creative archers with access to machine shop equipment to produce a variety of mechanical releases. The archery magazines were loaded with advertisements for the latest designs, all touted to make it easy to shoot a perfect score.

I met a young archer at the 1972 NFAA Southern Sectional and, if my memory is correct, I sold him a release. Here, reproduced with his permission, is a recent letter from him:

Dear Roger,
Just a brief letter to try and give you some insight on releases. Releases started some 3,000 years ago with the Chinese. They were used as catch mechanisms on crossbows during medieval times. Releases actually came

into the archery industry as ropes, straps, or thongs in the early 1960s. There were several being made in garages or hobby shops in 1971.

Roger, I began in earnest to supply releases to the public at a reasonable price to improve shooting and accuracy in the early part of 1972. The two big advantages of using a release is the advantage of surprise—not knowing when it will release, and to eliminate "archer's paradox" (arrow whip).

Sincerely,
Keith Stuart

Stuart's group of Hot-Shot releases (two for hunting and two for target) quickly gained notoriety and popularity. Today, they set the standards by which all other releases are judged. Virtually all bowhunters who use a mechanical release have shot or owned a Stuart Hot-Shot.

Total Shooting Systems also produces a popular and complete selection of releases with features desired by both tournament and bowhunting archers.

The mechanical release can be a shortcut to more accurate shooting, but only if correct shooting form is maintained. The archer who simply punches the trigger of a release and expects to score is in for a big disappointment. Good shooting form is essential. Emphasize shoulder tension as you start your squeeze. This is where most release shooters go wrong. The release itself is not a cure-all for poor habits.

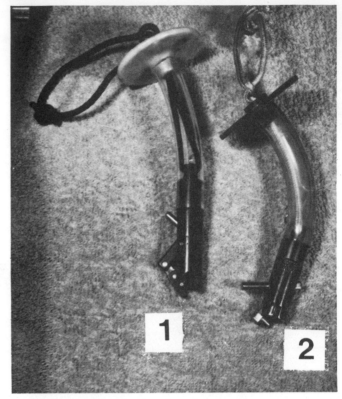

1. The Fletch Hunter Concho release.
2. Total Shooting Systems SY-1 Concho release.

The Model A Hot-Shot mechanical release by Stuart. Possibly the most popular release in use today.

The classic way of shooting a mechanical release has been—draw, aim and squeeze—as long as the sights are aligned until the release unexpectedly fires. Frankly, some bowhunters still shoot with a tab or glove because they have never learned to "trigger" a release.

Check out a Total Shooting Systems SY I or a Fletch Hunter release. Notice that the SY I is a concho-type release that transfers the draw weight of the bow to the heel of the hand.

The Fletch Hunter is a wrist draw release that utilizes a strap around the wrist to support the draw weight of the bow.

Eliminating the weight of drawing the bow from the fingers gives you a choice to squeeze or to trigger your shot. It takes very little practice with the proper equipment to master the instant shot.

There are also sound medical reasons for using a release which reduces strain and tension at the finger joints. Archers afflicted with arthritis in the hands may still continue to shoot with the aid of some form of mechanical release. Arthritis is a vicious crippler with absolutely no regard for age.

Stuart Model C Hot-Shot. A combination trigger and rope release.
Rope reduces string wear and release torque.

The Wilson tab. This model is suitable for any anchor point,
and for both tournament shooting and hunting.

The Wilson target tab. Note the white plastic anchor support.
Developed for an under-the-chin anchor point.

Total Shooting Systems shooting glove. A form of
finger protection preferred by many instinctive bowhunters.

But, it doesn't always have to mean an end to archery for the unfortunate sufferer.

THE TAB AND SHOOTING GLOVE

The use of a tab or similar finger protective device probably dates as far back as the development of the bow itself in some cultures. Shooting gloves came along much later after the needed designing, cutting and stitching skills had been acquired.

Modern tabs have gained in popularity as bowhunters changed from instinctive to a precision style of shooting. Tournament target archers are devotees of the tab.

It makes no difference as to the material from which the tab is constructed or the treatment given the tab if you do not have proper shoulder tension and complete relaxation of the release hand as the arrow is fired. This is the key to proper use of any release aid.

The Wilson tab has long been considered the standard of shooting tabs and is available in several versions for either target competition or bowhunting. Trim the flaps of the tab to suit your hand. It is my feeling that short flaps produce a more natural and cleaner release.

Shooting gloves are available from several different manufacturers with the major differences being

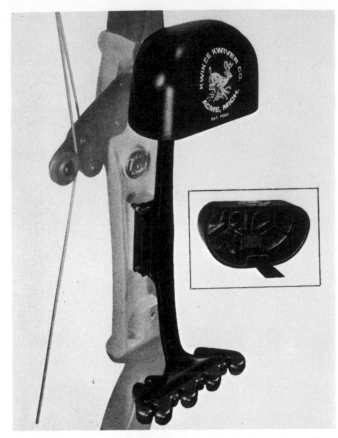

A well designed bow quiver affording good protection to the archer and his sharp broadheads.

Author's leather shoulder quiver is over 30 years old and still going strong. Note the large accessory pouch.

either a snap or velcro fastener. Next to shooting barehanded, the glove is the fastest way of nocking and shooting several arrows in succession.

Hill, Pearson and Bear all used the glove because it was the most common protective device in use at the time.

The user of a glove must wear it constantly while he is hunting or he may find himself having to shoot barehanded to make an unexpected shot. He will also find himself constantly in search of a glove that won't form a crease in the leather where the bowstring and the glove make contact.

QUIVERS

The Bowhunter Silhouette Course makes a good case for the shooting glove and the shoulder quiver. There is no better or faster way to handle a dozen arrows while shooting this course.

The bow quiver in its present form owes its popularity to Fred Bear. It is a very convenient way to carry a few arrows while hunting. A bow quiver provides the possibility of a rapid second shot at game, requiring the least hand and arm

movement which might attract the attention of the animal. A deer hunter rarely needs more than six arrows. On the other hand, the roving archer or small game bowhunter sometimes needs ten or more.

Each bowhunter will decide on a preferred way of carrying arrows as he gains field experience. He can choose a bow quiver, a back quiver, a shoulder quiver, hip quiver or a belt quiver. There is no best way to carry arrows—pick the way that suits your personal preference.

Judge a quiver by its capacity, its convenience, the protection afforded your arrows and how safely it carries sharp broadheads. Test your quiver for quietness. A bow quiver should hold your arrows very securely or they can vibrate as you make your draw. Arrows can rattle around in a shoulder quiver as you move through the woods. Hip and belt quivers are notorious for snagging on

When slipping through heavy cover with a shoulder quiver, slide it under your arm and hold it to your body.

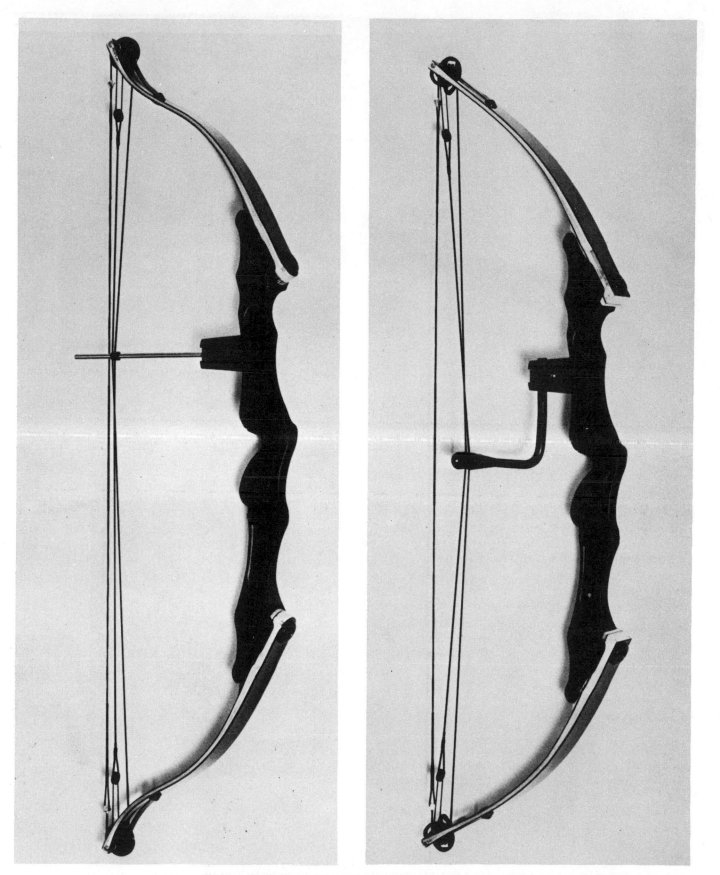

The Mark III Hunter (left) and the Firebird Hunter (right) compound bows from Golden Eagle Archery.

Golden Eagle offers a 13-ounce hunting stabilizer that will fit most standard compound bows.

Handle riser weights, five or eight ounces, are available for archers who like a bit more heft in the handle.

A 30-inch World Class Easton stabilizer mounted on a Bear Tamerlane tournament bow; also equipped with a Killian tournament sight and a Zero string peep. Fine for the competitive shooter but impractical for the deer woods.

brush and messing up arrow fletching. Whatever your choice in quivers, most can be modified and improved. Foam rubber and rubber cement can work wonders in silencing a quiver.

I like a shoulder quiver. It carries my arrows, my spare bowstring, and has room for any other assorted items that I feel will help.

My young friend Bill Hogue uses a bow quiver attached with a quick release device. He packs his ancillary equipment in a belt pouch around his waist. The pouch and the bow quiver both hang from a convenient limb while he is on stand. Remember that a bow quiver full of arrows can change the feel, balance and the tuning of your bow. If you use a bow quiver take these factors into consideration and practice accordingly.

STABILIZERS

Over 30 years ago Earl Hoyt equipped his target bows with a couple of long, horn-like projections and called them stabilizers. Ever since, the bow

A short stabilizer from Easton for use on hunting bows Its effectiveness is limited by its size.

stabilizer has proved to be a valuable aid to accuracy on the target range.

The modern hunting bow stabilizer is simply too short, in my opinion, to fulfill the intent of stabilizers in general. If you want to change the weight and balance of a light hunting bow, stabilizers work quite well. However, putting a short stabilizer on a heavier weight compound set up with a bowsight, bow quiver or other accessories will be of little help.

ARM GUARDS

The arm guard serves two functions. It protects the inside of the bow arm from the bowstring, and it keeps loose shirt or jacket sleeves from deflecting the bowstring as the bow is fired.

The inexperienced archer has the greatest need for an arm guard because he makes the most mistakes with his shooting form. The first time an archer heels a bow and rolls the elbow of his shooting arm towards his bow he will have an

unforgettable experience. The pain and large black and blue bruise caused by the string slapping his arm will be remembered as long as he shoots a bow. This bruise looks more horrible than serious with full recovery in about four days.

Almost every school archery class issues a full length arm guard to prevent this type of injury. Most major archery equipment manufacturers list these full length arm guards in their catalogs and they are wise investments for cold weather bowhunters. Don't let the bulk of a down jacket sleeve deflect your bowstring and cost you a deer.

Every bowhunter needs two arm guards. Warm weather shooting requires a light, ventilated arm guard for comfort and protection of the veins and arteries on the inside of your forearm. Hot weather shooting is short sleeve weather and there's no lower sleeve length to offer some protection or interfere with the bowstring.

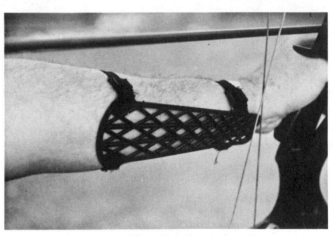

A warm weather arm guard from Saunders Archery Company.

A long arm guard for cold weather use from Pearson. Guard keeps bulky jacket sleeve out of the way.

ARROW RESTS

An arrow rest may be small but having the proper rest on your bow is essential to good shooting. It is an integral and vital part of your bow. A good rest serves two functions: it supports the arrow as it is drawn and fired; and it assists in absorbing the shock transmitted to the arrow during firing. This is important to optimum arrow flight.

A good rest must also support an arrow in the same manner shot after shot without the shaft binding and making noise, plus keep the arrow in place regardless of whether it is shot straight down

A carpet rest is fine for shooting instinctive style.

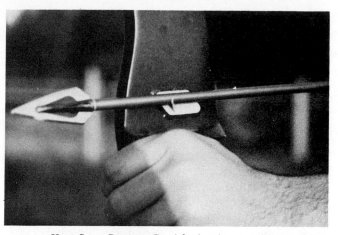

Hoyt Super Pro rest. Good for barebow precision shooting.

The Accra-Springy arrow rest is available with three different spring weights to match weight of your bow.

The standard factory rest on the York Tracker. This rest may be used with a cushion-plunger.

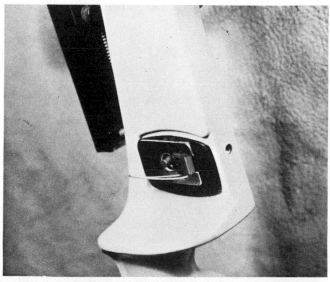

A Flipper cushion-plunger. A popular rest for hunting and tournament shooting, with compound or recurve bows.

The Star Hunter adjustable rest from Golden Key-Futura for high performance bows, installed on a Quadraflex.

or out at an angle. A rest that keeps dropping an arrow is of no use to a bowhunter.

A longbow starts an arrow with its maximum thrust which decreases as the string comes forward. We found that a simple carpet rest and leather arrow plate were best when shooting longbows or recurves instinctive style. The arrow shaft was kept close to the top of the archer's fist. Proper arrow spine and arrow plate thickness was about all that was needed with these bows. Finger pressure at the nocking point kept the arrow from falling off the shelf. At times friends and I experimented with plate thickness by adding pieces of Band Aid. Like most everything else, archery was simpler in the early 1950s.

An archer with a recurve bow who wants to shoot with the bow vertical and follow a precision archer's technique should use a stick-on rest, like those from Hoyt or Bear Archery. Shooting with three fingers under the arrow nock means he can't hold the arrow on the rest by string pressure rotation. The precision archer and the mechanical release user both need a rest that will hold the arrow in place.

With a compound bow, an adjustable rest with some shock absorbing ability is a necessity. The Flipper cushion-plunger is a very popular type, functioning in a horizontal plane and, to some extent, vertically as well.

The best results with an adjustable plate rest are achieved when the sight window is cut past center and drilled and tapped for secure installation of the rest.

A modern, high performance bow like the Delta-V or York Tracker starts an arrow at the minor draw weight, then increases sharply through the major draw weight for several inches, finally diminishing in thrust until the arrow clears the string.

This sustaining and varying shock-thrust places quite a strain on an average arrow spine. To compensate, you can choose a different arrow spine able to cope with the shock-thrust, or load down the bow to the point where it becomes sluggish.

Or, a better solution is to use an arrow rest designed to absorb shock-thrust. An appropriate rest will allow you a much wider choice of both spine and shaft weight. This enables you to reach the velocity and flat trajectory potential of a high performance bow.

The same applies to the newest eccentric cam bows. Don't even consider a non-adjustable rest. Our experience with these bows showed the Accra-Springy rest to be outstanding. It is dependable, simple and inexpensive, and provides good shock absorbing ability both vertically and horizontally. Should the spring portion be damaged it is a simple matter to install a new spring and go right on shooting.

There are a number of arrow rests being marketed today that are complicated in design and often involve moving parts. These are sometimes satisfactory for tournament shooting. Should you elect to use one of these rests for hunting may I point out that they are susceptible to damage not easily repaired in the field.

CABLE GUARDS

I believe that the Jennings Compound Bow Company was the first major supplier of the cable guard. This device was soon duplicated by many other manufacturers.

A cable guard, in its many variations, serves to offset or deflect the cables of a compound bow to allow adequate clearance for the passage of your arrow's fletching.

These guards range from inexpensive and simple to expensive and elaborate. They all do the same job. Use just enough cable offset to clear your arrow fletch. As long as the guard offsets the cable without signs of cable wear it will give good results.

Almost without exception, the two-wheel compound requires the use of a cable guard. Stay with the cable guards recommended by your bow manufacturer.

BOWSIGHTS

Sights on hunting bows were uncommon during the 1950s and early 1960s. Almost all bowhunters

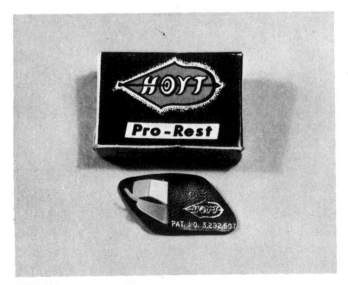

Hoyt offers a stick on arrow rest.

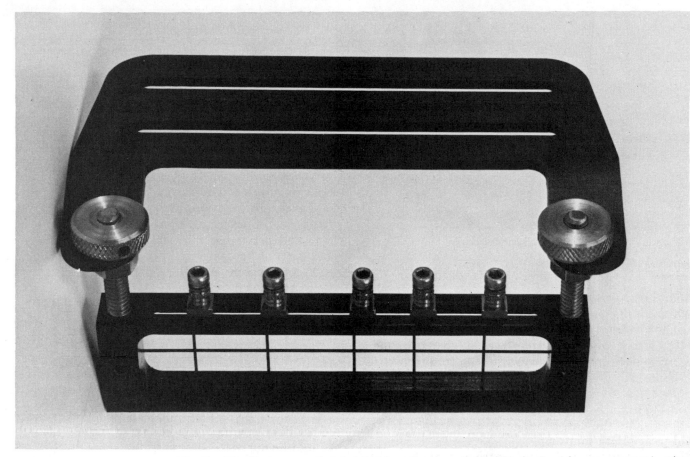

The Fine-Line Hunter, a practical deviation from the conventional sight pin. Good for open country hunting.

considered them as handicaps rather than attributes. After all, the leading bowhunters of the day did not clutter up their bows with sights and they did very well. The general feeling was that no game animal was going to stand around while the archer fiddled with a sight. Formal target archers recognized the advantages of sights and used them extensively.

Late in the 1960s the trend in shooting style turned toward the precision method and the multi-pin bowsight gained in popularity. By 1970 many bowhunters had discovered and were using sights.

The compound bow really helped bowsights take off. Beginning archers had no preconceived notions to overcome and readily accepted modern bow designs and with them, bowsights. They just assumed the two went together.

The majority of today's bowhunters use bowsights. Most proshops use sights and releases in their teaching programs. The use of a bowsight builds confidence and allows a novice to concentrate on the basics of shooting. Early shooting mistakes are easily identified and corrected. This allows the beginner to work on one phase of his shooting form at a time.

The mastering of basics is necessary for accurate shooting whether you use sights or not. Master the basics and it will surprise you how easy it is to change from one bow to another and move from one shooting style to another.

A consistent anchor point is a vital part of sight shooting. Let's start our discussion of sight equipment with anchor points and the equipment installed on our bowstrings. Most bowhunters simply draw to a familiar anchor point and use a sight pin as a means of controlling elevation and windage.

We were taught to use a consistent anchor as one of our basic archery instructions. Combining the use of a bowsight and anchor point is the simplest form of sight shooting. It is reasonably accurate and some bowhunters are satisfied with it. Many bowhunters have had bad experiences with string peeps and other devices and have returned to the original anchor point/bowsight system because of its simplicity. Its advantages are

A kisser button helps achieve consistent anchoring.

reliability, unobstructed field of view and speed while aiming. However, you are restricted to one anchor point for that awkward position shot. Most users of this system would give up some aiming speed in exchange for more accuracy.

Another group of bowhunters uses a small device on their bowstrings called a "kisser button." This idea originated with the formal target archer. On the target range it is a very definite aid to accurate shooting.

The kisser button, firm consistent anchor and simple sight pin is the legal sighting equipment of members of the National Target Association. This is Olympic-legal equipment, and the sight equipment used to shoot the York Round.

Incidentally, one part of the York Round consists of shooting 36 arrows at 90 meters at a target slightly larger than a dinner plate. The shooting distance is about two arrow lengths short of the length of a football field. That's tough shooting even for a rifleman using open sights from the offhand standing position.

A real kisser button is a small plastic disk seven millimeters or less in diameter. It is secured to the bowstring a short distance above the archer's anchor point, positioned to contact the archer's lips at full draw and normal anchor. The button is a confidence-building check on both draw length and anchor point. Most bowhunters improvise a kisser button by using wraps of dental floss or a clamp type nock point.

Kisser button users are pretty much restricted to the old target type low anchor with the bow string centering the tip of the nose and chin and a firm anchor under the chin. This is a favored anchor setup for archers with sight-equipped recurves and the longer compounds.

The most accurate method of sighting, and the only real archery rear sight, is to use a string peep. Many bowhunters tried the older style peeps and abandoned them because of the problems involved. They should take another look.

Most peeps are simple plastic or aluminum disks with an aiming hole in the center. The peep sight is positioned between the strands of the bowstring high enough above the anchor point to allow the archer to look through the hole and align the sight pin with the target. It serves the archer as the rear sight on a rifle serves the marksman.

Under hunting conditions some peeps sometimes failed to rotate properly in line with the archer's eye, and prevented him from seeing his sight pin and game as he completed his draw.

Fine-Line has solved the rotation problem with their Zero Peep by connecting the peep to the face of the bow with a length of rubber tubing. This device may look unusual on a bow but who can argue with success. It does not affect accuracy in any way. It aligns that peep correctly time after time without deviation—a prime requirement for bowhunting equipment.

Another problem was a much restricted field of view caused by a very small diameter peep hole. It is still an erroneous common belief that this hole should be very small for accurate shooting. Not so.

To increase the field of view use a 3/32 inch drill bit and open up the sight hole in a Zero Peep. Use the factory hole as a pilot guide. There is enough material in the peep to go to 5/32 inch

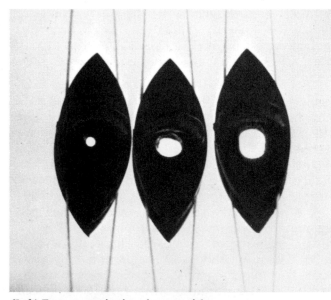
(Left) Factory opening in string peep sight.
(Center) Opened to 5/32" with hand held drill bit.
(Right) Elongated 5/32" diameter with pattern file.

The author sighting through a mechanically oriented string peep from Fine-Line.

diameter if desired. If you have a long draw and a short bow you may elongate the hole with a small pattern file. Your objective is to get that peep opened up so you can see through it quickly, comfortably and with a good field of vision.

The Zero Peep comes with a small diameter hole leaving it to the discretion of the archer as to the final hole size. String angle and anchor point both affect the hole size needed. The closer to your eye the smaller the hole you can use without restricting your field of view.

Don't worry about hole size or a slight hole elongation affecting accuracy. It is a proven scientific fact that the human eye will automatically seek out the center of a small opening. Enlarging the peep hole to your requirements will not affect good hunting accuracy and will almost always make the sight more useable. All the peeps on bows shown in this book have been opened up to 5/32 inch diameter, and the Zero Peep on the York Tracker has a slight elongation.

Don't work on any peep while it's on a bowstring. You may damage your bowstring. Use a tap handle or other means of holding the drill bit and using the factory hole as a pilot hole gently open the hole by hand. I would not exceed 5/32 inch with the Zero Peep. To do so may structurally weaken the perimeter.

The Zero Peep is the one peep sight that I can recommend for bow hunting. It is the only peep on the market with a positive means of controlling rotational alignment, and the only commercially available peep that will line up dependably on the new cam-equipped bows.

Installing a Zero Peep is not difficult. Separate your bow string into two equal parts using a pencil as a divider. Be careful not to damage any of the strands. Slip the peep between the strands with the rubber post pointing away from you toward the face of the bow. Pull your bow to a normal anchor and have someone slide the peep up or down to locate your approximate line-up point. Make

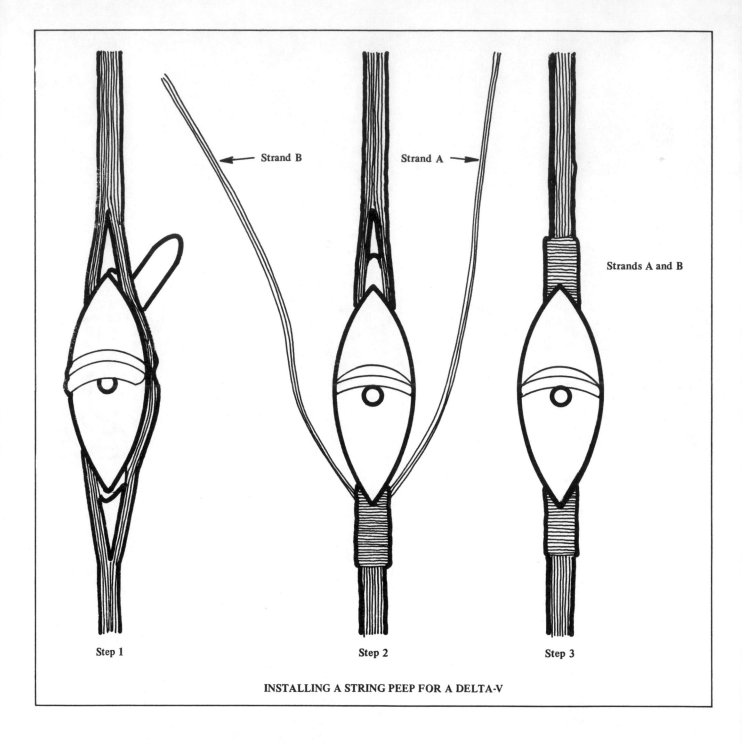

Strand B

Strand A

Strands A and B

Step 1

Step 2

Step 3

INSTALLING A STRING PEEP FOR A DELTA-V

temporary lashings with dental floss and install the pad and the rubber tubing. See the instructions provided with the Zero Peep for installation on a conventional bow. Follow the instructions given here for the Delta-V.

Draw your bow and adjust the peep up or down until you have precise alignment. After determining a comfortable peep hole size make your permanent lashings. I recommend securing both lashings together to prevent their spreading from the

vibration of shooting. This is necessary for cam-equipped bows.

The use of a string peep is legal for National Field Archery Association free style competition. It is not legal for National Target Association or Olympic competition. Peep sights are legal hunting accessories in all states.

The string peep and bowsight combination is the most accurate sighting system in general use for bowhunting. It is made to order for the precision

Closeup of the Zero Peep. The disk end attaches to the face of the bow, and rubber tubing keeps sight from rotating as bow is drawn.

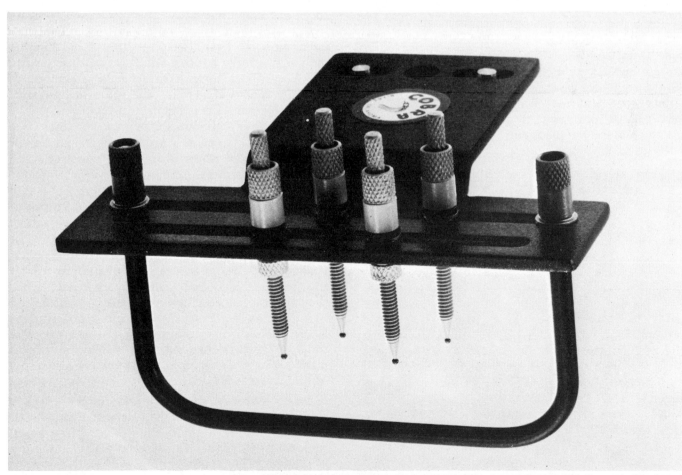

A four-pin, dual-slotted bowsight from Cobra. Note the sight pin guard. This is a typical basic unit.

archer. An experienced peep man can float his anchor with very dependable accuracy for that awkward position shot. A peep is a disadvantage on fast moving game. However, when set up properly its advantages far outweigh its disadvantages.

Most bowhunters use a dual-slotted, four fixed-pin unit permanently mounted on the side of the bow. As a start I suggest that you stay with this basic unit. It seems as though there are as many types, colors and variations of bowsights as there are fishes in the sea. There are scopes, pins with circles, pins with rectangles, big dots, little dots—the choice is bewildering. Stick with the basic fixed-pin sight until you know exactly what you want.

Proper setup of the fixed-pin sight can produce very accurate shooting. Prices of these sights range from inexpensive to moderately expensive. All modern sights are designed for Archery Manufacturer's Standard installation. All late model metal-handle bows are drilled and tapped for sights. Some wooden-handle bows have factory installed bushings for sight and other accessory installation.

Base your selection of a fixed-pin sight on the following features:

• The sight pin mounting bracket should be very strong. These sights are considered to be a permanent installation. A flimsy bracket can bend and cause missed shots. It should accept or be equipped with a sight pin guard. It should take No. 10-24 screws for rigid mounting. This bracket should have two or more slots to accommodate close pin spacing and easy adjustment.

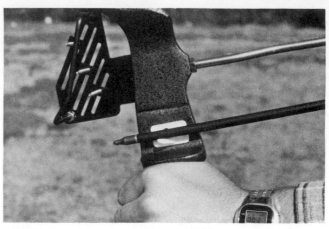

The TSS three-pin, three-slotted Model 1000 on a York Tracker.

• Check the bracket, with sight pin guard installed, for adequate arrow clearance. Bows with short sight windows can be a problem with broadhead arrows.

• Ease of pin adjustment often accounts for the price difference between sights. This is a convenience when sighting in on the range. Ironically, the more expensive "ease of adjustment" pins are the pins that come loose while hunting. Simple brass pins are best. Jam two brass nuts together on a sight pin to control and lock windage length, and use a star lock washer and a brass nut to regulate elevation. Lock your pins to the sight bracket by using a small ignition wrench.

Mount your sight bracket with a 1/32 inch neoprene shim between the sight bracket and handle riser. This shim absorbs shooting vibrations and helps keep mounting screws from vibrating loose.

Your hunting territory, average length of shot and light conditions should govern your choice of sight pins. If you hunt primarily in heavy timber or brush country the chances are your shots will be shorter, and lighting conditions usually poor. Under these circumstances a set of pins with large tips provide increased visibility, especially when they are colored with light fluorescent paint.

A Testors Fluorescent Kit from a hobby shop is very handy for outdoor uses. You can use it to touch up muzzleloading rifle sights, bowsights, pistol sights, fishing lures and anywhere else a spot of brightness is needed.

Paint your first pin a light fluorescent green. It stands out like a neon light against a dull background. The second pin should be a fluorescent pink and the third a fluorescent yellow. This mix of colors helps avoid aiming with the wrong pin during the excitement of seeing game within range.

The TSS three-pin, three-slotted Model 1100 on a Quadraflex.

Ignore the darker reds, blues and greens as these colors tend to fade and disappear in dim light. White gives poor contrast and definition, contrary to what most people assume.

The more experienced an archer becomes in the use of sights the fewer pins he will need for reference. The latest compound concepts, such as the Dynabo, produce flatter trajectories resulting in the pins being closer together on the sight, commonly to the point of being crowded. This situation demonstrates a need for improvements in sighting systems. There is a definite trend toward the single-pin adjustable sight. Most of the members of my hunting group have made the change.

This is how we do it:

• Install a Killian, Accura Sight or other high quality adjustable sight.

• Choose a pin to your liking. I like and use a simple homemade fiber optic sight. The plans and instructions for this sight pin are in this chapter. The Chek-It combination pin and level is another popular pin for this type of shooting.

• Shoot a group at 40 yards using broadhead arrows.

• Now, without changing sight settings, move up to 20 yards and shoot a second group. Measure the distance to the group center above your line of sight. What you have done is determined your midrange trajectory. If you are a deer hunter this midrange trajectory should be approximately 12 inches. This distance is a reasonable dimension of the thickness from the top of the back to the bottom of the chest cavity of a deer, or more if you are hunting elk. If your bow will stay under 12 to 14 inches at 45 or 50 yards that's good. If not move back to 35 yards. This still covers a lot of deer-killing yardage. The physical grain weight of your arrow will have an important effect on this distance.

• Start thinking in increments of the thickness of your principle game animal above or below your line of sight. This is the key to better use of a bowsight. Become familiar with the measurements of the animal that you are hunting. Deer and elk come in large and small sizes. They don't always stand around broadside, either. The ability to hold off your target is equally important as holding dead on. Become flexible and don't get in the rut of having to hold dead on. Start thinking and practicing in terms of holding so many deer bodies high, or one half a deer body low. This is good mental conditioning.

The trajectory of my 50-pound Dynabo is seven inches high at ten yards, 12 inches high at 20 yards, dropping down to ten inches high at 30 yards, dead on at 35 and ten inches low at 40 yards.

It takes little imagination to realize that we can judge or estimate 20 yards a lot more accurately than we can 35 or 40 yards. The longer shots require a more accurate range estimate. Usually you will have more time to estimate range, set sights if necessary and mentally prepare for a longer shot. One of your most important decisions concerning a long hunting shot is guessing whether that animal is passing through or just wandering around your area. Sometimes passing up a long shot pays off later with a close, sure kill.

Setting your adjustable sight or first fixed pin to a 12-inch midrange trajectory will prove to be very efficient. You have control out to 60 yards. It's a fast and accurate technique.

I use a sight pin enclosed within a one-inch round hood painted a light fluorescent green on the end facing the archer. It stands out in extremely

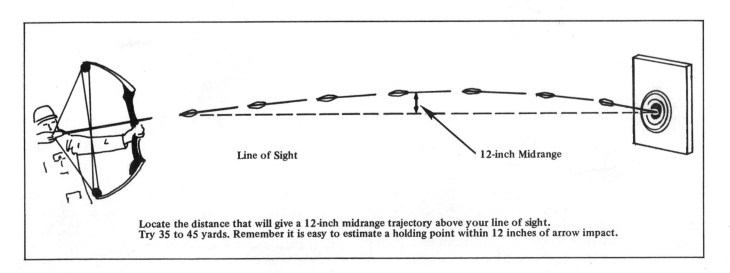

Line of Sight   12-inch Midrange

Locate the distance that will give a 12-inch midrange trajectory above your line of sight.
Try 35 to 45 yards. Remember it is easy to estimate a holding point within 12 inches of arrow impact.

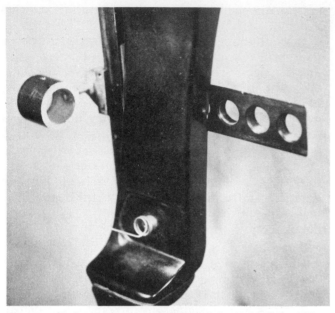

The Accra-Springy arrow rest provides good shock absorbing ability. Shown here with author's homemade optic sight.

poor light. This fluorescent ring also serves as a simple range finding device. When I cannot see my pin I use the ring itself to center my game.

By the time I settle my anchor I know just how far it is to that deer or turkey gobbler and my between-the-ears computer has programmed me for a high or low hold aiming point.

I have never known a good sight-using bowhunter who couldn't relate his equipment to the game as a means of determining yardage. This is one reason some sight users are reluctant to change sight pins. They have built up an estimating relationship and don't want to disturb it.

Select your sighting equipment with care. Think of it as more than an aiming device. Rather, it is part of the "team" blending the sight, yourself and the arrow's trajectory together as a single functioning unit. The relationship must be harmonious for success in the field.

There are many substitutes for fixed-pin and adjustable-pin bowsights. All will work under certain conditions. Most pinless sights are basically attempts at combining range finding and sight pins. For instance, if the deer fits between these lines then use the red, green or purple pin or circle, or whatever references are built into the sight.

Most of these sights look good in the store but may be difficult to use in the field. Some red, green and blue colored rings, thin lines and many sight pins are impossible to utilize under poor light conditions. Be aware of the type of sight

you need for your hunting and make your choice accordingly.

The light emitting diode (LED) pins are very popular. These pins were first regarded as the answer to a bowhunter's prayer. Alas, some of the early pins shined like the tail lights on an old model Thunderbird. They were so bright that they blinded the archer at dusk and prevented him from seeing his target.

Later models of the LED pins use reostats to regulate light intensity. Fiber optics have also been used very sucessfully with light-regulating devices. These electronic sights are very practical and fine pieces of equipment.

Another practical sight is the Fine-Line Hunter. I have not used one but I have seen and examined one closely. There is real potential for this crosshair sight in hunting, silhouette shooting and other broadhead competition shooting. It is not a legal sight for National Field Archery competition.

Accra Manufacturing Company markets an interesting scope sight for bowhunters. They also produce an automatically compensating tree stand sight. This little device can be adjusted by use of a set screw for the velocity of your arrow. When sighted in properly this gadget will compensate for a straight down shot or regulate itself automatically for a shot at 30 yards.

We tested one of these tree sights. They come equipped to fit the Buckeye sight bracket. I would suggest using two brass nuts to regulate windage, and a brass wing nut for easy exchange with a conventional sight pin when not in a tree stand.

A reostat-controlled LED sight with two pins from Twilite Products. The sight is mounted on a Graham Dynabo.

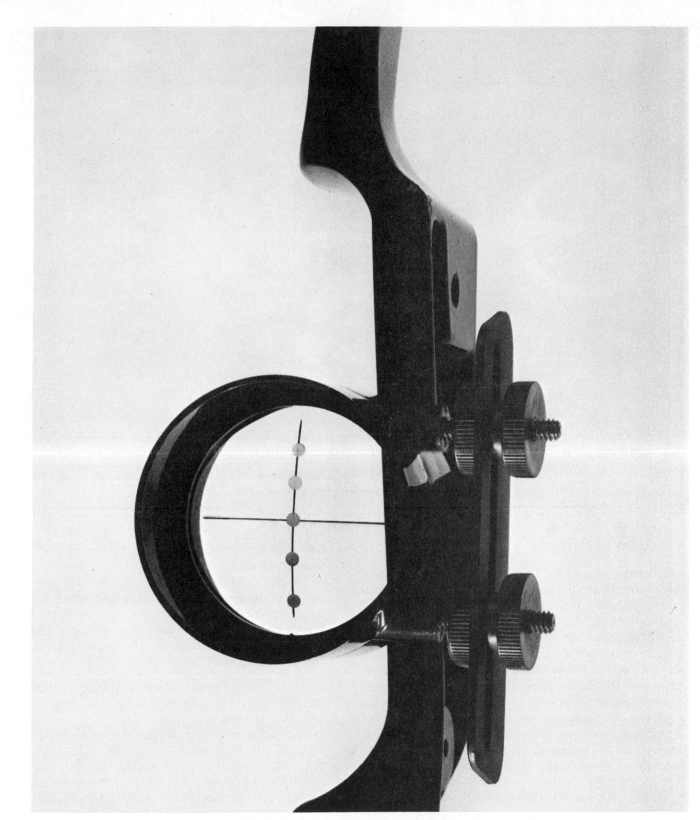

A scope sight for bowhunters from Accra. Available with zero, two or three power magnification lenses.

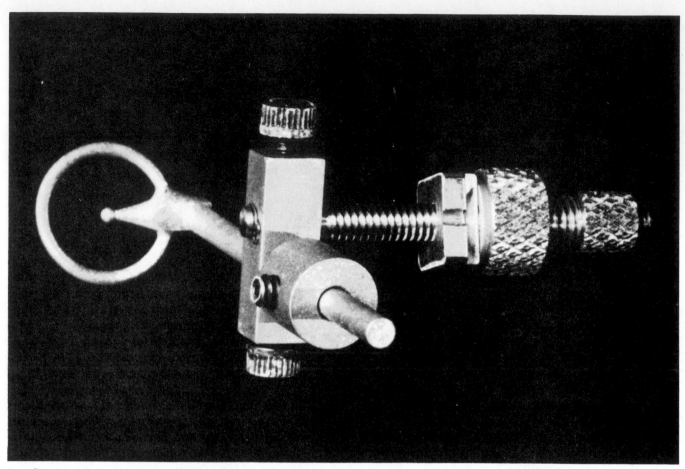

Accra's automatically compensating tree stand sight. Can be adjusted with a set screw for velocity of the arrow.

A HOMEMADE SIGHT

The sight I use for competition or hunting is a single-pin adjustable sight. My sight pin is a simple fiber optic pin inside a hood. Natural light illuminates the tiny fiber optic bud that is my sight reticle. Here is how you can make this simple sight:

1. You'll need a short length of extruded acrylic tubing. It's available in many sizes. I recommend a one inch outside diameter with a 3/4 inch inside diameter, leaving a 1/8 inch wall thickness for tapping. The tubing is inexpensive. If you decide to substitute something else for the tubing remember that lightness, strength and the ability to hold paint on its surface are important prerequisites. The heavier the material is the greater the tendency for it to come loose from shooting vibrations.

2. A good hobby shop should be able to supply a short length of .020 inch diameter fiber optic material. Model train hobbyists use a lot of fiber optics. It comes in several diameters, if you care to experiment. The .020 size seems to be the best for archery sights. While you're at the shop pick up a Testors Fluorescent kit.

3. At a hardware store, get a few two-inch No. 8-32 screws and nuts. You only need one set to complete the project, but it's nice to have spares on hand in case one gets damaged. Add a 3/4 inch wooden dowel, sandpaper, epoxy cement and a small tube of Super Glue.

4. Cut off a piece of acrylic tubing a little over an inch long. Square off both ends and polish with fine sandpaper.

5. Half way along the tube length drill a hole through the wall using a No. 29 drill. Then tap this hole for a No. 8-32 screw. The hole for the .020 fiber optic pin will be at 90 degrees to this mounting screw hole, and about 1/16 inch forward of its center line (see illustration). This allows for the centering of the fiber optic bud in the sight. Use a pin vise and a No. 74 drill for this tiny hole. Chamfer the small hole approximately 1/32 inch deep. Study the drawing thoroughly to understand the location of these holes.

6. Cut a right angle "+" in the end of the wooden dowel with a hacksaw. This serves as a centering jig for the fiber optic bud. Sand down the dowel pin until it is a snug fit inside the sight hood. One leg of the "+" will match the tiny pin hole and the other leg of the "+" will line up slightly behind the 8-32 screw hole.

7. Take a short piece of fiber optic material and touch it to a medium hot piece of metal. You will notice the fiber optic material start to swell and form a bud. Now, point the untouched end toward a light and notice how light will follow the fiber optic and illuminate the bud. It doesn't take much heat to form the bud. Use a clean, medium hot surface. I use a Hobbycraft wood burning tool. The cleaner the tool the brighter the fiber optic bud. An electric soldering iron at low temperature will work if the iron is clean. Practice making a few buds. Notice how the bud will continue to form after the heat is removed. Low temperature and removing the heat source at the proper time is important in making your sight pin bud.

8. Now to tax your patience. Bend a piece of fiber optic material very sharply about 120 to 130 degrees with the hot iron. Cut the material 3/16 inch from the bend. Gently touch the short end with the hot iron and start forming your bud. The trick is to remove the heat at the proper time for the bud to stop forming just before it starts tracking around the bend. The face of the bud should be parallel to the fiber optic stem. You will have to practice making this bud with a bend several times to get the knack of it.

9. Mount the acrylic hood on the wooden dowel with the pin hole lined up in the bottom of one leg of the "+." Using a pair of tweezers insert the fiber optic bud through the tiny hole inside the hood. Hold the bud centered in the "+" with your finger and snip the fiber optic approximately 1/8 inch above the hood.

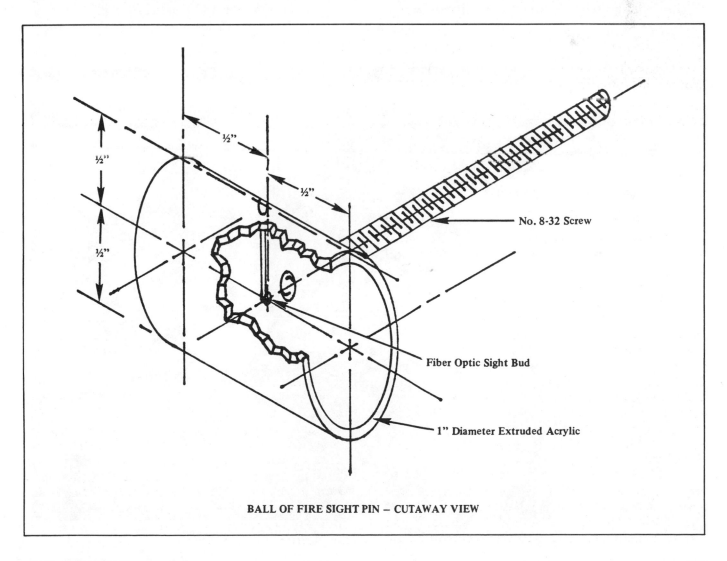

½"

½"

½"

½"

½"

No. 8-32 Screw

Fiber Optic Sight Bud

1" Diameter Extruded Acrylic

BALL OF FIRE SIGHT PIN – CUTAWAY VIEW

10. Next, apply a drop of Super Glue or fast-setting epoxy in the chamfered hole and form another bud on top of the hood after the adhesive has set. Another way is to slide the fiber optic stem up the centering jig "+" and form another bud. Make your touch with the iron light and fast. You are trying for a precise fit of the stem between the chamfered hole and the center of the hood. When the top bud fits in the chamfered hole and the other aiming bud lines up in the center of the sight apply a drop of Super Glue in the chamfered hole and seat the top bud. Be careful that you don't glue your finger to the sight. This last method results in a neater, more workmanlike appearance. It is also more trouble to make. Keep the Super Glue off the top of the bud as it reduces the light transmitting ability of the fiber.

11. Cut the head from the 8-32 screw and bevel the cut with a file. Insert the screw with a drop of fast-setting epoxy and seat flush with the inside of the sight hood. Run a nut against the hood finger tight and secure with another drop of epoxy.

12. Apply two light coats of white base paint from your fluorescent paint kit, letting each coat dry thoroughly between applications. This is the secret of good painting. Finish with a light color fluorescent paint that will contrast well in your hunting area for the final coat.

This little sight has several advantages. The hood serves as a simple range finder. The fiber optic bud takes on the color of the overhead sky. There is no blinding glare, or switches to turn on, or dead batteries to worry about. In the event you are under heavy overhead cover and your bud fails to illuminate then the fluorescent hood ring takes over. Just center that late afternoon deer in the sight hood and you are still in business. If it is too dark to see the bud or the hood it is too dark to hunt—go home.

Some experience with fiber optics may stimulate you to design your own sights. It is no problem to use LEDs if you desire, mount sight levels or create other variations. You are limited only by your imagination and handicraft skill.

Two Ball of Fire sight pins mounted on Chek-It Killian adjustable sights. The one on the left has a level attached.

Chapter 7
Shooting Style

A lot of people start bowhunting because of successful friends in the sport. Fortunately, I had some wonderful friends to learn with during my early years in archery. What we lacked in experience we made up for in enthusiasm. However, we helped each other and learned quickly.

Ours was a diverse group. Among its members were three doctors, a banker, a commercial fisherman, a realtor, a tile contractor, an office worker, a factory worker and a couple of farmers. We were all veteran gun hunters but only three members had any real bowhunting experience when the group was formed. And then there was Ben Pearson.

Pearson had booked a trip in 1952 to go after giant alligator gar in Arkansas' White River. Duane Holloway was his young guide on that expedition. Lifetime friendships were formed and Ben became part of our group as a result.

The attitude among our members was that Pearson was just another guy who put his pants on one leg at a time. I believe Ben really appreciated this casual treatment and he blended right in with the bunch.

Later, when Howard Hill joined the Pearson Company he was given the same reception while hunting with us. These two noted archers enjoyed these escapes from the celebrity status they were frequently forced to endure. You could see them relax and unwind.

Quite often Pearson would bring other famous archers to hunt the White River Refuge. Ann Markston, Jim Caspers, many national champions and other archery notables were among these guests.

You might assume that because of our contact with Pearson we had one continuous shooting lesson. That was not the case. Of course, if we had a shooting problem and sought Ben's advice it was cheerfully given. Most of us used his equipment and all of us tried to shoot as he did.

Pearson had other interests besides archery. He collected L. C. Smith shotguns, and was an excellent photographer. Ben could well be considered a mechanical genius. He designed and supervised the construction of much of the equipment used in his plant.

Pearson started his archery career entirely on his own with nothing more than a Boy Scout

Manual as a guide. He entered his first State Target Tournament and finished next to last. I believe that this was Ben's first experience around trained archers.

He left that first tournament with more than a resounding defeat. Now he knew what tournament archery was like. You didn't have to show this man twice. The next year he won the tournament.

After the formation of the Pearson Company, Ben was called on for archery demonstrations. Target archery has poor spectator appeal and, realizing this, Pearson developed his fast shooting style at moving targets that drew applause at sport shows and outdoor events across the nation. He was a combination sharpshooter and instinctive archer at close range. Later he adapted this shooting style to bowhunting. He never returned to competitive target archery.

The handle on his bow served as his arrow rest. In reality he was shooting off his fist. He gave this advice many times, "Learn to aim with your fist." Another clue to his aiming method was given to me while shooting the 80-yard shot on a Pine Bluff field range, "Try the top of your third knuckle for elevation."

Ben aimed as he made his draw and the instant he touched his anchor the arrow was gone. Many times while giving demonstrations that arrow was gone when the aim was right even before touching the anchor point.

He didn't stop to deliberate while shooting a running rabbit in a thicket, either. I watched the film of his shot on a javelina from the top of a cliff into the canyon below at approximately 130 yards and his draw, aim and release was one smooth, blended motion. Ben's knuckles served as a method of almost instant aiming for longer range shooting, and for him it worked well.

Instinctive shooting with the longbow. The arrow rest is as close as possible to the top of the fist.

This style of shooting was not competitive for field tournaments. It was not that precise but it worked on running, jumping game animals or birds in flight.

Another outstandingly accurate shooter in our group was William F. Clements. Bill picked up a new bow in my living room over 30 years ago and has since become a legend in Arkansas archery. Back when barebow shooting was at its peak, Bill won the Arkansas Bowhunters Annual Broadhead Shoot an unprecedented five times.

Clements has bowhunted in Arkansas, Texas, Louisiana, Mississippi, Alabama, Colorado and Mexico. He is both a skilled woodsman and an innovative archer.

If any one person helped Clements it was the late Jack Witt, one-time public relations director of the Pearson Company, and a nationally known archery authority. Witt, in his travels around the country, would spot a new idea. Clements would work on the idea and adapt it to bowhunting.

Clements progressed from the old space gap instinctive style as soon as he found out that there was another way to shoot.

Bill uses two anchor points. He feels that string walking (raising or lowering the anchor point) is too complicated for bowhunting. He varies his distances with different anchor points by using three fingers under the arrow to draw, or by drawing and anchoring with the arrow between his first and second finger.

Clements' high anchor is three fingers under the arrow and anchoring with his forefinger at the corner of his nose for a bull's-eye impact at 43 yards. Holding the arrow between his fingers and using this anchor point he is dead on at 58 yards.

He uses the corner of his mouth and three fingers under the arrow for 53 yards. By changing to a between-finger draw with the same anchor he is dead on at 65 yards.

Notice that his dead-on distances all fall between 43 and 65 yards. These are the harder to hit distances for a barebow archer. I asked Bill what he did out to 43 yards. "I can look at a deer under these distances and visualize the curved trajectory of my arrow to the target," was his reply. "Many times I have made shots when my arrow arched over or under a limb by just a few inches."

I have walked too many miles with Clements to ask how he determines yardage to his game while hunting. He estimates distances to key objects around him while on stand. He will pace off distances if practical before the game arrives. He is a good estimator of range and delights in saying, "Rog, how far is that stump?" This constant practice pays off.

Bill Clements' high anchor with three fingers under the arrow. Impact with the target at 43 yards.

The high anchor with the arrow nock between the first and second finger. Impact with the target at 58 yards.

Bill Clements' low anchor with three fingers under the arrow nock. Impact with the target at 53 yards.

The low anchor with the arrow nock between the first and second finger. Impact with the target at 65 yards.

Clements switched over to using a compound bow in the early seventies, but he has not as yet totally adopted a bow sight and mechanical release. All of our old bunch of White River bowhunters have taken up the compound.

Of the group, Bill Hogue of Bryant, Arkansas, has become something of a wizard with the compound. He was intrigued with the design the first time he saw one used. The fact that the shooter claimed he couldn't hit the broadside of a barn with it didn't discourage Bill. He figured he could make it shoot accurately, and he was right.

Hogue soon acquired the reputation of being the free-styler to beat on the tournament trail. While gaining this reputation he won every major broadhead tournament in the state. He is also one of the most successful bowhunters in this part of the country.

He is a student of archery with a genuine interest in any new equipment or shooting technique that comes to his attention. Hogue demands the utmost from his equipment in dependability and accuracy. He continually experiments with arrow shafts and broadheads to satisfy his expectation of good broadhead arrow flight and grouping.

Hogue shoots a mechanical release two different ways. If he is shooting in a tournament he squeezes the release. While hunting he triggers the release. He wants his release to go the instant that a deer presents the best exposure.

I have never seen Hogue or Clements shoot light bows. Both men are well over six feet tall and 215 pounds in weight. They are very powerful, active men. Hogue prefers a bow with a holding weight between 40 and 45 pounds.

Clements shot field archery with recurves holding from 45 to 49 pounds. His favorite hunting recurve weighted 70 pounds at his 29-inch draw length. Both men agree that it requires over 40 pounds holding weight to achieve the shoulder tension and feel that they want.

HOW MUCH BOW?

Here is a factor to be considered in choosing your bows—just what is your ideal holding weight? No one can answer this question without experience in shooting several different weight bows and having attained a fair degree of shooting skill. Somewhere there is a holding weight that is best for you. A compound's major draw weight can be controlled by your physical conditioning. A compound's minor holding weight controls your ability to shoot accurately.

A local indoor shooting range is an excellent place to gain some experience with bows of different let-offs and draw weights. Your first bow has a very important effect on your future as an archer. Very few bowhunters are content to shoot their first bow for more than a few months. For this reason pick an inexpensive model from any one of the major manufacturers that meets the following requirements:

● Select a compound with a minimum length of 45 inches when measured axle to axle. Short bows can be difficult to shoot while learning the basics of archery. If you are going to use a recurve choose a bow in the longer lengths. Don't assume that it takes a short bow to hunt in the brush. A 5'6" recurve is an excellent hunting length. You buy a bow to hunt with and to shoot. Rate a bow by its ability to perform on game, not its ability to be carried.

A long sight window allows you a choice of anchor points.

● Choose a compound with a full sight window. Measure from the arrow rest to the beginning of the radius in the sight window. Look for a bow with a minimum of five inches above the arrow rest. A long sight window gives you the option of anchoring under your chin or wherever you feel comfortable. If you prefer a recurve, a long sight window gives you the same options. Make sure the compound sight window is cut deep enough for adequate in and out adjustment of the arrow rest. You may decide to replace a stationary factory rest with an adjustable rest for better tuning. The handle riser of most hunting recurves probably will not be drilled for the installation of an adjustable arrow rest. If you buy a used, older compound be sure that the handle riser is drilled to accept an adjustable rest.

● Select a compound with draw-weight-adjustable limbs. Forty pounds is minimum legal hunting weight in many states. A compound peaking in the 40- to 50-pound range is an excellent choice for a first bow. This weight range can be handled by

A good, local indoor shooting range is an excellent place to gain experience in shooting various bows.

adult males, most women bowhunters and teenage youths. The 20- to 25-pound holding weight enables you to concentrate on learning to aim and develop proper shoulder tension. As you gain in skill and experience you will start forming some ideas about the equipment that you would like to own. Don't make the mistake of buying a heavy first bow with the idea that you will work up to handling it. Overweight beginning bows cause lots of problems, some of which stay with an archer for a long time. Results on the target will show you when you're ready to move up to a heavier bow.

• Some bows require changing the eccentrics to change the draw length. This can mean an added expense. Shooting experience and improved muscle conditioning often cause an increase in draw length over the length initially selected.

Every manufacturer with a full compliment of bows in his catalog has a bow with these features. These bows will have alloy handle risers and will be drilled and tapped to AMO standards for sights, bow quivers, arrow rests and stabilizers. The limbs will be solid fiberglass.

These bows may be just a little slower, a little rougher in the hand to shoot, and may be considered plain in appearance compared to more expensive, top of the line equipment, but they offer impressive shooting potential. In fact, their capabilities exceed the abilities of all but championship caliber archers to bring out their accuracy.

SIGHTING

There are three basic shooting styles used in bowhunting:

1. The instinctive archer uses no definite sighting aids but simply looks at his target and shoots when he feels that his sight picture is right. This archer directs his arrows in the same manner that you would throw a rock or snap shoot at a flying quail with a shotgun. He concentrates on his target and lets instinct acquired in practice direct the arrow. He prefers his arrow rest as close as possible to the top of his fist. He perfects his style until his arrow becomes an extension of his bow arm.

This is the style of the early bowhunter and the most enjoyable method of shooting the bow ever devised. It is a good method for a moving target; the rabbit bursting from the brush pile, and the pheasant in flight are fair game for this bowhunter. This is the province of the longbow or a good stable recurve. Hill, Pearson and Bear used the instinctive method to perfection.

2. The barebow precision archer was at the peak of his sport up until the compound bow came on the scene. These bowmen used recurves with full sight windows, along with shooting tabs.

The bow was held in a vertical position and aimed by aligning the arrow tip with the desired point of impact. Elevation was controlled by raising or lowering the anchor point in combination with how the arrow was nocked and drawn.

Field tournament archers refined this style of shooting to a degree competitive with all but the absolute top sight shooters. String walking, as it is called, is the most accurate method known of shooting a bow without the use of sights.

The bowhunter utilizes the tip of the arrow as a front sight or aiming device and draws with either three fingers under the arrow or a forefinger over the arrow in combination with a high or low anchor point.

The early compounds were not competitive with the recurve for barebow shooting. It took several years of compound development, and David Hughes, a young Texas archer, to place the compound in the winner's circle of barebow competition.

The bowhunter rapidly changed to a simplified version of the tournament archer's string walking techniques. The heavy broadhead arrows would not respond to string walking with the dependability and simplicity required for bowhunting.

The two-wheeled compounds shoot barebow with the ease and accuracy of a good recurve. Longer axle to axle length produces less finger pinch and a cleaner release.

There is an old axiom in archery that any improvement in one phase of a bow's performance will be at a sacrifice to another phase of that bow's performance. This is still a true statement but not to the same extent as it was years ago.

Practice for hunting with the bow quiver in place to get the feel of the total physical weight of the outfit.

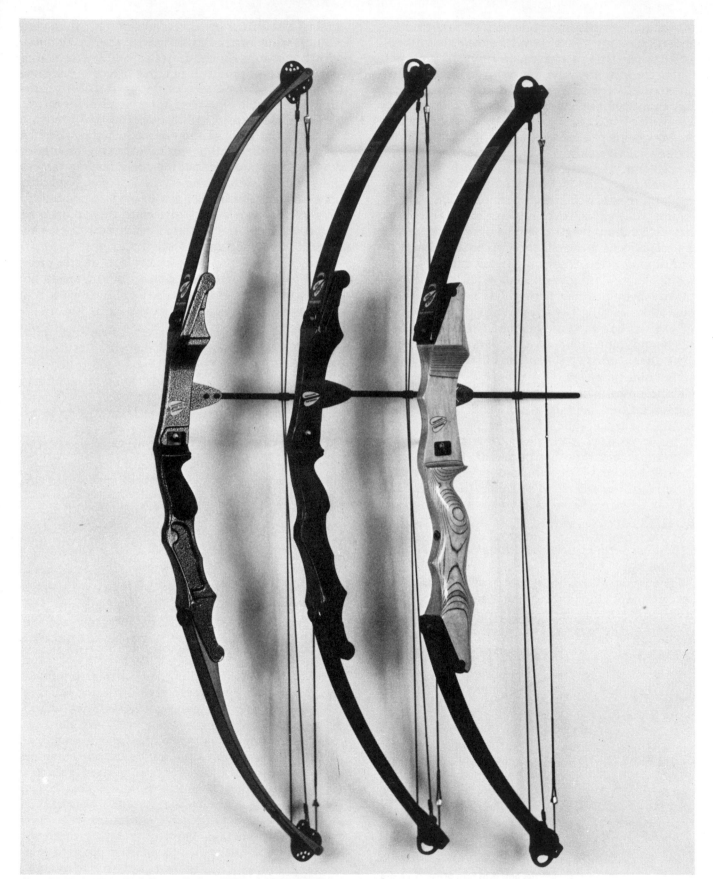

(L to R) ZB-1, ZB-2, ZB-3. Eccentric Cam "Z" bows from Ben Pearson Archery.

Better materials and engineering have produced the new concept in compounds yet the sharp string angle formed by drawing a short bow remains to haunt the modern barebow archer. Once we would have considered accurate shooting with bows as short as the Delta-V or the York Tracker to be impossible without using a mechanical release. Today you will find a number of barebow hunters shooting these short bows with gloves or tabs and doing a creditable job of it.

3. Nowadays, bowsights are virtually standard equipment. Most bowhunters use some sort of sighting device as an aid in aiming. Usually the bowsight is mounted on a compound bow, and the archer will use a mechanical release. This style of shooting fits the modern concept of archery for the new bowhunter, and also suits many of the old-timers. Bowsights are easy to use and extremely popular.

The mechanical release shooter should try both the under the chin, and the higher, alongside the chin anchor. The longer compound with the full sight window will permit you to anchor under the chin. The increased string angle of the shorter compounds makes it necessary to anchor alongside your chin in order to have a string peep as close as possible to your eye to obtain a wide field of view.

TUNING

The first step to tuning a new bow is to measure the bow in the following manner:

1. Use a bow square designed specially for measuring limb tiller, fistmele and locating nocking points. The Potawatomi bow square is a very popular scale made for this purpose.

2. Measure the fistmele or string height for a recurve. If you have a compound bow, measure the limb tiller at each end of the handle riser.

3. Check the draw length of the bow by measuring from the back of the bow when drawn to the minor draw weight.

4. Weigh the major and minor draw weights of the compound bow. Weigh a recurve at your draw length.

5. Record these measurements for future reference.

Install your arrow rest. Now place an arrow on the rest and have someone hold the bow in a vertical position by the tip of the top limb. View the bow from several feet behind the bow. Move the arrow rest until the outside edge of the bowstring and the inside edge of the arrow shaft at the tip are in alignment. This points the arrow slightly away from the bow.

Snap a bow square in place on the string with the bottom edge of the bow square touching the support finger of the arrow rest. Mark and serve a temporary nocking point with dental floss or a commercial clamp-on nock point 1/2 inch above 90 degrees with the arrow rest support.

Select an arrow indicated for your bow weight and draw length from the Easton shaft selection chart, or a similar arrow chart.

Install your bowsight, stabilizer, bow quiver and other accessories. Tune your bow exactly as you plan to shoot and hunt with it.

The setup mentioned should put you in shooting condition with reasonable arrow flight to permit the final fine tuning of the bow.

Have a friend stand behind you and if possible slightly above your arrow's line of flight. He can see the arrow in flight better if the sun is behind you.

Make your first shots at 20 yards to obtain an approximate sight setting, a feel for your new equipment and an idea of your arrow flight. Let your friend do the watching while you concentrate on shooting form. Don't attempt to do this job by yourself. Peeping to watch arrow flight can cause some severe shooting problems.

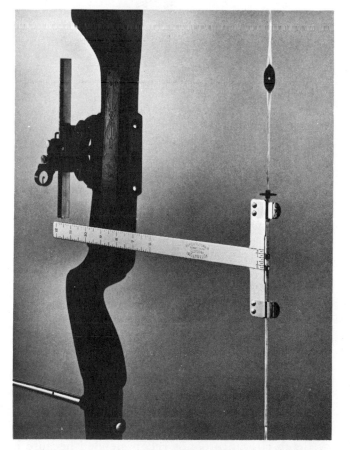

Using a bow square, in this case a Potawatomi, to measure and set the correct nock height.

Author uses a Potawatomi bow square to measure the limb tiller at each end of the handle riser.

Work on one phase of arrow flight at a time. If your arrow is porpoising (nock end of the arrow moving up and down in flight) then try adjusting your nocking point up or down the bowstring until the arrow flight smooths out. Correct this problem first before attempting any other arrow flight alteration.

If your arrow is fishtailing (nock end of the arrow moving from side to side in flight) move the arrow rest out no more than 1/64 inch and shoot again. If the fishtailing increases then retract the rest toward the bow.

If problems continue, go up or down one step in arrow shaft spine. If your arrow flight is still mediocre, sprinkle talcum powder around the arrow plate and sight window. Shoot an arrow and check for fletching contact. It may be necessary to rotate your fletching in relation to your arrow nock for good fletch clearance. Do this by removing the present nock and installing a new nock.

If problems continue, change your arrow rest to a rest with more shock absorbing ability.

You can adjust the plunger tension on the cushion-plunger type rest by increasing or decreasing the pressure on an internal spring.

Increasing plunger tension causes the arrow to shoot away from the bow. Decreasing the tension causes the arrow to shoot towards the bow.

The springy type rest is available in three different weight ranges. Use the light 15-ounce spring for bows up to 40 pounds, a medium 20-ounce spring for bows from 40 to 60 pounds and a heavy 25-ounce spring for bows over 60 pounds. The springy rest provides shock absorbing ability in both vertical and horizontal directions. This shock absorbing ability and simplicity makes this rest very practical for the new concept compound bows. The Accra-Springy rest is listed in the catalogs of all major archery suppliers.

The hunting recurves are usually supplied with a carpet or fixed rest. Drilling a handle riser or undercutting the sight window for additional shaft or fletch clearance is not recommended because it reduces handle riser strength.

These recurves have been shot instinctive style for years using the carpet type rest. Should you desire to shoot by string walking or using a multiple anchor point then a Hoyt Pro or Super Pro fixed rest is recommended. These rests are attached with adhesive backing. They are simple and inexpensive.

The first indication of over-spined arrows with the recurve will be a change in impact away from the bow. A further increase in spine will cause obvious fishtailing and slight porpoising.

The first indication of over-spined arrows with a well tuned compound will be a noticeable loss in arrow velocity followed by a change in impact, fishtailing and porpoising.

Under-spining with the recurve or compound causes an arrow to shoot towards the bow with erratic arrow flight and inaccuracy.

The latest concept in compounds has created some new problems in tuning. These bows are very fast for their draw weight. The Dynabo, Delta-V and the York Alpha Cam bows impart an unprecedented amount of peak weight thrust to an arrow shaft. These new bows handle heavy hunting arrows very efficiently.

The Dynabo was the first of the new concept in compounds and it provided a graduate course in tuning. My first Dynabo was one of the early one-limb Martin Cheetahs with a 42-pound peak weight.

Martin's instructions were to go up ten pounds in spine weight. To me, loading this little bow down with heavy arrows just to produce good arrow flight left something to be desired.

Tuning this bow with light arrows and a Flipper cushion-plunger rest proved erratic at best. Switching to a springy 20-ounce rest tamed this bow like feeding tuna to a tomcat.

Achieving fast arrow velocity with this bow was just half the battle. The bow shot a vertical group at 20 yards.

Drawing the bow provided a clue to the problem. This bow had an unusual feel as the cam sector broke over from peak to let-off weight. Any arrow not nocked tightly to the bowstring could shift away from the nocking point just enough to cause slight porpoising and a shift in vertical impact.

Securing the arrow to the bowstring by using a clamp-on nock lock above the arrow with a rubber

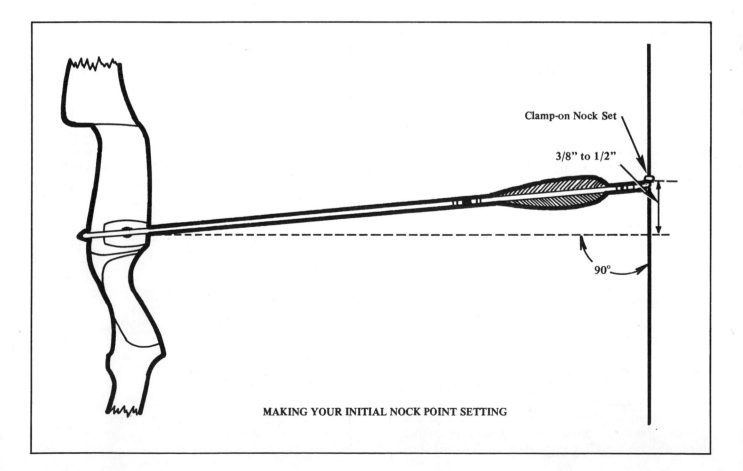

Clamp-on Nock Set

3/8" to 1/2"

90°

MAKING YOUR INITIAL NOCK POINT SETTING

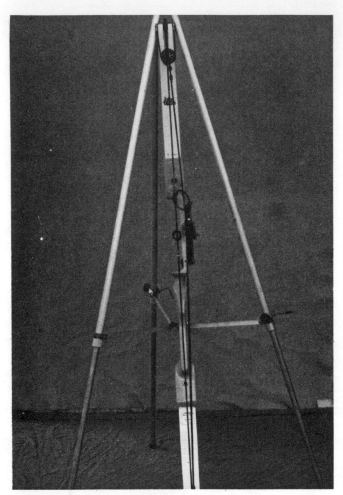

View your bow from several feet back to
determine the in and out adjustment of the arrow rest.

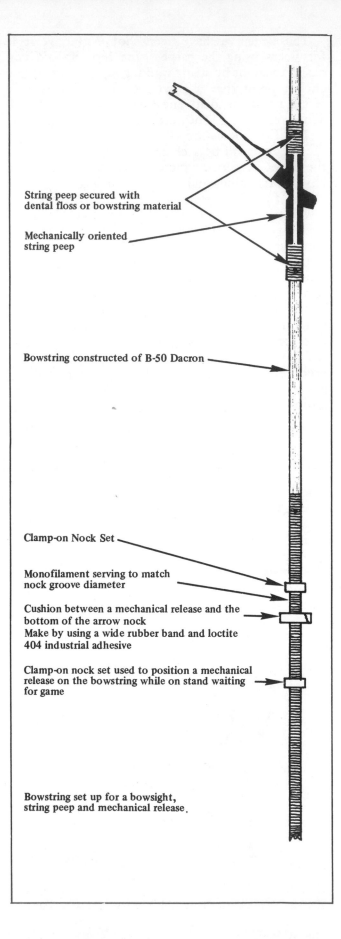

String peep secured with
dental floss or bowstring material

Mechanically oriented
string peep

Bowstring constructed of B-50 Dacron

Clamp-on Nock Set

Monofilament serving to match
nock groove diameter

Cushion between a mechanical release and the
bottom of the arrow nock
Make by using a wide rubber band and loctite
404 industrial adhesive

Clamp-on nock set used to position a mechanical
release on the bowstring while on stand waiting
for game

Bowstring set up for a bowsight,
string peep and mechanical release.

cushion just under the nock provided a lower
nocking point and a cushion between the arrow
and the mechanical release. This setup has worked
on several different Dynabos by both Martin and
Graham with excellent results.

Two of my sons, Bill Hogue and I shot the
Delta-V right out of the box with nothing more
than a dental floss nocking point 1/2 inch above
the Bear Weatherest support finger. We shot both
a tab and a mechanical release with very acceptable arrow flight.

Next, we shot the Delta-V using 8.4 metric
magnums with vane fletching off the Weatherest
using a mechanical release. After several hundred
shots there was a slight rub mark caused by the
upper hen vane. Arrow flight and accuracy were
very acceptable.

Using the Delta-V Flipper rest and a cushion-
plunger was no problem. I would recommend
rotating the fletch to form a "Y" configuration

with the nock, and the use of a right helical spiral for a right-handed archer.

This right-wing/right-hand, left-wing/left-hand fletch arrangement works for me. I like the idea and can find no fault with the setup.

I installed a springy 20-ounce rest on the Delta-V. Nocking points were installed above and below the arrow nock. The top of the arrow nock was 7/16 inch above the rest support finger. The inside edge of the arrow tip was aligned with the outside edge of the bowstring when viewed from behind the bow. The arrow fletch was rotated to a "Y" configuration with the arrow nock. This setup worked well for us shooting with both the tab and mechanical release.

I would not recommend going lower than 7/16 inch above 90 degrees nock height for either tab or mechanical release. You should approach true center with caution when using field or target points and a mechanical release. Stay with a little offset for better grouping with broadheads.

The York Alpha Cam Tracker responds very well using the same tuning setup described for the Delta-V. The Tracker shot well with a tab and the factory rest in spite of a very sharp string angle at full draw.

An Accra-Springy rest was installed, along with double nocking points and a Zero String Peep. The Total Shooting Systems Model 1000 bowsight had to be reversed to allow clearance for broadheads under the sight pin guard. Experience to date indicates easier tuning and less sensitivity in shooting when using the spring type rest.

Nock height is more critical with these new compounds compared to the old conventional compounds. You should experiment to obtain the lowest possible nock height. Once good flight is established install your permanent nock points. The use of double nock points is definitely recommended for these high performance bows.

Light snap lock tension as the arrow is nocked helps provide good arrow flight. Using two nock points insures that the arrow stays nocked in the proper place on the bowstring as it is fired and until it is ready to leave the bow.

PRACTICE

My dictionary offers a definition of practice—"To do something repeatedly so as to become proficient." Applying this definition to archery requires that you do the *right* things repeatedly or you'll never gain proficiency.

I have heard many archers vow to practice religiously until they can hit with a bow. Some-

A group of archers competing in a broadhead tournament shooting at lifesize animal targets. Note the backstop.

times they will shoot several hours a day thinking that they are really learning to master the bow. This is doing things the hard way.

A new archer should start under close supervision. As in developing any physical skill, getting started the right way is very important. Accuracy will come sooner, and with it, confidence. The chance of acquiring bad habits is less if someone is there to point them out.

Unfortunately, many self-taught archers have already placed limits on their shooting ability through repeating inefficient movements until they become ingrained. Some of them can be retrained with the help of a competent coach. They may not become Olympic material, but are sure to be better archers. It depends on the extent of the problem and the skill of the coach. If you seem to have reached a plateau in your shooting skill and are dissatisfied, look for help.

Engage the services of a local indoor shooting lane operator to analyze your shooting form. Most of these operators are excellent archers with considerable coaching experience. Discuss your incorrect shooting habits and plan an approach to improve your shooting. Sometimes correcting one bad habit will be helpful in overcoming other habits.

Have a professional make this analysis. Your friends may not have enough experience to spot shortcomings. Again, even skilled friends often make poor instructors. Just one hour spent with a skilled professional can show you a great deal about improving your shooting technique.

Work and practice alone until an improved shooting form starts to develop. Shooting in a group is fun but you may fall back on old habits under the stress of friendly competition.

Once correct shooting form is firmly imprinted it is still a good idea to check yourself out. Develop a check list and if your shooting starts to slip go through the list and review what you're doing. Bill Clements is a firm believer in using such a list. Here are some things to check:

• Stand at 90 degrees to your target. Nock an arrow and check your stance. Your weight must be evenly distributed on both feet with just enough spread to insure good balance.

• Raise and extend your bow arm to the target.

• Reach across your body to the bowstring with your draw arm. This establishes the right amount of opening to your stance.

• Rotate your head toward the target and draw to your anchor point. This sets up an aiming pattern and establishes aiming elevation by bending at the waist. Raising or lowering your bow arm to make an elevation correction causes a loss of shoulder tension. This can cause freezing.

• Maintain tension in your upper drawing arm and release your arrow by relaxing your fingers. Proper follow-through is accomplished by continuing the aiming process until after the arrow reaches the target. Follow-through provides a clue to improper shoulder tension, grabbing your bow, peeping, dropping the bow arm and improper release.

• Only the upper draw arm should have tension. Your wrist and release should be tension free. Tension in the wrist and release hand can be fatal to accuracy.

Don't think for one minute that I'm suggesting you should be a solitary archer. Hunting and competing with other archers is part of the enjoyment of bowhunting.

Once you have a good, basic shooting style down pat, then competition will provide the motivation necessary to produce a skilled tournament or hunting archer. A considerable number of the most successful bowhunters are tournament archers, or have a target shooting background. The bowhunter who shoots tournament field archery during the summer season will usually be a deadly shot on game that fall. No other form of competition provides the variety of ranges, the number of shots or the measure of your ability to place an arrow.

There has been an increase in the popularity of broadhead tournament shooting at animal silhouette targets. Shooting at animal targets has a natural appeal to the bowhunter. I believe that most bowhunters are target shooting because they love to hunt with a bow and not because they love to shoot a bow. They choose the type of target

The Bowhunter Silhouette Course is tough shooting.
Many competitors take this form of archery very seriously.

archery that they feel will increase their hunting success.

Just recently I watched a group of archers shoot the new Bowhunter Silhouette Course. If you feel that you are a red-hot archer try this course. It's rough, it's tough, it's fun and has genuine spectator appeal. You will see many competitors take this form of archery very seriously.

Silhouette shooting is regulated by Bowhunter Silhouettes International, and is patterned after silhouette shooting with a rifle or handgun.

The targets are in the shape of a chicken, pig, turkey and ram, all placed in groups of three at distances from 20 to 70 meters. The first target of each group is located on the left side of the course at a known distance, with the other two similar targets set at unknown distances.

The archer has a two-minute time limit to shoot one field-tipped arrow at each target, and must

Silhouette chicken, pig, turkey and ram targets, and a practice target from Stanley Hips Targets.

Fortunate bowhunters have a safe practice area close to home. Here, an archer practices from tree stand height.

take a minimum of one step to the side between each of the 12 shots.

The two-minute, 12-arrow time limit eliminates the characters who aim forever on a target. Now they have ten seconds to nock, draw, aim and shoot each arrow. This time limit brings back memories of the fast shooting style of Hill and Pearson.

Backyard practice provides many hours of enjoyment for those fortunate enough to have a safe area for their own private shooting range.

Stanley Hips Targets markets a complete line of ethafoam target butts including silhouette targets, life-size animal targets and a conventional square portable butt. One ethafoam target butt at a Texas university has absorbed the impact of over 736,000 target arrows.

Ethafoam is a very high density foam made by Dow Chemical Company. It has proven to be a very satisfactory arrow-stopping material. It is

light, portable and super-tough. This new foam handles broadhead arrows very satisfactorily.

Backyard practice keeps your shooting muscles in tone and allows you to shoot whenever you want. It's certainly more convenient than having to drive somewhere.

Your own range is a great place to check equipment and clothing. If there's a suitable tree try out your tree stand and practice your climbing. If safe, you'll also want to practice shooting from the elevated stand at measured and estimated distances.

PROBLEMS

Every archer has problems with his shooting. An important factor in correcting these problems is his mental approach established during his early training, and determination in wanting to improve.

There are three basic steps in shooting a bow. Each one of these steps must be completed properly before the next step can be successful. These three basic steps are: drawing, aiming and releasing the arrow. Each of these basic steps is made up of a series of smaller steps.

Shooting problems arise from violations of one or more basic steps, and your inability to recognize and correct the offense.

Let's discuss drawing the bow. Some of the smaller steps leading up to proper drawing of the bow are stance, draw weight, bow arm and heeling. Even snapshooting can be considered a phase of drawing the bow.

Your stance as you draw the bow directly affects the leverage exerted on the bow. This in turn governs the muscle coordination directly affecting shoulder tension, aiming and release.

Nothing in archery is more personal than bow weight. Don't kid yourself about how much weight you can comfortably handle. You're an archer, not a weight lifter, remember. Pick a practical bow weight and learn to shoot it well before considering something else. A bow that's too heavy causes snapshooting, freezing, heeling and many other accuracy problems.

Your bow arm governs the stability of your overall shooting platform; namely your bow, arrow rest and bowsight. Proper movement of the bow arm resulting from the release of shoulder tension is vital to accurate shooting.

Heeling is caused by putting the heel of the palm behind the grip of the bow. Heavy bows and poor physical condition of the archer contribute to this problem. Heeling a bow causes unexplained high flying arrows, and holding problems while aiming.

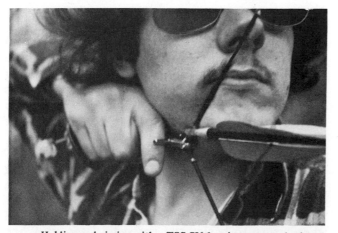
Holding and aiming with a TSS SY-1 wrist supported release. Note that the finger is not on the trigger.

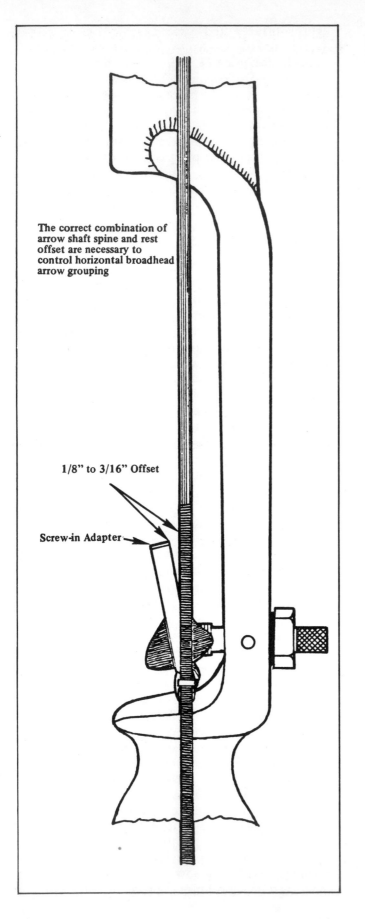

The correct combination of arrow shaft spine and rest offset are necessary to control horizontal broadhead arrow grouping

1/8" to 3/16" Offset

Screw-in Adapter

Poor physical condition and over-bowing have obvious causes and corrections. Poor visibility is corrected by changing sights or sight pins, or enlarging the hole in your string peep. Improper shoulder tension is often corrected by improved stance and mentally increasing your draw at the instant of release. You should continue the draw as the arrow is released for correct follow-through. Improper shoulder tension is an easy problem to correct.

Freezing is a mental problem that prevents an archer from aiming precisely. He can still draw, aim and hold but he cannot hold on a specific point of aim. He may try forcing a hold, or release as the sight passes the target, neither of which results in accurate shooting.

It seems to the archer that there is a solid wall enclosing the aiming point. Ironically, the key to breaching the wall is the fact that you can still draw, aim and, if you don't attempt to shift your aim, shoot with good form even if you can't hit the bull's-eye. The problem is not insurmountable. Return to the basics.

Have a professional check out your shooting form. Shoot at a large, blank target butt at ten to 20 yards. You must be free of the mental and physical stresses of aiming at a specific spot.

Work at correcting the minor flaws in your shooting form. Strive to shoot each arrow well. Don't try to shoot a lot of arrows at first. Concentrate at a slow but steady pace, grateful for slight improvements. Continue to shoot at the large target area, which you can hold on with ease.

When your arrows start grouping in a small area of the large target, add an aiming mark and hold on it. If you start to freeze again, take down the mark and go back to the plain blank target. Soon you'll feel secure enough for another attempt at an aiming mark. As your basic form is corrected, the tendency to freeze will be less and less.

You can play a mental trick on yourself by telling yourself that you are going to draw, aim and then let down without shooting. Chances are you can align the sight pin in the center of the aiming point and hold for a reasonable length of time, as long as you realize that you are not going to attempt a shot. If you can do this then try a Total Shooting Systems SY I Wrist Draw release, or the equivalent.

Now return to drawing, aiming and letting down. Sometime when you are on target and holding well hook your finger over the trigger and see if you can squeeze a shot off. If you fail then return to basics and try again later on. When you start succeeding don't overdo it. Shoot a few

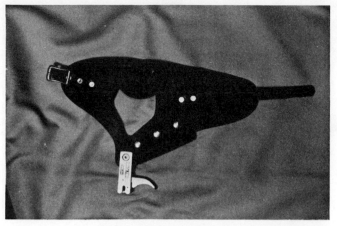

The Free Flight release system. A wrist supported trigger release from Winn Archery Equipment Co.

well aimed shots at a time then quit for a while. Avoid competition or shooting under the stress of scoring.

Freezing is the toughest problem to correct in archery. Probably most bowhunters who have quit the bow did so because of freezing. There is a good chance that one of the methods described will help you correct your problem and make you a stronger and more proficient archer.

A crisp, clean release is obtained by good shoulder tension and a proper grip of the bowstring, or by squeezing a mechanical release while increasing shoulder tension.

Grip a bowstring in the crease formed by the tip joint of your first three fingers. Drawing a bow with the string crossing the tip of each finger will place every finger joint and muscle in your hand under stress while holding at full draw. There is no way that you can obtain a crisp, clean release in

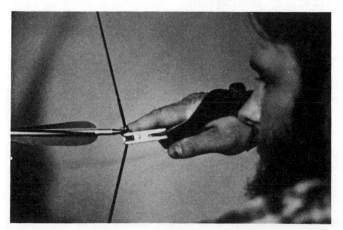

The Winn Free Flight release in use.

this manner. Draw a bow by grasping the bowstring exactly as you would grasp the wire bail handle on a water bucket as you pick it up.

Should you attempt to shoot an arrow by flipping your fingers open the flight of that arrow will vary from shot to shot. The release will be very sloppy. Your draw fingers will drag off the bowstring one at a time rather than the clean, instant release obtained by a complete relaxation of the hand as you increase shoulder tension just as if you are going to draw the arrow back through the arrow rest.

Shoot a mechanical release the same way. Squeeze off the trigger just as you increase shoulder tension.

JUDGING DISTANCE

Between 20 to 30 yards seems to be a jinxed shooting distance for bowhunters. More deer are probably missed at those ranges than at shorter or longer distances. Why, is a mystery, but excitement certainly has a lot to do with it. When a deer comes by and the hunter's adrenalin starts pumping it takes steady nerves to keep from shaking.

Yet every bowhunter who uses a sight can judge distance by utilizing portions of the sight relative to the size of the game. A close estimate of the distance will give the archer confidence in making a sure, clean shot; and helps tame those shakes.

A hunter with a multi-pin, dual-slotted bowsight has two good options built right into his sight. Learn to use either the sight pin knobs or the space between two sight pins for a practical method of estimating distance out to 40 yards. Past 40 yards your ability to hold and define will limit its effectiveness as a gauging system. It is still more accurate at longer distances than guessing.

Deer do not always stand broadside, neither are they all the same size. A big eight-point buck I took one year measured 15 inches from top to bottom of the chest cavity; does and fawns are proportionately smaller, usually 10 to 12 inches across that vital aiming area. Use these references to establish a range-finding relationship with your equipment.

The big advantage of using your bowsight to judge distance is that it's always right there in front of you. There's no searching or fumbling for another piece of equipment. To get a better idea of how this method works, try this:
● Set up a life-sized deer target and put up distance markers every ten yards out to 60 yards.
● Starting with the closest ten-yard mark, draw your bow and aim at the target. Now, at each ten-yard marker record the percentage of the deer's chest area that was blotted out by the sight pin ball.

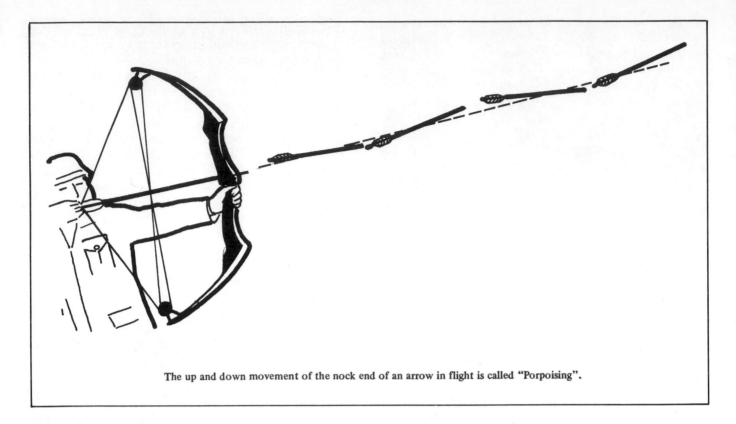

The up and down movement of the nock end of an arrow in flight is called "Porpoising".

● Or, you can use the space between your first two sight pins as a gauge if the sight pin balls are too small to be practical for this purpose.

● If you are a barebow shooter, then determine what percentage of the deer's chest was blotted out by the ferrule of your broadhead.

You can see that the potential is there. It is a simple and proved triangulation system. Always use the system at full draw to maintain an accurate relationship between your eye, your sight pins and your target. Changing equipment can disturb your relationship and your estimating ability.

Establishing this relationship is something you will have to do for yourself. Using your equipment to your advantage improves your chances for success. Choose a system that gives you confidence.

The following table may give you a better understanding of how this is done. My son Travis called the sight picture for me while using a Bear four-pin sight with large diameter sight pin balls for measuring. Here are his estimates:

Distance	Amount of Deer Chest Covered
10 yds.	10%
20 yds.	15%
30 yds.	30%
40 yds.	50%

He had problems determining how much of the deer chest was blotted out this side of 20 yards. However, at that short distance it didn't really matter. Just knowing that the deer is under 20 yards should give the hunter confidence and keep him from choosing the wrong pin.

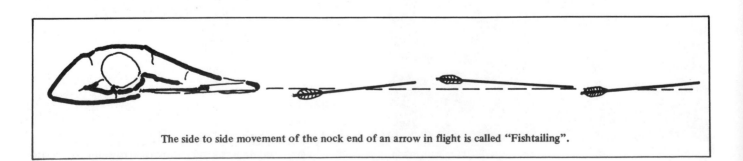

The side to side movement of the nock end of an arrow in flight is called "Fishtailing".

Between 20 and 40 yards the definition is more accurate. Over 40 yards holding can cause problems because any bow movement is magnified out at the aiming point, just as in using a scope on a rifle when shooting offhand. But, he was still able to come up with a working, practical estimate.

Next, Travis used a Delta-V bow set up with a four-pin sight for broadhead tournament shooting. We made up another table, this time using the space between the sight pins for measuring. The pins were set at 20, 30, 40 and 50-yard increments for tournament work. Travis concentrated on the 20- and 30-yard pins for his estimates.

Distance	Amount of Deer Chest Covered
10 yds.	20%
20 yds.	60%
30 yds.	100%
40 yds.	140%

The gap between the sight pins was much bigger than the diameter of the sight pin ball used in preparing the earlier table. The definition was much more accurate, easier and quicker to establish.

My youngest son, Rayburn, assisted me with one of my all-time favorite bowhunting combinations — an early Martin Dynabo set up with a single adjustable fiber optic sight pin; my homemade ball of fire sight.

Distance	Sight Picture Viewed Through One-Inch Ring
10 yds.	75% of deer chest
15 yds.	Full deer
20 yds.	Deer chest fills 66% of sight ring
25 yds.	” ” ” 60% ” ” ”
30 yds.	” ” ” 55% ” ” ”
35 yds.	” ” ” 50% ” ” ”
40 yds.	” ” ” 45% ” ” ”
45 yds.	” ” ” 40% ” ” ”
50 yds.	” ” ” 35% ” ” ”
55 yds.	” ” ” 30% ” ” ”
60 yds.	” ” ” 25% ” ” ”

Notice that the larger the sighting ring used the easier it is to define. At 35 yards my fiber optic sight pin bud is sitting on the deer's back. From previous shooting experience I know that my point of impact at 40 yards is ten inches low. By gradually raising my hold as the range increases to the point where the inside bottom of the sight ring is held on the top of the deer's back, my proper holdover out to 60 yards has been established.

Even the barebow archer can use a similar system. When he looks at a target and says to himself, "This looks about right," he is relating to something in establishing his aim, whether he is aware of it or not.

To make a rubber cushion under the arrow nock, begin by fastening the end of a rubber band to the bowstring using Loctite 404 industrial adhesive.

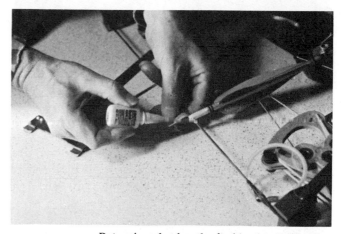

Determine what length of rubber band will roll to approximately 3/8 inch diameter. Unroll and apply Loctite 404 lightly along the rubber.

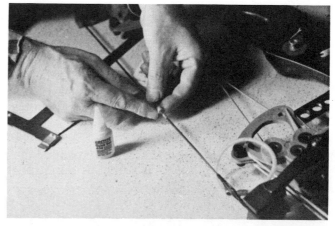

Follow the manufacturer's instructions very carefully when handling Loctite 404. Roll the rubber band around the bowstring to the predetermined cushion diameter.

A small, durable practice target from Calmont Archery Co.

I used my old Palomina recurve bow and the ferrule of a Black Diamond Eskimo broadhead to work up the following table:

Distance	Amount of Deer Chest Covered
10 yds.	Too close
20 yds.	40%
30 yds.	90%
40 yds.	130%

At ten yards it is hard to relate the ferrule diameter to the deer's chest. At 20 yards everything begins to fall into perspective. The system is beginning to tell me something. At 30 yards the deer is almost blotted out. This distance is very important to a high anchor barebow shooter. Under 30 yards he has been holding low under his target. At 30 yards he is approaching or has reached his dead-on point of aim. An accurate check on target distance is very important. At 40 yards he may be beyond his dead-on hold point. It helps to be able to establish this distance.

I have suggested several ways to establish or estimate distance while using your normal sighting equipment. You may choose to work up another system more adaptable to your shooting style.

Whatever system you use, jot down your information and practice using it until it becomes automatic. Then you can say, "Hey, that looks just right."

RANGEFINDERS

There are optical rangefinders on the market for the bowhunter. Ranging Measuring Systems can fill any need for this equipment.

A common mistake with stand deer hunters is to wait until a deer is sighted before they use a rangefinder. Instead, use that rangefinder to determine the distance to key or prominent objects around you before a deer arrives — then you don't have to do a lot of moving and shifting and risk spooking the animal.

Ranging is a bowhunter-oriented company. Their latest catalog lists two split image units made to order for bowhunters. The Ranging 50 is a woods whitetail unit that is color coded for use with their model 20/20 bowsight. This is a 15-50 yard measuring unit.

The Ranging L/R 80 rangefinder is for open country bowhunting. It is accurate to plus or minus one yard at 75 yards. Its ability to measure from 19 to 400 yards makes it ideal for the bowhunter who also hunts with a rifle. This company makes a top quality product.

I know one very skilled archer who specializes in mule deer and elk hunting in the Colorado

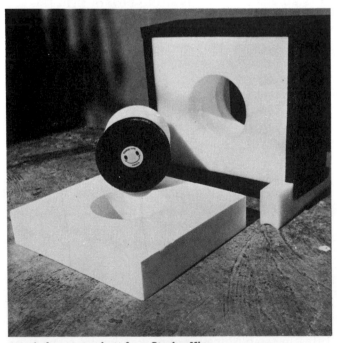

An ethafoam target butt from Stanley Hips.
Note the replaceable target center. Ethafoam is super-tough.

The Ranging Model 50 rangefinder for normal bowhunting.

Rockies. This fellow has shot professionally for several archery companies, and really knows his equipment.

His hunting method is to walk the high country until he finds a concentration of game, and then he builds a blind overlooking an elk wallow or feeding site. He makes himself comfortable and waits. A typical kill for him was the nice bull elk he arrowed at 65 yards one season.

This hunter enjoys success year after year on elk and mule deer. He is highly rated among the most accurate long range archers in this country and has made exceptional shots on elk and mule deer. He hunts bedded and feeding deer by stalking to a concealed point, and after determining the range with a rangefinder he puts an arrow through the animal's rib cage.

This bowhunter uses a 65-pound, two-wheel compound, Lamiglas arrows and Razorbak Five broadheads.

The successful oldtime bowhunter who had no range estimating devices to rely on was an excellent judge of distance. He had to be. He prided himself on his ability to look at a tree and remark, "That big oak is 63 yards away." Such statements were often challenged and had to be proved, and they were — by pacing them off step by step.

Teaching the art of estimating range is like trying to teach someone how to run fast. Some people just run faster than others. The same applies to being able to judge distances. Some archers have a natural affinity for it; others don't.

A bowhunter can learn to estimate 20 yards fairly easily. He lives with that distance at the local indoor range. It is a little wider than the average city lot; and it may also be the distance from your carport to the street, or some other familiar length.

Pick a 20-yard measurement that you can see and study every day. Visualize it firmly in your mind and start looking for other 20-yard stretches elsewhere. Perhaps you jog or walk for exercise. This is a good time to develop and practice your distance estimating skill.

Don't be surprised if you find yourself over-estimating distances in open country. For some reason, open country brings on optical deceptions. By contrast, estimates made along a wooded path are likely to be closer to the actual distance. You'll have to learn to compensate, and this comes with practice.

Once you have 20 yards down pat, look at 40 yards. Don't think of it as 40 yards; think of it as two 20-yard lengths, or two 20-yard strips laid end to end.

The 20-yard distance is important to a bowhunter. When you can estimate a perfect 20 yards, and can double 20 yards with good accuracy, move on to 60 yards. Think of it as three 20-yard lengths. Think of 80 yards as two 40-yard lengths. Always think and estimate in increments of 20 yards for bowhunting.

How are some people able to estimate long distances? Usually by having a lot of exposure to these distances and the objects involved. Many times they pick a point halfway to the object. Then they half the remaining distance, and so on until they have a distance that they can estimate accurately. Finally, they estimate the overall distance in multiples of their shorter, accurate distance.

Ranging Model L/R 80, for bowhunting and rifle shooting.

The skill or art of estimating range will require practice. Once you acquire some degree of skill it must be maintained. Use it whenever practical. You could wind up impressing your friends, but be prepared to back up your estimates.

Stanley Hips (left) and a young archer check their target. Note the belt quivers, convenient for tournament practice.

Chapter 8
Hunting Aids

Up to now we've been concentrating on the equipment and techniques dealing with actually shooting a bow. The primary responsibility of any bowhunter is to be able to shoot accurately, with properly sharpened broadheads. Assuming he can hit what he shoots at, the next step for the hunter is to assemble gear that will help him find and bag game. That's the ultimate goal.

There are many items on the market designed especially for bowhunters; some of them worthwhile, others gimmicks. We'll try to sort through the selection and discuss items that we're personally familiar with. New items are being introduced all the time, and after a few seasons of experience you'll be making your own logical choices.

TREE STANDS

Ask any group of bowhunters what item of equipment best helps their chances of success and most would say the compound bow. Few would name the portable tree stand, yet this simple seat gives them a big advantage in their pursuit of deer. Being up high lets the archer see more of the woods, and keeps his scent away from approaching game.

Deer do not expect danger from above and seldom search the trees above their line of sight unless some noise or commotion attracts their attention. Occasionally, in heavily hunted areas you will find tree-savvy deer, who have been spooked by hunters in tree stands. In this case, use total camouflage and move your stand into thicker cover.

In general, however, the hunter sees the deer first in plenty of time to anticipate its movements and get into position for a shot if all goes well. Of course, you can't dance a jig up there and expect deer not to notice. Keep quiet and still. After a while you become part of the forest and can watch small animals and birds go about their activities. That's part of the fun of bowhunting, too.

The use of tree stands is legal in every state, subject to local restrictions:
• The use of spiked or permanent stands on public lands and wildlife management areas is prohibited.

• Some states specifically require that the tree stand be of the type that does not penetrate the bark of the tree more than one half inch.

• A few states merely refer to "the tree stand shall cause no visible damage to the tree."

As to private land, the type of stand is left up to the discretion of the landowner.

The first tree hunters simply looked for a climbable tree with comfortable limbs. If they could shoot 180 degrees around that tree it was known as a really good bow tree. However, there were too many times when deer entered that unshootable area under the tree and then walked off. We still had much to learn.

The next step in our tree hunting equipment was the addition of a pair of climbing irons. Very few of us knew that there was a difference between the short-spiked pole climbing iron used by the local telephone and power companies, and the longer tree-climbing spike.

Broken legs and necks should have been common during this period of early bowhunting. Enough of us experienced a short and sudden trip "burning" a tree to spread the word that bowhunters should keep their fannies out from the tree and use irons with long spikes.

Once we were up there we needed something to sit or stand on. The homemade tree stand was born. These early stands were constructed of heavy plywood and metal conduit pipe. The rear of the stand was attached to the tree by short spikes pulled into the bark with a short length of chain and a chain dog. The front of the platform was supported by the conduit and a spike driven into the tree trunk by downward pressure on the front edge of the platform.

Tree Steps from Martin Manufacturing Co. The cam-equipped step is attached to a chain wrapped around the tree. Downward pressure secures the step. Tree limbs, if not rotted or brittle, become extra steps.

The method of attaching these stands served as a pattern for a number of commercial models that soon appeared in archery shops and sporting goods stores. But these stands still posed the same problems of getting them up and securely positioned.

Much of our hunting is on public land and land owned by the timber industry. Forestry commissions and other professional foresters recognized the rapid spread of the tree stand hunting and pointed out the danger to the forest caused by these spike-equipped stands. Every time the outer bark of a tree is penetrated, it allows access to the inner bark and possible infestation by parasites, insects and disease.

Game and forestry commissions concerned with protecting timber soon outlawed the use of spike-equipped tree stands in many states.

The Baker climbing stand appeared in the sixties, and to the best of my memory they were the first self-climbing stands on the market. At last here was a stand that was light, portable, safe and would climb a tree. It was an important contribution and welcomed wholeheartedly. Today, there are more than 20 firms making tree climbing and tree hunting-oriented equipment.

The tree stand industry is very innovative and highly competitive. This competition has worked in favor of the tree hunter by producing the lightest, strongest and safest equipment ever available.

Look for future legislation to restrict all tree hunting equipment to the "no visible damage" type on both public and private land. An outbreak of tree disease on private land can spread across boundaries to public land.

Using a set of tree-climbing irons. Check your state regulations. Spikes may be banned in some areas.

The major manufacturers are very much aware of the "no visible damage" trend and are producing equipment meeting this specification.

What to look for in a tree stand:
- It should be easily transported.
- It should be simple, quick and silent to assemble. Avoid stands with nuts and bolts to lose.
- There should be a separate climbing unit with a climbing stand.
- A strong stand is usually a safe stand, and will be less likely to squeak.
- It should be able to withstand weathering.
- It must be comfortable during hours of waiting.

Total Shooting Systems offers a well engineered selection of climbing stands. Their stands are very light, stable and the quietest stands that we have ever used. The locking system utilizes thick rubber grippers on the platform and holding pads. These pads protect the tree from damage, and form positive non-slip gripping units.

The TSS Climbing Unit is a very cleverly designed fabric strap. It is a fast, easy to use unit that doubles as a deer drag. It weighs less than eight ounces.

The Amacker is a sit and stand climber. The climbing unit is a combination climber and tree seat. To operate this stand you sit down on the seat and raise the stand with your feet then you stand and reposition the climber for another step. Keep repeating and you climb up or down the tree.

Wood and Water produces a very light, all metal stand. This is a well designed and sturdy stand. One big advantage is that squirrels can't chew on the plywood should you leave the stand unattended. I have seen plywood stands badly damaged in one weekend.

Many hunters who hunt private land, and some of the older hunters, prefer the ladder type portable stand. Usually these stands are heavier than a self climber but they allow very easy access to an elevated stand. Many hunters feel more secure on a ladder stand, and I don't blame them.

The Crow's Nest by Impact Industries is another very practical light stand.

Baker Manufacturing also offers a ladder stand in their extensive line of products.

The self-climbing stand requires a limb-free tree trunk. Either you stop at the first limb or you cut the limb off. Recognizing this disadvantage, Martin Manufacturing Company of Hephzibah, Georgia, markets a unique tree climbing system.

Martin's tree steps consist of a cam-equipped step attached to a piece of chain. Invert the step and wrap the chain around the tree trunk and hook it to the inverted cam step. Returning the step to

The Baker climbing stand is light, portable, safe and efficient. Similar stands are made by over 20 firms.

its normal position dogs the step and the chain to the tree. Any limbs encountered as you climb merely serve as additional steps.

When you reach your desired height, pull your stand up with a rope and attach it to the tree. Pull up your bow and quiver and you are ready for business.

These tree steps are very portable and practical. Anyone with physical problems should give them consideration.

Tree stand hunting can be very uncomfortable without a good seat. Get a tree seat to go with your stand. You will stay more alert and hunt longer. The hunter who leaves before the deer arrives is not going to eat any venison.

Total Shooting Systems TRC-30 tree stand and seat.

A simple, portable tree seat from TSS.

The Patsco tree seat utilizes a chain for security.

Arrowhead Manufacturing Co. offers its Quik-Rest seat.

The Baker and Amacker climbing units also serve as seats. Total Shooting Systems markets a variety of seats. By all means make your stand as comfortable as possible.

Climbing should always be approached with caution. There is always the possibility of falls, muscle strains and overexertion. Be aware of this to prevent these serious accidents before they happen. After all, you hunt for pleasure.

Buy yourself a commercially manufactured, tested and approved safety belt and use it. I have said many times that a rope used properly is better than a fall. Recognize the dangers involved in the use of makeshift safety belts. They can become strangling devices instead of safety devices.

Baker, Total Shooting Systems and Amacker all make good safety belts. There is no question that one of these inexpensive belts could save you serious injury. This is no place to economize.

Get settled safely in the stand first, then pull up your bow and quiver with a length of rope. You can't climb safely carrying them.

The stands erected on private land are the most dangerous of all elevated stands. Too many of these stands are made of used scrap lumber and erected carelessly as permanent stands. They are never maintained or repaired until they break.

Design and build your permanent stand in such a manner that it will last for 3 or 4 years between maintenance, and build it so that it can be moved.

The illustration suggests some construction ideas.

• Build the ladder supports of western cedar or other rot-resistant wood. Notch these supports to accept the crosspieces of the ladder.

• Spot drill the crosspieces to reduce splitting. Use aluminum nails.

• Make the platform of exterior grade plywood. A thickness of ¾ inch is recommended.

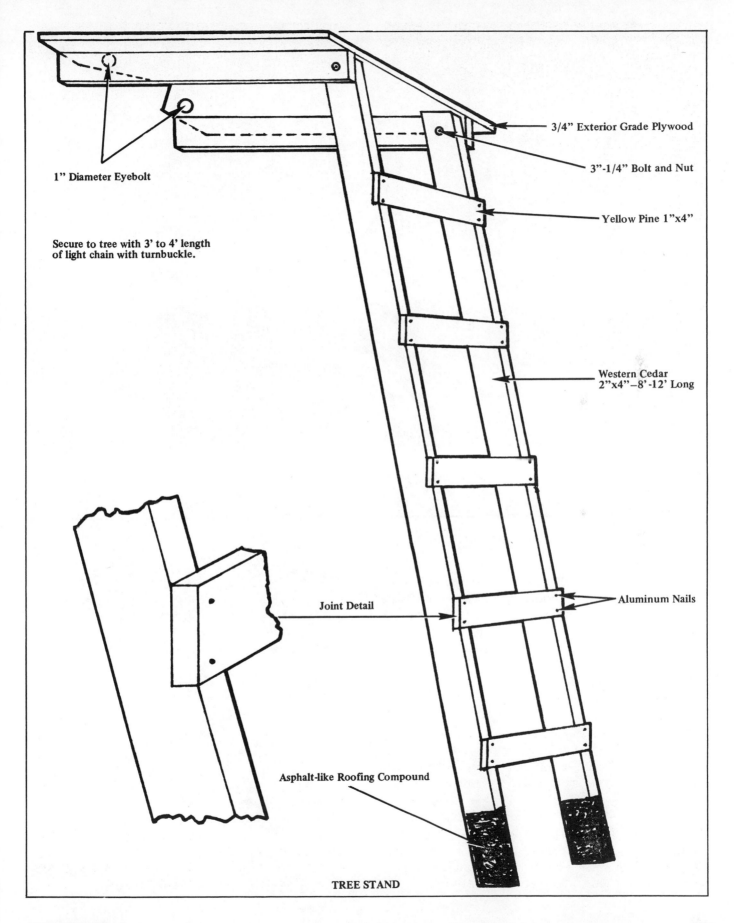

1" Diameter Eyebolt

Secure to tree with 3' to 4' length
of light chain with turnbuckle.

3/4" Exterior Grade Plywood

3"-1/4" Bolt and Nut

Yellow Pine 1"x4"

Western Cedar
2"x4"—8'-12' Long

Aluminum Nails

Joint Detail

Asphalt-like Roofing Compound

TREE STAND

This interesting tree stand from Crosman Airguns is made of heavy-duty polyolefin structural foam.

Binoculars, a spotting scope or a telescope are handy for locating game far away and planning the stalk.

Rayburn Maynard using the Total Shooting Systems climbing strap and the TSS TM-30 tree stand and seat.

Before building a permanent stand on private land make sure that you have the landowner's permission. Also, choose the stand location carefully. Does it overlook a well traveled deer trail, feeding or bedding area, or will conditions change drastically from year to year? A portable stand eliminates these worries.

Remember that climbing a tree is a strenuous activity. A climber must be in good physical shape, or he better stay on the ground. Don't climb too high. You're there to hunt, not cling to a swaying treetop.

If possible, locate your stand in the shade. You'll blend in better and there's little likelihood of reflection flashes off your equipment.

It's best to check the stand location before the season opens. Simulate shooting and see if any

• Coat your stand with a penetrating wood preservative.
• Secure the stand to the tree with a short length of chain and a turnbuckle or chain dog.
• Coat the bottom of each ladder support with roofing compound. This prevents moisture from working up the supports and causing decay.
• Loosen the chain turnbuckle at the end of the hunting season to allow for tree growth.

Many bowhunters still make their own climbing tree stands. I have seen some well designed homemade stands; however, I know of two homemade, slap-together stands that collapsed while in use. Both hunters took falls, but fortunately, their injuries were minor.

Few hunters realize the terrific leverages exerted upon the structure of a self-type climbing tree stand. For this one safety reason I am advising against the construction of home designed climbing tree stands. The material cost is always higher than anticipated, and the end result is less than expected, and could be tragic.

Total Shooting Systems and Baker Manufacturing both supply kits for the bowhunter who prefers to build his own. These kits contain all hardware, templets and instructions. You supply the plywood and the work and wind up with a fine, safe stand.

But just being up in a tree won't guarantee you a shot at a deer. You have to be sitting in the *right* tree. Using a portable stand allows you to go where the game is, so to speak.

This nine-foot aluminum ladder from Baker is another way to climb. A three-foot extension is available. Note safety strap.

TSS and Baker both supply kits for bowhunters who prefer to build their own stands, and save money doing so.

interfering branches have to be removed. Can you swing your bow freely left and right? Can you get a clear shot at the ground? Cut off obscuring brush at ground level. If you do this early enough the deer will become used to the change by opening day. However, don't machete your way through the underbrush the night before the season opens and expect the deer not to notice. They know their woods better than you know your kitchen, and will avoid any sudden, stark defoliation.

If your stand is on a hillside remember that deer going up or down will be eyeball to eyeball with you at a certain level. If a deer spots you, remain absolutely still. The old doe with fawns is usually the most suspicious.

A doe will often snort and stamp her foot in an attempt to get the strange object (you) to move. Sometimes she'll signal her fawns and they'll take off. Other times she'll relax and go about her business.

A comfortable, well-made rifle stand on private land can also serve for bowhunting with modifications.

With my stand on flat ground, I've had deer look up at me, probably trying to figure out where that "giant squirrel nest" came from. Some will give you a wide detour, or go back the way they came. Others seem to accept you and pass by unconcerned.

Each deer reacts differently, and that's part of the fascination of the sport.

CAMOUFLAGE CLOTHING

The amount of camouflage needed by a hunter depends on the game he's after. For example, turkey hunting requires total concealment. A wild turkey can distinguish colors as well as any human. And, it can tell the difference between brown and green-hued camouflage, so choose an appropriate background when hunting these wily birds.

My old turkey hunting buddy, Bill Clements, goes one step further. If he gets a response from an old gobbler, Bill will cut off two or three small bushes and stick them up in front of his sitting position as an instant blind to help break his outline. Of course, he'll be sitting against a broad tree to blend in with the background. A net face mask and camo gloves are routine, along with camo tape hiding the weapon. When possible, he sits in the shade. A gobbler can spot any slight movement from 50 yards, and is super-cautious when coming to a hen call.

Deer also have good eyesight, but it can't compare with a turkey's. As long as you remain motionless deer have difficulty picking you out from the background. They are said to be colorblind, but can distinguish variations in shading fairly well. For this reason, wear neutral, darker colors in lieu of camouflage. Personally, I like camouflage.

The camouflage pattern breaks up the solid expanse of torso, arms and legs into many small patches of random shadings, just as in nature. One of my favorite bowhunting outfits is a chamois cloth camo shirt and pants sold by Cabela's of Sidney, Nebraska. I find it just right for early fall hunting. It is also quiet. This is very important. Any clothing that rustles or scrapes as you walk or draw a bow has no place in the deer woods.

There are two basic types of camouflage clothing. One type is fairly light and meant to be worn alone on warm days, or pulled over heavier garments when the weather turns cold. Camo cloth is not meant for bulling through briars so if your hunting is rough on clothes you may be better off with regular hunting clothes made in a camouflage pattern. They can be found in heavy-duty canvas or insulated material for severe conditions, and many variations in between, including rain gear.

(Above) Without camouflage clothing a bowhunter stands out against the background and is more likely to be seen.
(Below) The effectiveness of a camouflage pattern is shown here. The hunter blends in with his surroundings.

You'll find camo clothing sold in most sporting goods stores. Don't overlook army surplus stores. They may not have the variety, but sometimes the prices make up for it. You can even get camo long sleeve T-shirts, which is not a bad idea in very hot weather. If the chamois cloth shirt gets too hot slip it off and you're still "in disguise" but a lot cooler.

Himalayan Industries can supply virtually any sort of camo garment you may need. There are others, of course. For instance, Bowing Enterprises markets their own unique cloth pattern design resembling the bark of a tree.

Two important parts of your anatomy that need camouflaging are your hands and face, especially the latter. There's a lot of square inches of surface area to shine. A thin pair of dark cotton gloves solves the hand hiding problem. You can hide your face behind a net mask or under camo makeup. Mosquitoes and gnats can make you wish for a head net in a hurry. Camo makeup runs when you sweat and is messy. Take your choice.

Whether you use camouflage outerwear or not, the rules of natural concealment apply:
• Eliminate all light-reflective surfaces on equipment, or cover them. This includes your own person. Hide that wrist watch.
• Avoid presenting a silhouette against the sky on a ridgetop or in a tree stand. Try to pick a tree thick enough to help break your outline.
• Even when you don't see game in the vicinity, make any movements slowly and smoothly. A sudden jerky movement can be noticed from a surprising distance.
• Make sure that your body and equipment odors don't give you away. Some hunters use Camo Soap, a special product, to neutralize odors.
• If possible, stay in the shade.

Deer hunters who go afield during the firearms season are used to wearing blaze orange. It is required of them in many states, and it does save lives. Only in rare circumstances, such as in restricted hunting areas, are bowhunters required to wear blaze orange.

When this bright color first came on the scene there was much discussion as to whether deer could see it. Our first encounter with its effects upon deer answered that question. Being a Hunter Safety Instructor, I was in favor of it for gun hunters for it was sure to reduce the number of "mistaken for game" accidents, and I was right. This type of deer hunting accident has all but been eliminated in Arkansas and elsewhere.

Just before firearms deer season I bought several inexpensive vinyl plastic blaze orange vests for myself and my sons in keeping with the new regula-tion. It didn't take long on opening day before we realized that we were being spotted by every deer that came within sight.

This happened to a large percentage of our deer hunting group that morning. Some members reported no apparent change in deer behavior. However, those hunters wearing the shiny plastic vests reported the opposite. Those vests looked to be blaze orange in the store but were a reflective bright silvery-orange color in natural sunlight. They reflected light like mirrors.

However, those hunters wearing blaze orange fabric did not alert deer. This fabric does not reflect light; yet other hunters could see it distinctly.

Since that first blaze orange firearms deer season most of our group have switched to high quality vests made of Burlington's 10-Mile Cloth.

A bowhunter using a Crow's Nest portable ladder stand from Impact Industries. Camo clothing also works in the winter. The hunter's outline is broken by the tree trunk. However, any movements should be made slowly and smoothly.

ANIMAL SCENTS

Fur trappers have used scents to attract animals for centuries. They have it down to a science. Depending on the animal species sought, the scent can allude to food, sex, territorial rights or merely arouse the creature's curiosity. The fur trapper has a host of scents to pick from; and many trappers blend their own secret lures. By comparison, the deer hunter is a rank amateur in the use of scents.

The post-World War II increase in deer populations across Texas and the southern states was accompanied by an invasion of deer hunters into the woods. This stimulated a whole new industry dealing with products geared to deer hunting. Included were various "buck lures."

Deer hunters have a well-deserved reputation for trying almost anything to bag a buck. The stories surrounding the use of these early deer lures run from the humorous and odorous to success and dismal failure. Anyway, scents were something new to deer hunters and many bowhunters tried them. Results were mixed, to put it mildly.

The Amacker Deer Thief sit and stand climbing unit.

The lure manufacturers had no reason to do extensive research. Their products were selling, so why pursue it any further. The lures were packaged with a few general instructions, leaving it up to the imagination of the hunter as to specific application.

If you bought several different brands you might find instructions and information about the product such as the following:
"Taken from captive doe deer at the peak of estrus."
"Use sparingly — Just a few drops — One bottle lasts all season."
"For best results, use generously."
"Sprinkle a few drops on your clothing or boots."
"Never place on your person. Deer seek the scent source."
"Squeezed from choice fermented apples."
"Contains doe urine, animal glands and musks, and other secret ingredients."

It's obvious from these often contradictory statements that the early scent products were not well researched, and the hunter was pretty much on his own.

The first-time user of a bottle of deer lure usually buys the stuff just to see if it works. If he kills a deer, fine. He credits the lure. If he doesn't get a deer he says the lure is worthless.

Bill Hogue summed up the use of scents very well with one statement: "Some of my worst failures and my most brilliant successes can be directly attributed to the use of scents."

Before using any deer attractor, consider the following:
• Prepare yourself, your clothing and your equipment to be as odor free as possible. Your chances of success are diminished if your immediate surroundings are flooded with odors that will make deer suspicious.
• Understand deer habits, and recognize that scent is an important means of communication for deer, as well as a natural alarm system.
• Choose the proper scent for the right place at the right time.

A mature buck is one that has survived one or more hunting seasons. Perhaps he was just lucky the first year, but now he's older with more experience and better prepared to avoid hunters. A deer knows its territory intimately; what it smells like and where those odors can be expected. Any deviation from the normal pattern is suspect. A deer encounters many different smells in its home habitat. All have been classified in the animal's memory banks as to potential danger.

Many deer smell human scent every day without becoming paranoid. They go on the alert until they pinpoint the source, and then continue on their way or fade back into cover. Most of the time human sounds and odors such as a farmer working in the field, vehicular traffic, car doors slamming in a driveway, dogs barking, and so forth are accepted parts of that particular environment. The deer pay no attention as long as the sounds are concentrated where they are encountered during the animals' normal routine.

The thing that makes deer nervous is when they receive a strange unidentified scent on the breeze, or a familiar scent where it's not normally found. The same applies to sound. Slam a car door a half mile from any farmhouse before dawn on opening day and every deer within earshot is alerted. Some may even remember that the only time cars park there is during deer season. I have no way of verifying this, of course, but I wouldn't put it past them.

Some examples of out-of-place scents that put a buck on guard are:

• Cypress scent up on a high ridgetop, when all the cypress is down in the swamp on the other side of the deer's territory.

A Patsco tree stand folded for carrying.

A bowhunter using a Patsco tree stand and seat.

• Human scent around the farm in places where the farmer does not normally go every day.
• Skunk scents where there are no skunks. Skunks are usually common in deer habitat, but not always. Your deer may have never smelled a skunk before in his life.
• Using pine or cedar scent in an area where these trees are not found, or where these scents are not normally encountered in the animal's daily travels.

The point is obvious. Use something indigenous to the immediate area.

The bottled scents of use to the bowhunter can be classed as sex scents, curiosity or calming scents and cover scents to blank out human odor.

Right at this point I want to give a word of caution: never place an animal urine scent or any scent containing animal glands or musk on your clothing, boots or equipment.

These scents can be detected by domestic animals for days and weeks after you think the scent has dissipated. These scents can bring on a

Regardless of the stand, a safety belt is recommended.

works, but other times all the hunter hears is a snort and the crashing of brush as the buck clears out of there fast.

The best place to use a sex scent is on a very active scrape. Make sure that you have a true sex scent. The label should refer to the rut and the estrous cycle. Beware of animal gland and other secret ingredient lures near a good scrape. You don't want to mess it up with some junk. Give that buck what he expects to find on his scrape. And he wants it right there, not scattered all over the mountainside. Remember, you are trying to imitate natural conditions.

With the start of estrus instinct begins to control that doe. She has only a few hours to establish contact with a breeding buck. She is going to make her urine deposit on that buck's scrape and then stay close for a while. Sure, a buck will sometimes follow her trail but he'll be on the alert while looking for the doe. Sometimes a strong "doe-in-heat" scent away from a scrape is alarming to a young, immature buck or doe. Sprinkle that hot scrape with a pure sex scent and you will have the most natural magnet to pull them in. Adding a urine scent to a scrape merely tells the buck that a "passing doe" has honored his scrape. It could serve as a curiosity or calming scent in this instance. If your stand is positioned properly and you are on the ball you might fill your tag. Straight doe urine is the most natural and useful scent available to the gun and bowhunter. Use this scent to attract, to calm, or position a buck for a shot.

It is perfectly natural for a buck to check out urine deposits as he comes across them. This is a means of communication, and a way of keeping track of the other deer in his territory. A mature buck recognizes the odor of the resident deer. He

seemingly unprovoked attack from cattle or horses and cats or dogs a long time after you have forgotten about applying the scent.

A friend of mine told me that he could smell a sex scent on his boots on moist days for three years. Max Zeiner and I once watched seven Texas range bulls go into a rage over a bit of scent. Bill Clements and I had an afternoon hunt messed up by some cattle that we did not know were around until they appeared suddenly. There can be very real danger from the use of these scents. Be careful.

The sex scents are the most popular scents on the market. The labels generally read, "Taken from doe deer at the peak of estrus." Today people feel that anything containing or pertaining to sex should be the best so this is the one hunters buy.

Many hunters lay a trail with this scent, and some simply open the container and put it on the ground hoping that an amorous buck will home in on it. This haphazard use of scent sometimes

Closeup of a good, commercially made safety belt.

Carry scent in a small glass jar with a wide screw on top.

For example, bobcat or coyote urine has value, assuming that they are found regularly in your deer hunting area. A passing deer will often stop and sniff the urine deposit of another animal species; except that of humans — that gives them a fright.

Food scents have little value to the bowhunter. The urine scents are far superior for attracting and calming jittery deer. Remember that urine is an animal's calling card. Skunk scent is the latest addition to a bowhunter's bag of scents. There are

will be alerted by and frequently investigate the odor of a ncw doc on his "home turf." This is why your doe urine scent must be the real thing. A buck rarely follows some odd-smelling concoction.

The odor or a recent urine deposit can calm and reassure a nervous buck. He knows that everything is all right, or else that urine would not be there.

When I say "a urine deposit" I'm not talking about half a pint. A dozen or so drops go a long way. Put them on a small piece of dark rag and position it so the buck will offer a good shot as he stops to investigate. I tie it about knee-high on a piece of brush.

The odor strength of bottled urine seems to increase with age. A dozen drops should easily retain their potency for a full hunting day.

Whatever scent you use be sure to carry it out with you when you leave. You don't want the animals coming to it when you're not there. They'll lose interest and further use of scents at that stand site will be ineffective.

Use a small glass jar with a wide screw-on top to transport your scent cloth. Remember, don't get the scent on your clothing, boots or equipment.

The use of other animal urine scents sometimes pays off for the few seconds necessary to make a shot. A good bowhunter needs imagination and initiative. If there are lots of other hunters around, and all using scent, try something different. Or, if the deer are not responding to the regular scents, give them something new.

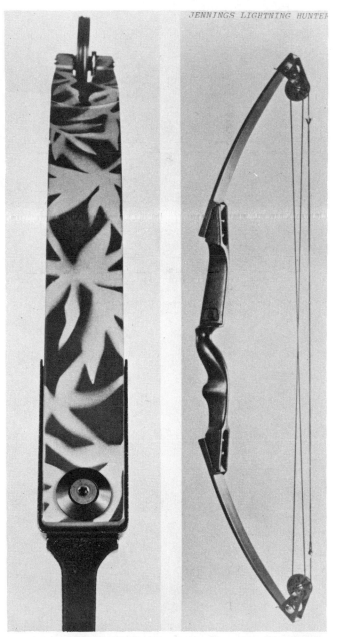

JENNINGS LIGHTNING HUNTER

The Jennings Lightning Hunter bow in a camouflage pattern. Most makers will supply similar finishes on special order.

The Trebark camouflage pattern from Bowing Enterprises is different and especially useful against large trees.

some experimenters who say that skunk scent cannot cover human scent, and others say that it is the only scent that will. I say that you can't argue with success. Many hunters swear by the stuff. This is one scent that you can use to cover your trail. Tie a rag to a short piece of string and let it swing in the air as you walk to your stand. Position this rag ten to fifteen yards downwind of your stand and opposite a scrape or the spot that you have sprinkled with doe urine. Make sure that you have a clear shot at the skunk rag for it often receives a thorough checking.

Keep upwind from the odor of skunk scent. Continued exposure to this scent has made some bowhunters sick.

Never open a container of these animal scents in your home, car or hunting camp. Just one little accident with an open bottle and you have a major problem. Try selling a used car that smells like a zoo.

In any industry there is always a leader. The headman in the animal scent industry, and enjoying every whiff, is Tink Natham, owner of Safariland Archery Corporation, and a bowhunter with years of experience with North American and African game. Tink has researched the use of scents for the bowhunter very well, and markets a complete line of pure basic scents.

Bowhunting does things to people. I have never met a successful bowhunter who wasn't continually searching for a better way to improve his method of hunting and increase his knowledge of nature.

Tink Natham combines these bowhunter traits in a very successful business. Tink recognized the usefulness of the chlorophyll pill for the bowhunter. Natham's firm markets these pills especially for the bowhunter under the brand name, Tink's Non-Scent.

The chlorophyll pill has been known to the medical profession for many years. Medical uses of this drug are to eliminate the powerful odors from patients suffering from some dreaded diseases. Another use is to control bad breath from gum diseases, and eating strong foods.

Some people have a very strong personal body odor. They can take a bath, wear fresh, clean clothes and still smell as if they had never had a bath, all within an hour's time. The chlorophyll pill is a blessing to these unfortunate people. The pill is taken internally for several days before and throughout the hunt. It does not stop you from perspiring, but serves to control the odor of the perspiration as it occurs. It does not eliminate the need for a bath because bacterial action on your perspiration will eventually cause an odor build-up. Anyway, who wants to go several days without a bath?

Dr. Jim Smith introduced our bowhunting group to the chlorophyll pill more than 25 years ago. Our experiences with the pill have been encouraging. As long as we kept ourselves, our clothing and our equipment clean the pills worked, as far as we could tell. I don't know of any controlled experiments to prove our assumption, and it would be a very interesting project for science. We do know that the pill does control odors beyond human ability to detect them, but an animal's sense of smell is far greater than ours.

Tink produces a number of bowhunter products. One of them is his advertising publication called "Tink's Tigerskin." This newspaper is full of technical advice, hunting tips, product updates, and makes for interesting reading. Sure, Old Tink beats

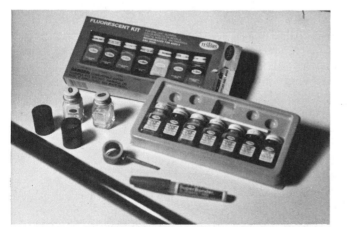

Although not overt hunting aids, bright paints are handy for touching up sights on bows and guns.

Many manufacturers offer animal scents, including lures to attract deer, and skunk scent to disguise human odors.

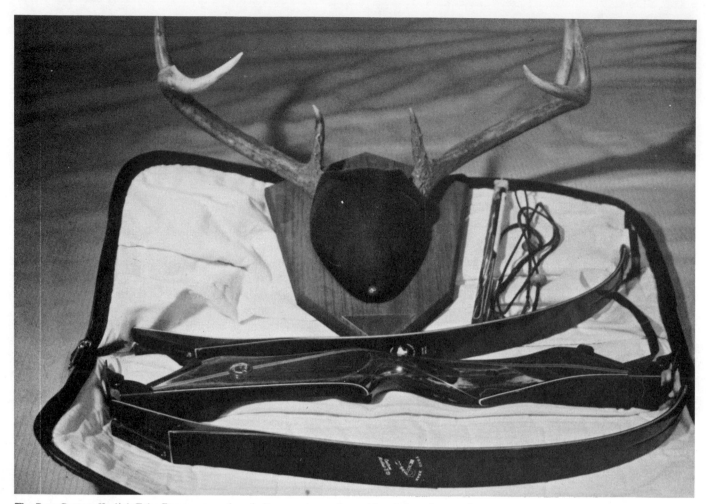

The Bear Custom Kodiak Take-Down recurve bow in its case. A popular and handy bow for travelers.

his own drum but there is a four letter word used on the front page upper right-hand corner — FREE.

Insect pest activity is the curse of warm weather bowhunting. Sometimes hunting in the early fall without the use of insect repellents is an impossibility.

I have thought of the Indians many times and wondered how they handled the insect problem. We assume they had some kind of a natural repellent. If their repellent could be duplicated it would be much more compatible with bowhunting than the unnatural odor of modern chemical repellents.

Each time this problem is discussed with other bowhunters we wind up agreeing that they prob-

ably used a natural repellent made from the crushed leaves of local plants. Rubbing yourself with crushed mint, cedar or pine leaves does a fair job against insects, and to a degree is a reasonable cover scent as well.

A word of caution: oils placed on the skin from the crushed leaves of many wild plants can irritate and cause skin rashes, and even allergic reactions with some susceptible people.

When insect infestation is heavy you have little choice but to use head netting and climb a little higher. If you have to use a modern repellent use towelettes and you can prevent saturating your hunting area with repellent spray as you would with a pressure can.

Chapter 9
Game Contact

Many of the bowhunters in this country first started hunting with a gun. A large percentage hunt with both the gun and the bow. The attractions of bowhunting are many: lengthy seasons encompassing good weather conditions; special archery hunts in areas of high game populations; and just being in a quiet and uncrowded woodland with a capable sporting weapon testing your skills and strategy against a great game animal.

Beginning bowhunters feel that a high degree of skill with the bow should be the first step to early success. Shooting the bow is fun and it is only natural to concentrate on learning to shoot well before taking to the woods.

Being a highly skilled archer and using the very best of equipment will contribute only a small amount to your success as you start your bowhunting career. Later, as the conversion from gunhunter to bowhunter occurs, and you learn other bowhunting skills, the use of top performing equipment combined with topnotch shooting skill will contribute very much toward your being a skilled and successful bowhunter.

The ability to travel the woods and locate areas containing game, and the hotspots or concentration points of the game within those areas, is the first real step to serious bowhunting.

You cannot be a successful bowhunter without game. However, just being a good woodsman and having access to game concentrations can be a frustrating experience to a new bowhunter.

Too many new bowhunters substitute a bow for a rifle and continue to hunt as if they were using a rifle. These hunters quickly discover that this doesn't work. An easy shot for a rifle is often an impossible shot for a bow. A small twig that would be brushed aside by a bullet presents an insurmountable obstacle to a bowhunter. Any arrow contact would send the shaft off target. A buck could be standing broadside 20 yards away and yet be perfectly protected if there's no way an archer can get an arrow through the intervening foliage. It's not enough to get close to a deer. The animal must present a clear shot for the bowhunter to stand a chance.

Pre-season scouting and pruning can open shooting lanes from the stand to well traveled deer trails. Preparedness pays off.

If you're a stalk hunter you accept each opportunity as it comes up. If luck is with you there'll be a clear shot. Most of the time there won't be, but if the animal hasn't been spooked it may move to your advantage. Stalk hunting is a real challenge.

A stand hunter can help his own cause by pruning interfering brush. Move up into a tree stand and direct your partner on the ground. Well used deer trails can be exposed by judicious trimming. Just a few limbs or dead branches removed here and there can make an important difference.

Also, don't forget that the woods are constantly changing. A good clear target slot last year may have saplings blocking it this year. This is another good reason for pre-season scouting. Just as important as finding game sign is checking the actual shooting scene. Limbs fall off trees, entire trees get blown over and the trail may now take a detour, possibly away from last season's favorite tree stand.

Checking a familiar area will reacquaint you with the lay of the land. It's easy to forget from year to year. It's also very embarrassing to walk into the woods before dawn on opening day and not remember your way to your stand. By going over the route in the daylight certain landmarks can be marked fresh in your memory to guide you on that all important morning hike.

Let's assume that you'll be hunting in new territory, or just getting started in bowhunting. What do you look for? Right off let me say that here's where an experienced partner can be worth his weight in gold; and add in his cousin's weight as well.

Sometimes it takes a keen eye to pick out tracks, droppings, rubbed trees, scrapes, nipped off tree buds, places where deer fed on acorns, where they crossed over, under or through fences or rock walls to reach croplands, where they bed down and their most likely travel routes. And, an experienced hunter can estimate how many deer are in the area. So, if at all possible, go with an old hand at the game.

Lacking this option, you're still not lost. If there's a bowhunting club nearby, apply for membership. An active, hard working club probably maintains its own shooting range. If it's a field range that's okay; shoot field points. You're there to improve shooting form, range estimating skills and other hunting techniques.

Many clubs have put in facilities for shooting broadheads, and that's very useful. However, I think that the 14-target field range with marked yardage is a fine training ground to learn distance estimation.

Membership in an active club can improve any phase of your archery technique. Good instruction is readily available, the motivation is there, and fellowship and fun are a big part of such a group. You'll find that these people not only talk a good game but practice what they preach. If you want to become successful at bowhunting, associate with experienced bowhunters.

Along with joining a bowhunting club, I would suggest contacting the Hunter Safety Coordinator of your game and fish commission and taking the Hunter Safety Course, required in some states. The National Field Archery Association Bowhunter Education Course is also very worthwhile. These courses will expand your knowledge of game habits and add to your confidence in the woods.

My next suggestion is that you do a lot of research. Libraries and book stores are stocked with references on woodcraft, hunting and outdoor survival. They also have books dealing with how to

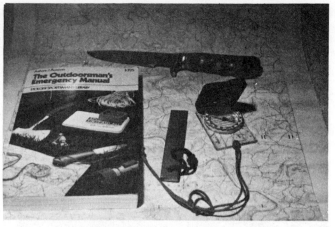

A topographical map, compass, knife, sharpening steel and reference manual contribute to becoming a better woodsman.

hunt for specific animals with both the gun and bow. The gun hunter is looking for the same clues as the bowhunter. After all, you're both after the same animal. So don't dismiss books written for gun hunters.

Part of your research should be reading maps of your hunting area. Topographical maps and U.S. Corps of Engineers quadrangle maps are very handy for showing how your hunting spot relates to the surrounding landscape. Maps showing contour lines and marshes are particularly useful. Deer, like humans, like to take the easiest route through the woods. Often you'll be able to predict logical runways and potential stand sites.

In addition to the printed map, make your own detailed record on a hand-drawn map. Indicate trails, farmland with crops attractive to deer, sites of active scrapes, where you've seen deer, creeks, springs, cliffs too steep to climb, saddles between ridges, swamps and the thickest cover patches, abandoned orchards, stands of oak and beech trees (or other mast-producing species in your region) and in general all the facts you can assemble about this particular deer habitat.

By the time your map is filled out you'll have no fear of getting lost or losing your bearings, It's surprising how many hunters hate to go out of sight of a road or their four-wheel-drive vehicle. They're either too lazy to hike back in a mile or more, or they're afraid of getting lost, or both. We've seen some good stands that were a bowshot away from a paved road, but usually the best hunting areas are reached by walking a fair distance.

When possible, talk to local farmers and landowners. Some of the finest deer racks come off of private land. You may be turned down flat, but

Associating with experienced bowhunters is an excellent way to learn hunting techniques and sharpen your skills.

Bill Hogue with a trophy Arkansas whitetail. Seeing a rack like this come by is almost guaranteed to give anyone buck fever.

VITAL AREAS OF A DEER

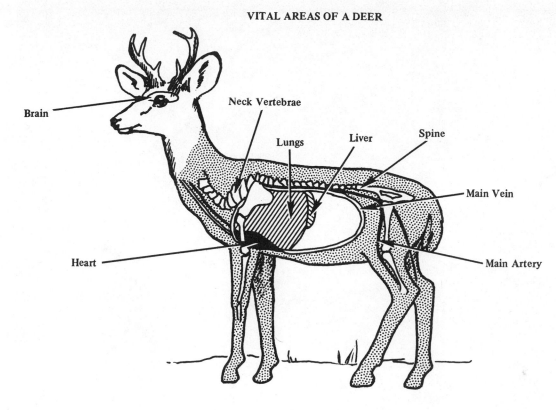

Brain

Neck Vertebrae

Lungs

Liver

Spine

Main Vein

Heart

Main Artery

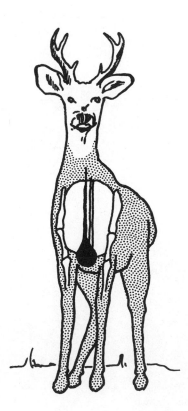

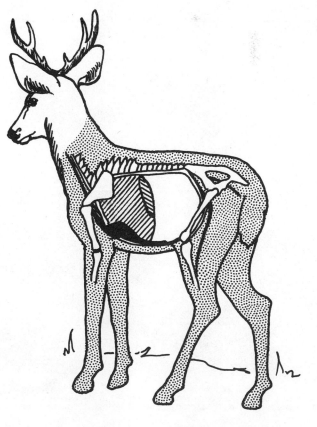

When an animal looks directly at you, freeze. If it does not catch your scent it will probably relax and move off.

don't hesitate to ask permission to *hunt with a bow.* Emphasize the outstanding safety record of bowhunters, and explain that bowhunting poses no danger to livestock or people. It's quite possible that the farmer has suffered crop damage from deer, or the homeowner has seen his ornamental shrubs nibbled to nubs by hungry whitetails, and will be glad to have a few animals removed. Obviously, should you receive permission to hunt, respect the owners's property and privacy. Tell him when you will be on the property. When you arrive before dawn do so quietly. Nobody appreciates slamming car doors at five a.m.

Should you bag a deer, it's a good idea to offer to share some of the venison. Even non-hunters enjoy an occasional venison steak. If you conduct yourself in a gentlemanly fashion the chances are that you'll also get permission to hunt deer there during the firearms season, which is a big bonus considering how crowded some public hunting lands can be at that time. Contacts like this are invaluable.

You don't need a huge parcel of land to hunt on either. I know a fellow back in the crowded state of New Jersey who once had permission to hunt on a meager 25 acres behind the owner's house. The catch was that the 25 acres were smack dab in the middle of thousands of acres of heavily posted land. And, the acreage stretched down along a hillside between the ridgetop and a big open field in the valley below.

It was a "country gentleman" situation with large houses all along the ridgetop. Any deer moving across that mountain stayed below the houses and above the field. This resulted in their passing through those crucial 25 acres at one time or another during the day. To summarize: my friend and his buddies took seven deer off the property in five seasons. Fortunately, the owner realized that taking a few deer wouldn't hurt the herd, and in fact agreed that there was a surplus of deer in the region.

Talking to people gives you a chance to make a pitch for sound wildlife management practices. There is more than enough anti-hunting propaganda around these days; all of it quite false and based on emotion rather than scientific facts.

As you scout your hunting spot keep an eye out for deer foods. Deer are not hesitant about helping themselves to apples, winter wheat, soybeans or corn. However, if the field crops are rotated or the land allowed to remain fallow for a year, the deer will have to look for alternate handouts or rely solely on natural foods. Keep track of what's been planted in nearby fields because a sudden change there could mean a change in deer habits.

We keep using the term "woods" but whitetails are actually "edge" animals. Where sunlight can reach the ground, such as along the boundary between woods and field or in a natural clearing in the woods, is where the browse deer prefer grows the best. A mature forest of giant trees that shut out the sunlight will have very little undergrowth and food for deer. Ideal habitat is farmland interspersed with woodlands. Deer are amazingly adaptable creatures and make themselves right at home within sight of a busy farm.

In the West, mule deer can be found from the sagebrush flats up to the timberline, and they are much more migratory than whitetails. Hunting

Rabbits offer many small game opportunities for bowhunters.

methods for mulies, elk and pronghorns all differ, but the basics remain: look for the animals' food supply, regular travel routes and signs of sexual activity. Plan to intercept them during the course of their daily movements. All game animals are creatures of habit and unless disturbed by humans or natural traumas such as severe weather or fire tend to follow defined patterns of behavior. The more you know about that behavior the better your chances are.

Male members of the deer family start their rut in the fall, as early as September in some places. Their antlers have hardened and they're standing at stud. Whitetail bucks will begin sparring with saplings. You'll come across rubs where the animal has scraped the bark off as he worked his antlers against the tree or bush. These rubs are easy to find and indicate bucks in the area.

Scrapes are more serious sexual signposts. A buck will paw the ground bare and urinate in it. He's marking his territory. Sometimes a scrape is so active that you can smell it from yards away. That's a good spot to set up a tree stand. Very possibly the buck will return. However, if he's running with a doe in estrus it may be days later. In the meanwhile other bucks may stop by the scrape; does, too. A scrape will often be under a badly scarred larger evergreen that has been battered in mock combat. Branches will be broken off and the ground torn up. Other trees may be

Western bowmen are fortunate to have a variety of big game to hunt. While hunting methods for mule deer, elk and pronghorns differ, the basics remain: look for the animals' food supply, regular travel routes and signs of sexual activity.

Not all deer are shot from tree stands. A good ground level stand will produce, as will stalking, but the odds increase.

used but whitetail bucks show a fondness for cedars, young pines, hemlocks and other evergreens.

Good places to look for rubs and scrapes are old logging trails and cuts for power lines. If you find an active scrape near the junction of two or more well traveled deer trails you've found a hotspot with good potential.

Assuming that you've followed some of our suggestions for hunting preparation you should be all set. You're wearing camouflage or dull, quiet clothing; your face and hands are hidden; your bow is touched up with camo coloring; and you've squeak-proofed your tree stand.

Make sure your bow is also silent as it is drawn. A little touch of paraffin on an arrow rest quiets down a raspy arrow sound. Check out any squeaks from bow limbs, eccentrics or idlers. Bow limb squeaks can be difficult to eliminate, and you may have to seek help at a pro shop.

Remember, the sounds made as you draw your bow are much more important than the sounds made as the bow is fired. In my many years of bowhunting I have never had a calm, unsuspecting animal jump at the sound of my bow being fired in time to escape the arrow. On the other hand, I have had nervous deer, that knew I was there, jump at the flash of my bow limbs as I shot.

Deer often travel in pairs or small groups. Many times I have prepared for a shot and had another deer spot me and spook the primary animal as I made the draw.

If you feel that string silencers help, by all means use them. Critics say that silencers reduce bow speed. True, but not enough to make much of a difference.

You may also want to try your hand at using scents. If you're hunting from a ground stand, or

stalking, remember that as the morning air warms up it will rise uphill, carrying your body scent with it. The reverse is true in the late afternoon.

Don't get the idea that you have to use a tree stand to score. Plenty of deer are arrowed at ground level. You can't see as far and have to be more watchful, that's all. Pick a comfortable place to sit or stand, preferably against a tree, stump, boulder or something else to blend in with. Realize that you are much more noticeable to deer at their level. But if you spot them first you can get a shot if the wind is in your favor and there's an opening for the arrow to fly true.

Whether up in a tree or down on the ground move as little as possible. Rely on your peripheral vision. Then turn your head slowly to see more cover. Also, tune up your ears. You'll often hear a deer approaching long before you see it. Birds and squirrels will give you false alarms but be alert for any crunching leaves or rustling of brush. Many times deer seem to materialize out of nowhere, but when the leaves are dry and crunchy, or covered with crusted snow, you can hear deer coming. Keep your cool and try to determine the direction. Anticipate more than one animal. If that's the case there will be extra eyes to catch any slip-up you make.

If it's a single deer moving slowly in a stop and go fashion get ready to draw when it stops, offering a shot, but don't move until it looks away or its head is behind a tree or other obstruction.

If the animal is moving deliberately or rapidly with no sign of stopping a sharp whistle will often stop it long enough to get off a shot, all other things being equal: distance, clearance, etc.

A tree in your backyard will serve as a place to squeakproof your stand and other equipment before the season.

Arrow shafts with a dull finish are preferred for bowhunting.

When there is no cover between you and the deer you have no choice. Make your movements super-slow and super-smooth, freezing the instant the animal looks your way. You can move, draw and aim on some animals as long as they are moving, even if they are glancing your way. But if the deer stops and you continue to move it's generally goodbye. You'll hear a snort and watch a white tail bounding away.

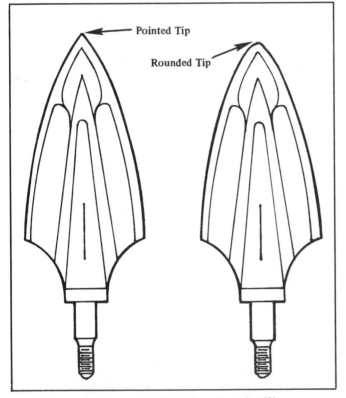

Pointed Tip

Rounded Tip

A slightly rounded tip on a flat-bladed broadhead is stiffer for better penetration and less likely to dig into a bone.

If all goes well, hold and time your release for the instant the deer's attention is diverted. The movement of the bow limbs can cause an alert animal to jump your arrow unless it's a very close shot.

AIMING POINTS

I do not advocate taking a shot at moving big game. It's difficult enough to place your arrow perfectly on a stationary target. You want to keep your margin for error to a minimum. A miss of a few inches can mean a crippled animal leaving little if any blood trail and escaping to perhaps a lingering death.

Given a choice I'll try for the basketball-sized chest cavity. This is a deer's boiler room that keeps the rest of him going. The heart and lungs, plus vital arteries, are concentrated there.

Broadside, a high lung aiming point is good; just below and behind the shoulder, but not too far forward. If the hit is a bit high there's a chance of hitting the spine; low and it goes through the lungs or heart; and a little back from the aiming point is the liver. However, if the hit is several inches forward the broadhead could glance off the shoulder bone doing little damage, or you might hit the foreleg if you shot forward and low.

Probably the best shot at a deer is when the animal is quartering away from you. The arrow can slip in behind the ribs and penetrate the lung area severing lung tissue and arteries as it angles toward the opposite shoulder. Deep penetration is almost assured.

If the animal is facing you and you have no other shot aim low in the center of its chest. Chances of a heart or lung hit are good.

Hunters disagree on whether to take a shot at a deer walking directly away. I'll hold my fire, hoping the deer will turn offering a quartering shot. Other bowhunters claim the rear end target offers femoral and aortic arteries in the legs and near the spine, and possible complete penetration the full length of the body cavity and into the lungs. Maybe so, but I'll pass.

No two shots are alike. The hunter must decide if a shot is feasible and then where to place the arrow so that it will prove lethal, preferably within seconds.

When aiming down at a deer from a tree stand visualize its anatomy, mentally tracing the arrow's path through the hide and into that chest cavity. The angles will vary greatly — another good reason for practicing these shots before season.

No discussion of game contact would be complete without mentioning "buck fever." I suppose there's also such a thing as "doe fever." Whatever you call it, it can and does affect all deer hunters, but some won't admit it.

Buck fever is simply the culmination of months of planning, and hours, sometimes days, of waiting on stand and suddenly the final act is about to be played out. It's no longer theory but reality. Can the hunter do his part and score a quick, clean kill? All sorts of messages and impressions are racing through his mind. No matter how many hours he's spent shooting at targets, drawing on a live animal is quite another thing.

There is no "cure" for buck fever, but it can be controlled for a few minutes, and that's all you need. Just as a professional golfer concentrates on a birdie putt in a big tournament, put everything else out of your mind. Family, friends, job and all distractions are shunted aside for the moment. If the deer is a buck, ignore the antlers. You can count the points later.

Turkey hunting with a bow is a special challenge. Bill Clements called this Arkansas tom into arrow range.

Decide where you want the arrow to go and tune your mind and body to getting the job done. Try to ignore your pumping heart, and keep your muscles under control. Your whole purpose for being where you are is about to be fulfilled.

AFTER THE SHOT

An arrow inflicts a lethal wound when the razor sharp edges of the broadhead slice through arteries and vital organs. Hemorrhaging results and, depending on the extent of the damage, the animal quickly dies, or runs off leaving a blood trail for the hunter to follow.

Unlike a bullet from a high powered rifle, an arrow produces little shock when it hits. A broadhead makes a clean cut and animals that have only been grazed, or even had an arrow pass completely through a non-vital part of their body, have a good chance of complete recovery.

You may know an instant after release whether you've hit or not. Always assume a hit until the arrow is recovered and verifies a miss. Bright fletching and fluorescent nocks made it easier to find it after the shot.

A word of caution: beware the animal that drops in its tracks from an arrow wound. It could be paralyzed, temporarily paralyzed or unconscious. Put another arrow into that animal. Do not approach closely until you know for sure that it is dead. It could regain consciousness and rear up to gore or kick you.

Watch the reaction of the animal. Some will give no indication of being struck, then take a few steps and drop dead. If the animal runs off, note exactly where it was standing at the shot, and which direction it took. Listen closely as the deer flees. Many times I've heard a mortally wounded animal crash to the ground and expire while running at full speed. I've heard air being sucked in and expelled from a lung shot deer. They can cover a lot of yardage in 10 or 15 seconds of life. Listen for any clues. They can be invaluable in recovering the animal.

Before you leave your stand pick out a reference so you can identify where the deer was standing and where it disappeared from view. If you were stalking, mark the spot from where the shot was made. This is important.

Now, settle your nerves and come down out of the tree safely. Of course if you heard the animal fall, proceed in that direction. Go over to where the deer was standing. Mark the spot. But if there's no reason to think the deer is down, look for clues. Look carefully for blood and deer hair.

The ultimate game contact depends on a sharp broadhead.

A sharp broadhead can clip a lot of hair on a raking shot. Hair color can help identify the kind of hit. White hair comes from the underbelly or inside the legs. Dark hair indicates a body hit. Don't be discouraged if you don't find any hair. The same goes for blood.

There may not be any blood at the site of the hit. This is why noting the direction of the deer's flight is so important. Sometimes blood trails can start out very faintly before large amounts begin flowing from the wound.

Next, locate the arrow if possible. If after careful searching you still can't find the arrow, assume that it's in the deer. If you find the arrow examine it for signs of blood. A clean arrow means you missed. A blood-smeared arrow confirms a hit. It's not unusual for an arrow to go completely through a thin-skinned animal like a deer or pronghorn.

Once a definite hit has been established, move slowly along the escape route to the spot where the animal disappeared. Look diligently for blood on the ground and on the brush.

If I find bright blood, a heavy blood trail, and believe the deer is hit in the chest area, I'll wait 20 minutes before going on.

If I find blood sprayed over bushes and a large amount of big blood splotches along the ground, I'll follow immediately anticipating a dead deer just ahead.

If I find small drops of blood on the ground and some smeared on bushes, I'll wait an hour before following the trail.

If I find dark blood, body fluids and partially digested food particles, it means bad news. A hit through the paunch or stomach calls for a long, difficult trailing job. I'll wait a minimum of two hours, ask for help from my companions, then proceed cautiously. If we jump the deer we'll try to shoot it again. If we can't, it's another two-hour wait. If it looks like rain any minute, we'll press on scanning ahead for a bedded deer attempting to rise. Every attempt will be made to anchor it permanently with another arrow.

As you follow a blood trail stick small pieces of toilet paper on the bushes to mark the route. Look for blood spots above ground level on leaves and grass. Be alert for a sudden change in direction.

Should you lose the blood trail, continue in the general direction the deer was taking. Make several short, cross-trail searches, and investigate any game trails you find. Follow them in the direction of heavy cover.

The trailing job is much easier when several trackers are looking for blood sign. Walk the woods in a definite pattern. Stop every 50 yards and look around for a fallen deer. Examine the cover on each side and behind you. A deer lying on the ground can be almost invisible, but looking from different angles may give a glimpse of white belly hair or antlers.

If you're forced to follow a blood trail after dark use a battery-powered fluorescent light or a miner's carbide lamp. These lights are very soft and cause blood spots to stand out brightly. Harsh incandescent light tends to blanch blood spots making them hard to see.

In many states it's illegal to be in the woods with a bow at night. If this is your situation, mark the end of the trail well, go home, and return at first light to take up the trail again.

There are several game-finding devices on the market. These utilize thin, strong nylon line attached to the arrow. The line is on a spool enclosed in a cone mounted on the bow. For example, the Game Tracker unit holds 2500 feet of 17-pound-test line, and the line pays out the same way it does from a closed-face spincasting reel in fishing.

I have not used one of these devices on game as yet, but I can see their potential, especially for close range shooting. However, no device can be considered an excuse for hasty or sloppy shooting. It is still the archer's primary responsibility to place his arrow with precision, or hold his fire.

GUIDED HUNTS

Sooner or later most bowhunters want to try their hand at other game in other regions. Let's say you've always hunted whitetails in Pennsylvania but have developed an itch to go after mule deer in Colorado or elk in Wyoming. If you're very fortunate you'll know a bowhunting buddy out there who will take you under his wing and act as your guide. From then on it's a matter of obtaining the necessary permits, following your friend's advice on what equipment and clothing to bring, and planning all the logistical details.

More typical, however, is the bowhunter who has no personal contacts out where he wants to hunt. He and his friends can still make a trip but the odds are stacked against them. In strange country they would have to be extremely lucky to score. When you're used to hunting in woodlots, facing an entire mountain range can be intimidating. Chances are there is lots of game, but it could be two valleys over, or 2,000 feet higher or lower than your camp.

Just knowing where to hunt is half the battle. And getting there is not always easy. Sure, there are vast National Forests out west, some of them as large as small states, open to public hunting. But where do you start? All the problems facing farmland bowmen are multiplied in the enormity of the wide open spaces.

Dr. David Bosma and a White River buck. When a buck presents a shot, don't be mesmerized by its antlers. Count points later.

A feral goat taken by Ben Pearson (Left) and Dr. James L. Smith near Bull Shoals Lake in the Ozarks in 1957.

The obvious answer is to hire a professional hunting guide — but not just any guide. Some guides are unsympathetic toward bowhunters; others simply don't recognize the special limitations placed on bowhunters. Before engaging a guide double-check his references to make sure that he either specializes in guiding bowhunters, or at least understands what's required for a successful bowhunting trip.

Getting a rifleman to within 150 yards of a bull elk is routine for a guide. That's a fairly easy shot with a rifle. Helping an archer stalk to within 40 (preferably 25) yards is another matter. The same goes for mule deer, pronghorns, caribou, moose, mountain goats and sheep.

The better known guides with solid reputations are commonly booked a year or two in advance.

You'll be paying a bundle and perhaps traveling thousands of miles so choose your guide with care.

If I were making a pack trip for mule deer or elk I would seriously consider arriving a day or two early and chartering a light plane to scout the prospective hunting area. The guide, too, would profit from such a reconnaissance.

I would rather spend one day searching out potential game areas and four days of actual hunting, instead of riding all over the mountains for days before finding game and then only have one day left to hunt. Using a plane for scouting may sound unsporting. Not so. Hunting time is very limited, and very expensive. Take advantage of every opportunity.

Of course, a plane may not be available. Then you have to rely completely on your guide's knowledge and recent experiences. Game can move considerable distances overnight so even when you're in good country it takes some searching to locate the herds.

And, don't be disappointed if you fail to take a record book trophy. Exceptional animals have always been rare. Be content with a good, typical specimen killed after careful stalking and proper arrow placement.

Giant brown and polar bears have been taken by bowmen, but black bears are the staple species for American archers. Some bears are killed by deer hunters, but these are chance encounters.

Organized bear hunts normally take place over bait, or by following a pack of bear hounds that will tree the animal or bring it to bay. The latter method is very popular in the western states. Sometimes the hunters will be on horseback. In other places, such as the dense rain forests of Washington state, the only way to keep up with the dogs is on foot. You'd better be in top physical condition, and you'll earn your bear with sweat and blisters.

Shooting a bear over bait requires planning and patience. Again, if you're unfamiliar with the procedure, hire a guide. Archery magazines carry advertisements offering this kind of hunt in many states. Remember that bears are big, powerful animals and should be considered potentially dangerous. It's nice to have a guide as a backup with a heavy rifle in case of emergencies.

Check the classified sections of outdoor magazines for a variety of guide services. Pay particular attention to those catering to archers. Ask for references and spend a few bucks and call and talk to people who have hunted with these guides in past seasons. Ask about the outfitter's camp facilities, food, how many hunters are assigned to each guide, nature of the hunting area, and how they hunted, general attitude of camp personnel and guides, numbers and kinds of game seen, and would they book with him again?

Some guide services are like a production line or fast food joint — quick turnover is their style. They often employ local ranch hands to serve as guides. Each "guide" may have four or more hunters in his party. He'll pass out skimpy box lunches after breakfast, then take his charges to "hotspot" stands scattered along the mountain. Frequently this is done with a pickup truck. The guide returns to camp to perform chores until evening when it's time to round up the hunters. After four days of this the hunters are transported back to town, where a fresh group will be picked up and the process repeated many times throughout the season.

Compare this kind of operation with that of a dedicated outfitter who takes fewer parties, each for a longer stay, and who works with the hunters to help them get their game. It's a matter of personal involvement and caring. As you might expect, it costs more but if you can swing it, it's the way to go.

There is another way that you may be able to enjoy a trip within your budget, especially if you've had camping experience and are used to being self sufficient.

Some outfitters provide drop-type hunts. They'll pack you into hunting territory and help you get set up in camp. Normally they supply the tents and cooking gear, and stock up on food of your choice. You'll get a map of the immediate area and suggestions on where to hunt. Then you're on your own for a set number of days. You do your own cooking, guiding and camp chores.

A strictly do-it-yourself hunt might be arranged with an individual rancher. Here, you're paying a daily or weekly access fee. Some ranchers offer boarding facilities, or you'll stay in your own tent, trailer or camper. The advantage of this situation is that you're on private land with some idea of where to hunt. The rancher wants you to succeed and will steer you in the right direction.

These less expensive hunting arrangements are all right for mule deer or pronghorns, but serious efforts are needed for a realistic chance at elk, moose, sheep and goats. These are wilderness animals, often difficult to reach and to bring out. Elk, for example, are huge beasts, and horses are standard equipment for carrying hunters in and quartered elk out. Seldom can you drive into really good elk country.

Regardless of the type of hunt that interests you, the first step is to contact the appropriate fish

A group of rope-spike and slip releases in common use during the early seventies, and still useful today.

and game department. They can supply maps, license information, season data, applications and other pertinent facts. Ask about guides and outfitters, and ranch hunting opportunities if you want.

One thing you're sure to discover — these days, non-resident big game licenses don't come cheap.

Lewis Rush is a firm believer in using shadows, natural cover and fallen tree tops for concealment when turkey hunting.

Chapter 10
Field Dressing

Big game hunters and newly elected politicians often ask themselves a common question — "Now that I have it, what do I do with it?"

The first thing a hunter must do is make sure the animal is stone cold dead. Absolutely, positively, no question — dead. Examine the animal's eyes from a distance and look carefully for any signs of breathing. The eyes should be glazed. Normally, any animal struck fatally with an arrow will have expired by the time you come up to it. But it still pays to be cautious. Wounded game or "dead" game that suddenly comes to life can be very dangerous.

Most states require that you fill out and attach the big game tag immediately upon taking an animal, so that's your first step. Next, you'll have to field dress the carcass so it can cool. This means removing the intestines, bladder, liver, heart, diaphragm and lungs. Then you can transport it out of the woods.

Because of the presence of ticks and other external and internal parasites found on deer, some hunters carry a pair of rubber gloves and slip them on before handling the animal.

Start by positioning the deer on its back so its head is uphill, if possible. This causes the innards to "flow" down and to the rear, along with the loose blood in the body cavity. There's no need to cut the deer's throat to bleed it. That was done by your arrow. And, if you plan to have the head mounted a slice through the hide in this region creates problems for the taxidermist.

Spread the deer's hind legs. If they won't stay apart use your dragging rope and tie them to some brush. Or, if someone is with you have him hold the legs apart as you work.

About this time, remember to roll up your sleeves and take off your watch and any jewelry you don't want to get bloody. Also, you should know where the broadhead is so it can be removed safely during field dressing.

Straddle the deer, facing toward the rear. At the sternum, or base of the rib cage, make a small cut through the skin and thin abdominal wall. Insert the point of your knife, blade up, and two fingers, one on each side of the blade. The fingers guide the knife tip, pull up on the hide and also

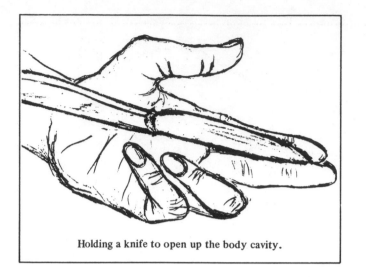
Holding a knife to open up the body cavity.

A bone saw, Wyoming saw or pistol grip saw with a bone cutting blade are handy for opening the sternum. A small belt ax hit with a stout stick or rock will also work. It isn't necessary to cut up through the center of the main bone. You can cut one side of the rib cage free where it joins the sternum. A strong hunting knife, tapped with a club, will do it. The junction of the rib bone is slightly softer than the bone itself.

With or without the sternum split you'll see the diaphragm, a thin wall of muscle between the intestinal and chest cavities. Cut the diaphragm where it joins the body. Then reach up into the chest cavity and grasp the windpipe and esophagus with one hand. Being very careful not to cut yourself, bring your knife hand above the grasp and cut both tubes. All the organs should be free from the chest cavity. Untie or let go of the hind legs.

Roll the deer on its side and finish the cut around the diaphragm. Pull out the lungs, intestines, heart and liver. If the intestines do not come free, feel along the backbone for a bit of connecting tissue. Cut this carefully, avoiding the intestines. The whole mess should flop out.

Drag the deer to a clean patch of ground and prop its body cavity open with sticks. If the air is cold you can see the body heat coming out. Flip the deer onto its belly and raise the head so the blood can drain out of the body cavity. Then roll it belly up again.

Separate the heart and liver from the innards and set them aside to cool. They can be transported in a plastic bag after cooling, but get them refrigerated as soon as possible. Back at the car, take them out of the plastic and lay them on top for further cooling. Fresh, sliced, fried venison liver and heart are immediate delicacies you can eat that same day, and traditional in many deer camps. If you don't care for these parts, save them for friends. You won't have to ask twice.

Back in the woods, it isn't necessary or recommended that you wash out the body cavity, unless the bladder or intestines have been ruptured. Then you have no choice and should flush it clean at the earliest opportunity. Handfuls of snow will also work in late season hunting.

Clean off your hands and wrists and relax for a while. The next job is getting the deer to the road and loaded on a vehicle. The secret of easy deer dragging is manpower, the stronger the better. A pair of Razorback defensive linemen on the end of the drag rope would be ideal. Just point them in the right direction and stand back out of the way.

push the intestines down out of the way as the cut is made.

You want to avoid cutting into the paunch, intestines or bladder. Use only the first inch or so of the blade point. Continue the cut from sternum to anus, cutting to either side of the sex organ. Some states require an attached sex organ on the carcass for positive identification. Check your state's regulations before going hunting.

This cut in the pelvic area exposes the pelvic bone and the bladder. Tie off the bladder canal with a piece of string to prevent spillage and contamination. Some hunters prefer to split the pelvic bone for easy removal of the bladder and any remaining fecal matter. I make two cuts about one inch to one and a half inches apart through the pelvic bone.

Other hunters ream the anal opening like coring an apple, but must be careful of the bladder. Any tubes are tied off with string and the "plumbing" pulled inside the body cavity to be rolled out with the intestines.

Back at the sternum, you have a choice as to how to proceed. If you plan to have a shoulder mount of your trophy, cut no further. The taxidermist will need plenty of hide to work with. If you're just dressing out venison, you can cut the hide up the chest and split the sternum allowing better access to the lungs, windpipe and esophagus, the feeding tube that connects the throat with the paunch. Or, you can leave the sternum as is. Some hunters prefer to leave it whole to protect the meat while the deer is being dragged out. However, in hot weather splitting the sternum allows body heat to escape faster, lessening the chance of spoilage.

Slit the skin from the breastbone to the anus.

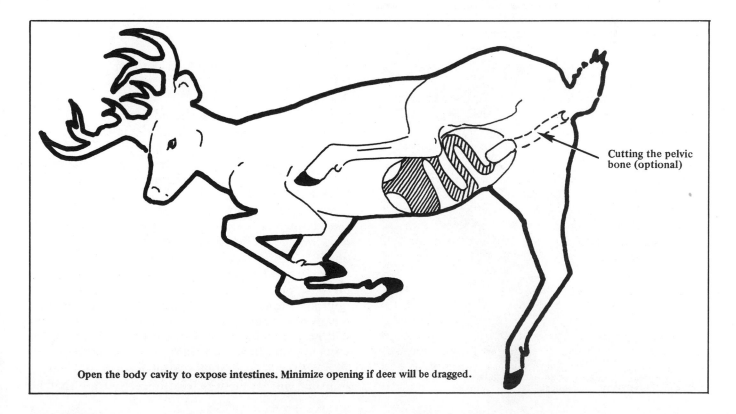

Cutting the pelvic bone (optional)

Open the body cavity to expose intestines. Minimize opening if deer will be dragged.

Lacking outside help, one man in reasonably good physical condition can drag a deer. Take it one step at a time and pause frequently to catch your breath.

How you tie the drag rope to the deer makes a difference. A popular method is to lasso the buck's antlers around the base, or around a doe's neck just behind the ears. Then take a half hitch around the deer's nose. This lifts the animal's head and neck off the ground as you pull, and reduces friction.

Some hunters like to tie the front legs with a wrap around the nose so these, too, are off the ground. The idea is to streamline the deer so it will slide over brush without the front legs hanging up on obstacles.

Use a stout stick about two feet long as a tow handle. After determining a comfortable rope length, secure the handle so it doesn't roll in your hands under tension.

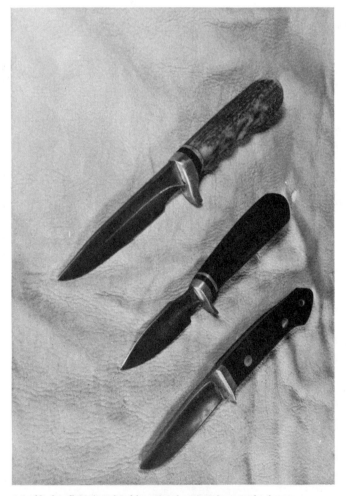

A knife for field dressing big game does not have to be large. A four-inch blade length is about right.

When going through brush you might find it easier to face the deer as you pull and guide it through the openings. Over a clear stretch you can face forward with your arms behind.

There are various shoulder harnesses meant for dragging deer and these are worth considering. Deer hunters are ingenious. We've seen homemade wheeled contraptions used if the woods are not too thick. On private land, some hunters cache a wagon, wheelbarrow, baby carriage chassis or cart with bicycle tires in the general vicinity. Wheeling a deer along a trail sure beats dragging one out. And, you can put your bow and other equipment in as part of the load.

The stereotyped picture of hunters returning to camp shows them carrying a deer suspended on a pole. This is all right but the pole digs into your shoulder and the deer sways and throws you off balance. A better way is to use two poles like a litter arrangement. It's more comfortable and efficient.

Some states require that a deer be registered at a checking station before the animal can be skinned and butchered. Whatever the case, skin the deer as soon as possible. The hide and layers of fat are effective insulators and retard the cooling of the carcass. The sooner you skin a deer after death the easier it is to peel off that hide, and the quicker the whole carcass will cool down.

BUTCHERING

Fashion some sort of strong gambrel pole to spread the deer's hind legs. Make a short cut between the large tendon and the first joint of each leg. Insert the gambrel pole hooks and raise the deer.

If you plan to have a shoulder mount made, cut the cape generously well behind the shoulder and peel it down to the head and cut off the head with the cape attached. Some hunters take no chances — they give the taxidermist the entire hide, with the head attached, of course.

Whether at home, in camp or on a pack trip, a few simple tools are necessary for a neat, quick job of skinning and butchering. First on the list is a top quality knife with a five-inch blade for general work. A good lockblade folding hunting knife will do if it holds an edge — and a knife that won't doesn't belong on a hunting trip. Keep sharpening stones and honing oil handy. Even the best blades will need touching up as you proceed. Skinning an elk, moose or bear turns into work in a hurry.

An Alaskan guide who specialized in polar bear hunting when that was legal once told me that he

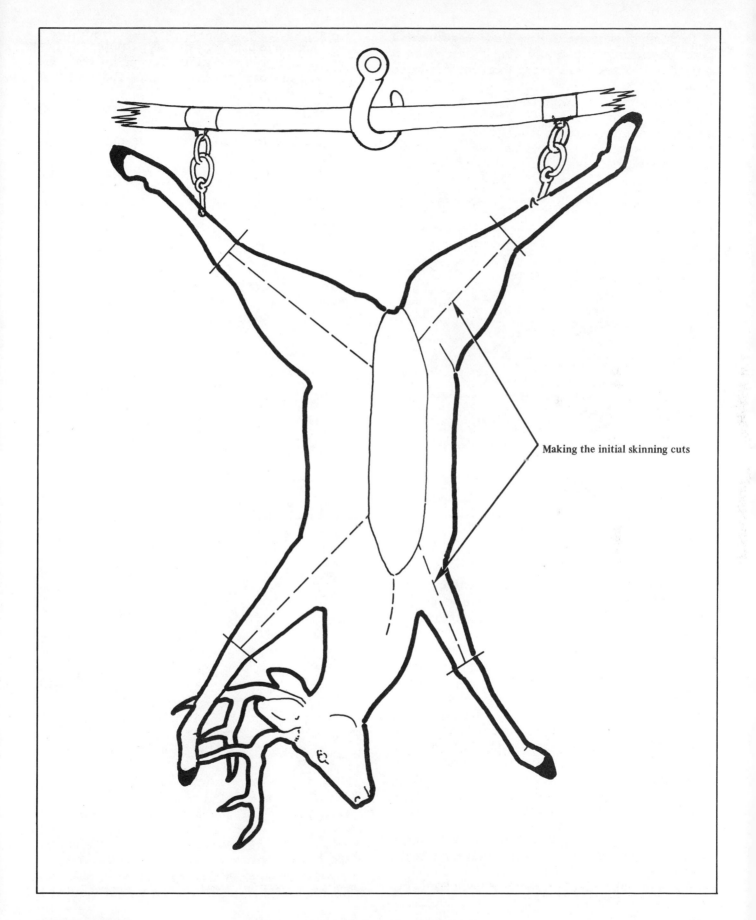

Making the initial skinning cuts

(Left to Right) A Green River skinning knife by Russell, a Rapala fillet model and a butcher's sharpening steel.

keep flies and other insects away in warm weather. There are game bags for just this purpose. The Ben Pearson catalog lists a game dressing kit complete with a game bag and instructions, and there are others on the market.

Take plenty of plain table salt to preserve capes and hides. Do not use iodized salt. I suggest that you check with a taxidermist for more detailed preservation methods.

A nighttime temperature of 30 degrees or less will help keep meat from spoiling for several days, provided that the meat is in the shade and hung so air can circulate freely around it, and if it is protected from night moisture or rain by a tarp. The temporary meat house should be open on all sides for air circulation.

With the deer hanging on the gambrel, and knives and saw at the ready, let's get on with the skinning and butchering.

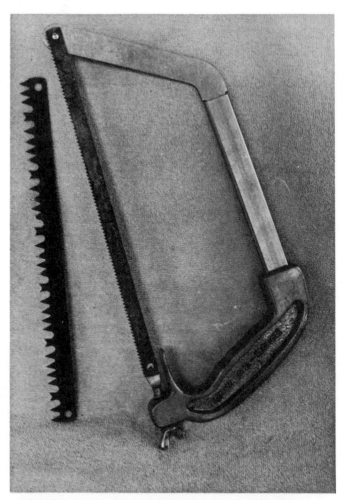

A Wyoming saw is handy for opening the sternum when field dressing, and later on for cutting bones during butchering.

had less than 30 minutes to remove the bear's hide, feet and head before the carcass froze solid. You can bet he didn't waste any time and had the tools to do the job.

He also had to be careful not to make any wrong cuts. His client was spending lots of money to get that trophy and expected it to be handled professionally.

Along with the five-inch blade, include a fish filleting knife for boning, plus a small caping knife.

You'll need a bone cutting saw. This can be a pistol grip saw, a Wyoming saw or, in a permanent camp, a regular butcher's saw.

An inexpensive, hand operated comealong is a very handy item in any hunting camp. Be sure to include plenty of rope.

Keep an adequate supply of cheesecloth, or mosquito netting as we call it in the South, on hand. Use it to wrap around meat to discourage insects. Sprinkling black pepper on the wrapped meat helps

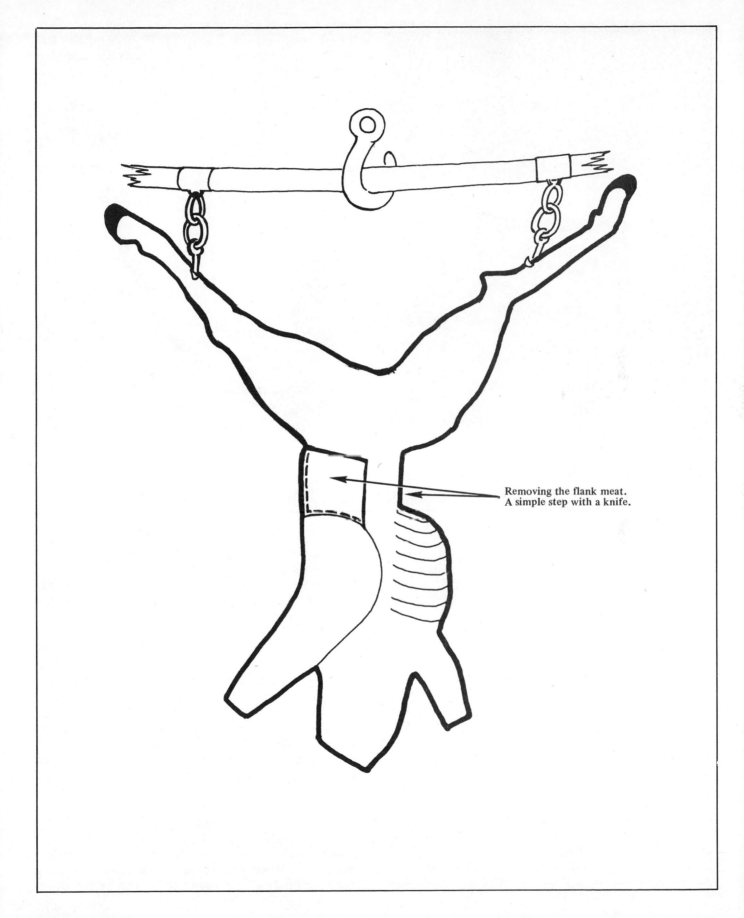

Removing the flank meat.
A simple step with a knife.

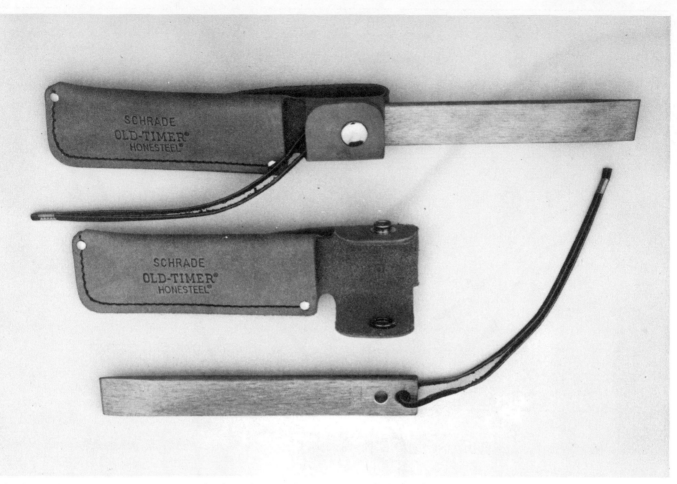

A honing steel not only keeps an edge on knife blades, but can also be used to split the pelvic bone on a deer if desired.

Cut the hide around each leg at the knee joints and cut down the inside of the legs to the body opening. Peel the hide away from the flesh, cutting connecting tissue when needed. Actually, there is more pulling than cutting involved. Cut off the tail at the base. If you're a flytier you'll want to bone out the tail and salt the tail skin well for bucktail material or bass bugs.

Continue peeling off the hide. Cut around the front knees and cut down each leg to meet the main opening. When you get to the base of the head cut it free between two vertebrae. The carcass is now ready for butchering.

My method is a combination of butchering and boning at the same time. I don't clutter up the freezer with unwanted bones, and I get the exact cuts of meat my family prefers. Here's how I do it:
• Slice off the flank meat. Remove and discard any fat. Set the flanks aside to be ground up for sausage makings or chopped meat.
• Remove each shoulder using your knife. There is no shoulder joint, just muscle. You can leave the shoulder intact for a barbecue, or bone it out for chopped meat.
• Remove the "tenders" inside the body cavity. These two strips lie under the backbone in the pelvic region. To my taste, these are the ultimate in venison. We reserve them for the smoker and serve them with salad, French bread, garlic butter and a good wine. You will never enjoy this delicacy if you have your deer butchered commercially.
• Bone out the ribs for ground meat, or saw them off high for barbecue ribs.
• Bone out the neck for ground meat.
• Now, working from the back, remove the two large backstraps by boning close to each side of the backbone. Remove any muscle sheath and visible white fat. This backstrap is really prime eating, second only to the tenders. You can broil, roast, smoke or cut this section into small butterfly steaks to dip into a good batter for frying.

Separate the hams at the pelvic bone using a bone saw. Make a knife cut all the way to the leg bone, following the contour of the pelvic bone.

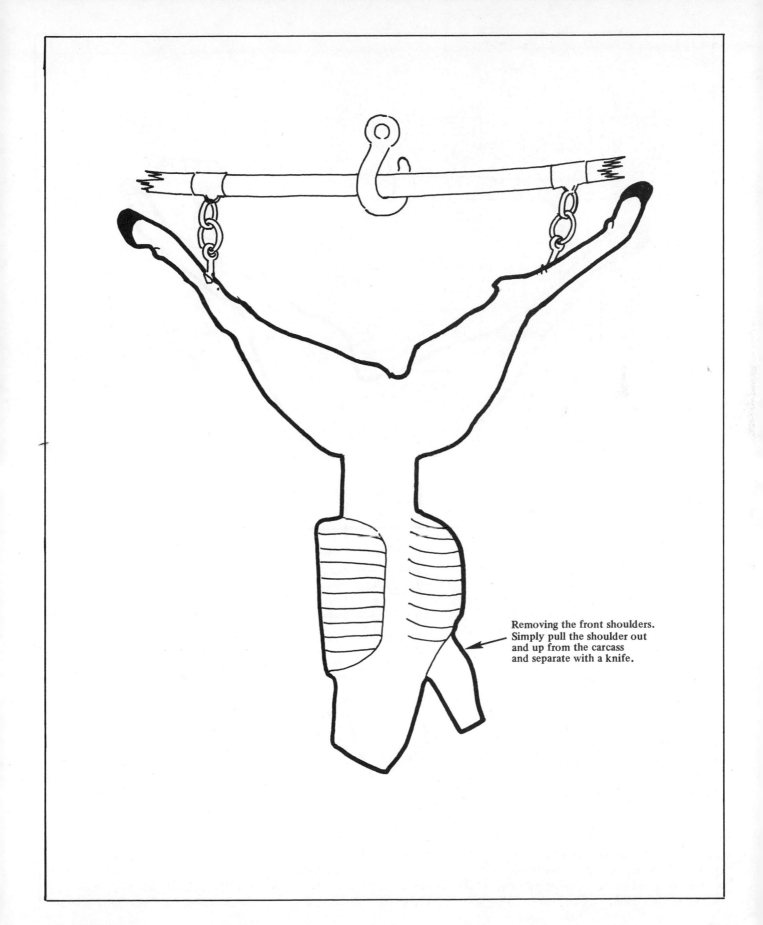

Removing the front shoulders. Simply pull the shoulder out and up from the carcass and separate with a knife.

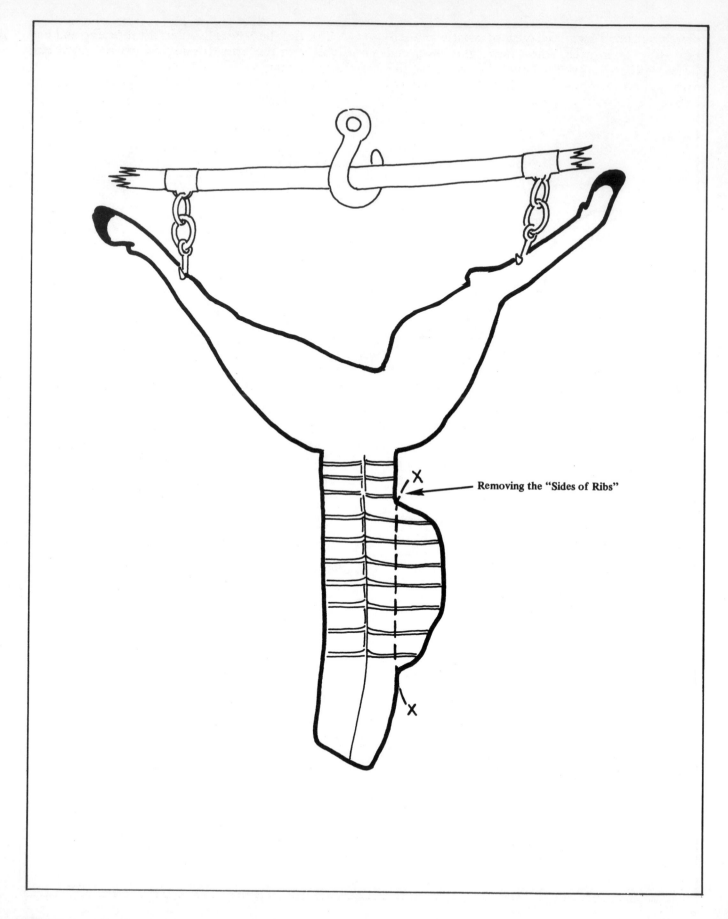

Removing the "Sides of Ribs"

Insert your hand into the layers of muscle and separate them from each other. Sever the lower end of these muscles from the bone. You will have five small strips of muscle from each ham. Be sure to remove the muscle sheath and visible white fat. Like the backstrap, these portions can be broiled, roasted or tenderized for butterfly steaks.

You may want to leave one ham whole for a large roast to serve at a party. A commercial butcher will usually slice the ham crosswise into oval steaks. I prefer my way.

One fall I skinned and butchered two whitetail bucks and kept records during the process.

The first buck was killed in the morning and had a full stomach after feeding during the night and early morning.

The other deer was killed the same day late in the afternoon and had an empty stomach. Compare the two deer weights as they were dressed and butchered.

Venison does not respond to aging in the same manner that beef does. Beef is a fat-marbled meat. Venison is not marbled. Beef fat is edible. Venison fat and muscle sheath are waxy and lard-like, tough and quite unappetizing. All of it should be trimmed off, leaving solid, lean venison. The only

Hunter: Tommy Moss
Location: Arkansas City Hunting Club
Whitetail: Six-point buck — 2½ years of age
Time of kill: 12/15/81 approximately 8 a.m.

Description	Carcass Weight	Weight Loss	Percentage of Total
Live Weight	162 lbs.	— 0 —	— 0 —
After Gutting	136 lbs.	—26 lbs.	—16.0%
After Removing Head and Hide	106 lbs.	—30 lbs.	—18.5%
After Removing Front Shoulders	84 lbs.	—22 lbs.	—13.6%
After Removing Ribs and Flanks	68 lbs.	—16 lbs.	— 9.9%
After Removing Back and Neck	42 lbs.	—26 lbs.	—16.0%
After Removing Both Hams	— 0 —	—46 lbs.	—25.9%
			99.9%

Hunter: Janet Moss
Location: Arkansas City Hunting Club
Whitetail: Spike buck — 1½ years of age
Time of kill: 12/15/81 approximately 4 a.m.

Description	Carcass Weight	Weight Loss	Percentage of Total
Live Weight	139 lbs.	— 0 —	— 0 —
After Gutting	124 lbs.	—15 lbs.	—10.8%
After Removing Head and Hide	94 lbs.	—30 lbs.	—21.6%
After Removing Front Shoulders	79 lbs.	—15 lbs.	—10.8%
After Removing Ribs and Flanks	67 lbs.	—12 lbs.	— 8.6%
After Removing Back and Neck	42 lbs.	—25 lbs.	—18.0%
After Removing Both Hams	— 0 —	—42 lbs.	—30.2%
			100.0%

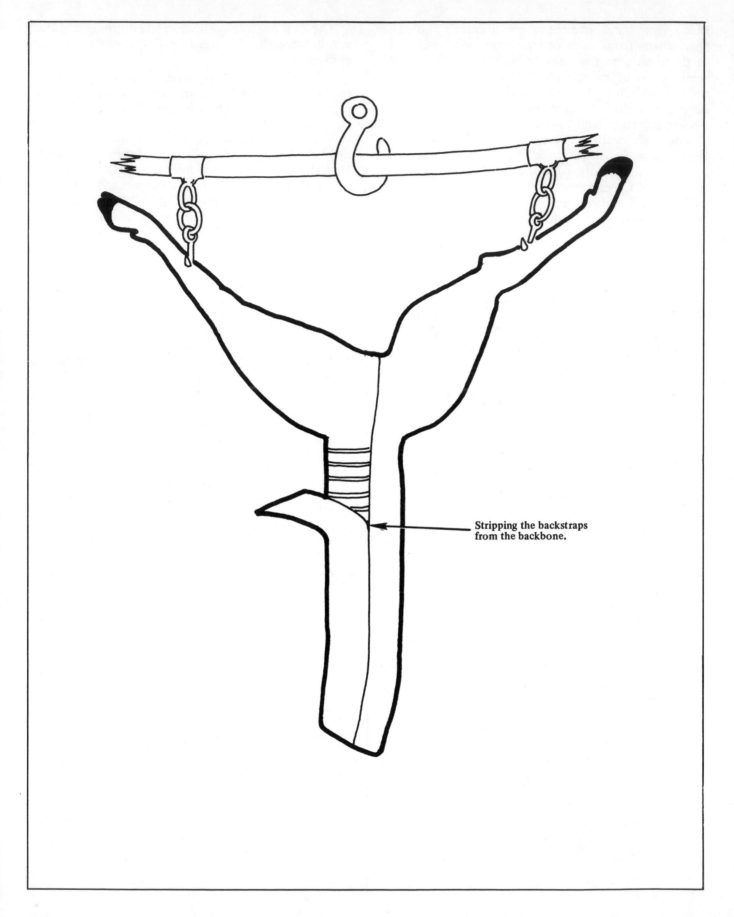

Stripping the backstraps
from the backbone.

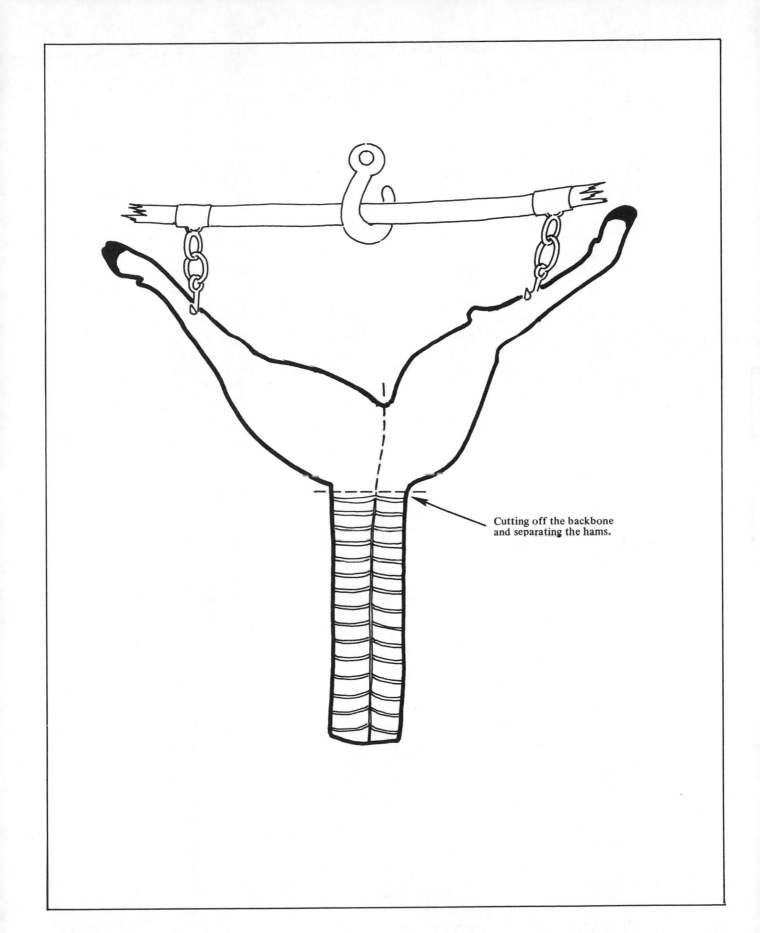

Cutting off the backbone
and separating the hams.

place where beef and venison can be handled similarly is in sausage and ground meat. A deer is a wild animal, and a steer is a domestic animal bred and reared under controlled conditions that determine the texture of its flesh. In no way can the two meats be considered comparable.

Place your cuts of venison in an ice chest and add about three bags of ice cubes. A 48- to 54-quart ice chest will hold a large boned-out whitetail.

Let the meat sit for 24 hours then drain off the bloody water. Add more ice cubes. This treatment will help clear blood clotted meat. The venison will be ready for packaging and freezing after the second draining. Any severe blood clots can be cut out.

You may have noticed during the description of my method of butchering a deer that very little bone stays with the meat. This becomes more important in a remote area on an elk or moose hunt. Because of their massiveness, these animals must be cut into manageable pieces before they can be moved. Trying to lift an entire elk or moose carcass into a pickup is a near impossibility, unless you have a crane standing by.

Elk and moose are gutted with the animal on its side. The intestines are pulled onto a seven-foot square of heavy plastic, then dragged off and dumped. The plastic is reused as a clean ground cloth to hold the pieces of meat during butchering.

One side of the carcass is skinned and the meat boned out. When this is done, the carcass is rolled over onto the hide already spread out and the second side of the animal is handled the same way. Boning is routine. It is much easier to leave the bones in the woods, and just about as quick in butchering as quartering and making additional trips to carry heavy bones back to camp. After boning there is a considerable weight reduction in the load the hunters or pack horses have to carry, and there's no loss of edible meat.

Deer are much smaller of course and can be managed much easier. There is even a shortcut method of skinning deer if its neck or back are not fractured. The method may seem strange, but it works.

Hang the field-dressed deer by its neck from a strong support. Cut the legs off just above the knee joints. Make the cuts down the inside of each leg, and cut through the hide around the deer's neck. Make sure all the cuts intersect the main cut from throat to anus.

Now, make two parallel three-inch cuts down the back of the neck and insert a hickory hammer handle, or similar strong hardwood stick. Loop a length of strong rope around the hide just under the hammer handle and secure it with a slip knot.

Then hand the rope to two strong men, tie it to a saddle horn, preferably with a horse under it, or tie it around a trailer hitch on a pickup. Put the power into motion and the hide should peel off like turning a sock inside out.

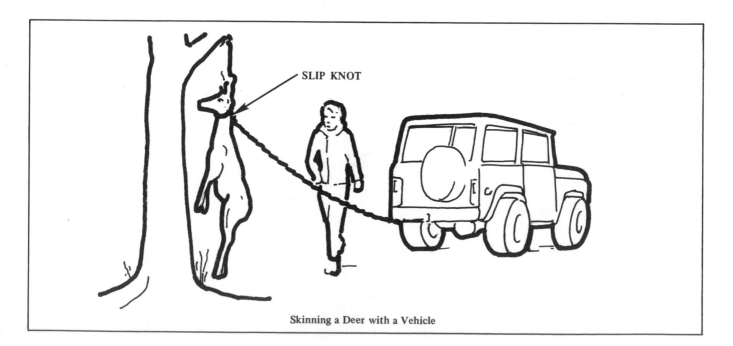

SLIP KNOT

Skinning a Deer with a Vehicle

Dragging out a blacktail buck in California. Having a partner along to help with the chore is a luxury we all welcome.

Western bowhunting seasons usually mean warm weather, and extra care should be taken to insure good venison.

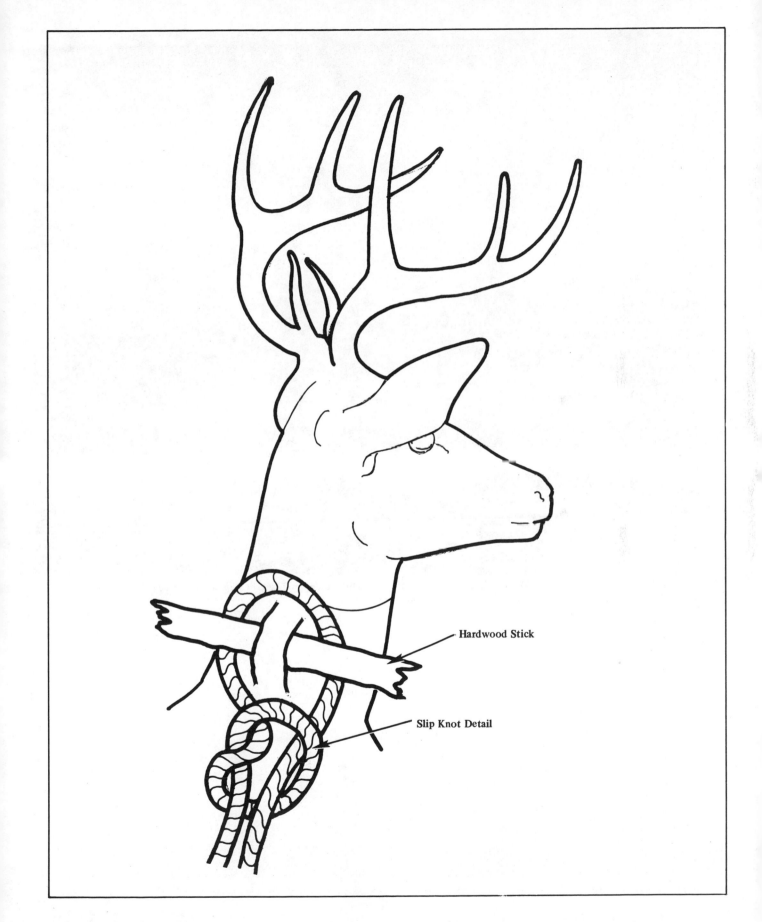

Hardwood Stick

Slip Knot Detail

After the fulfillment of the hunt comes the chore of field dressing. It needn't be sloppy if certain steps are followed.

Chapter 11
Cooking Game

Many hunters feel that prompt attention to field dressing and butchering is about all they can do to assure the good flavor of venison. This also applies to dressing out any game animals or birds promptly to allow body heat to escape. This is just part of the procedure resulting in outstanding table food.

Remember that the life of wild creatures is a cycle of extremes. Part of the year the living is easy; temperatures are moderate and there's plenty of food. In the northern states this is followed by lean, cold months accompanied by deep snow in some places.

To make it through the hard times many animals rely on stored fat reserves. Sometimes it's not enough and starvation occurs. This is commonly referred to as "winter kill" by game biologists. It's difficult to imagine a sleek, fat buck in October wasted away to the the point of emaciation by late February. Few sportsmen realize how this fat-to-lean cycle affects the taste of wild game meat. We associate a fat animal with tender meat and being in the best of condition. Deer, antelope, elk and moose all build up fat over the summer months.

Yet this fat is a major cause of the gamy, wild taste so many people dislike.

The method of cutting up a deer described in this book is the method used by pioneers many years ago. Any time one of these hunters had to pack his venison home on his back you can bet that he left the bones and other unusable parts behind.

Whenever housewives and hunters think of meat they have been conditioned to think of steaks, chops and roasts because of their everyday familiarity with beef, lamb and pork products. Unfortunately, many hunters leave the skinning, butchering and packaging of their deer to professional butchers, who treat the carcasses as they would domestic livestock.

Among hunters, including farm raised individuals, who butcher their own game the tendency is to duplicate farmland butchering methods. The result is a surplus of fat, bone and muscle sheath along with the meat. I know I've mentioned this before, but I'd like to emphasize it again; removal of as much deer fat as possible is essential to the best venison.

Other factors affecting how you react to a game meal include the manner in which it is served, the occasion, where you are and your mental and physical condition. Perhaps this is why venison always tastes better at a hunting camp.

The use of heavy-duty aluminum foil provides a self-basting method of cooking that adds to the flavor and tenderness of wild game.

As a general venison cooking tip, avoid adding salt until the meat is nearly done. Apply salt if desired during the last few minutes of cooking, or after you take the meat from the oven. Salt only takes a few minutes to permeate the meat, and it has a drying effect.

Coarse ground black pepper seems made to order for fish and wild game. It's definitely a hearty pepper and will get your attention. Diners who like their food seasoned on the snappy side will like it.

You can substitute elk, antelope or moose meat in the deer venison recipes. There will be some variation in texture and flavor but preparation is essentially the same.

I have not mentioned the cooking of deer liver in this chapter. There are localized infestations of liver flukes throughout the range of the whitetail. It is nothing to be alarmed about. Just check your deer's liver for signs of the parasites and if there's any question, discard the liver.

Keep in mind that we're dealing with wild meat here. Always cook game animals to the point of being well done.

Wild turkeys are delicious table fare but old toms can be tough. Try Bill Clements' method of cooking them.

SMOKED VENISON TENDERS

The ultimate in fine venison cuts lies under the backbone near the pelvic region, or loins. We call these two strips of meat "the tenders." If there is a better reward from deer hunting I don't know of it. Here's how we prepare tenders:

Bake two medium-large Idaho potatoes. Coat them with peanut oil and seal them in heavy aluminum foil. Allow one and a half hours cooking time in a 350-degree oven.

Set up your smoker for a medium-fast smoke. If you can find them, I recommend pecan wood chips as fuel. Allow about one and a half hours, depending on your smoker, to just cook the meat all the way through. Baste the two tenders often with peanut oil, and sprinkle on coarse ground pepper after the first basting. Don't let the meat dry out while cooking. Salt it lightly after you remove it from the smoker.

The potatoes should now be done. Serve them with chives and sour cream. As a side dish we like a green salad with vinegar and oil dressing. Serve the meat with a nice cherry sauce and hot rolls. As a beverage, we prefer a chilled bottle of Arkansas' Wiederkeher's Pink Cataba wine.

SMOKED VENISON BACKSTRAP

Smoking a thick piece of lean venison requires a degree of skill and experience. If you're inattentive the meat can come out too dry.

Prepare a slow smoke fire using pecan wood chips, if possible. Fat applied to the surface of the meat often fails to permeate, so use a larding needle to inject one or two strips of fresh pork fat the length of the meat.

Fix a baste of equal amounts of hot melted fresh pork fat and Planters peanut oil. Spread the baste with a swab or brush, and sprinkle generously with coarse ground black pepper.

Smoke the meat until it is almost done — about three to four hours depending on your smoker. Inspect the meat frequently and baste it often. Don't let it dry out.

Just before the meat is done, salt it lightly. Increase the heat and as soon as a crust begins to appear take the meat out. Do not precut this meat. Cut and serve as needed. Smoked backstrap makes a fine main course, and you can slice it thin across the grain for sandwiches the next day.

ELAINE'S VENISON BACKSTRAP

A venison backstrap consists of a two-inch thick strip of meat on both sides of the backbone extending from just behind the shoulders to the top of the hams. As opposed to the tenders, the backstrap is on top of the backbone.

Among many rural people it is still considered a privilege to have the local preacher and his family as guests for dinner after the Sunday morning services.

Naturally, the host makes every effort to see that his guests are served only the best cuts of chicken and home cured hams. In earlier times game was often on the menu. For generations children of host families have called the choice cuts of meat "preacher meat."

Venison backstrap qualifies as preacher meat. Backstraps should be cooked in foil or smoked. My wife enjoys this cut of meat because of the ease of preparation, and its outstanding flavor.

A 12-inch length of backstrap will generally feed four adults. Trim away any white fat and the silvery muscle sheath. Apply a generous sprinkling of coarse ground black pepper. Because this meat will be cooked wrapped in foil, you can salt it lightly beforehand. Anchor two strips of bacon along the backstrap with toothpicks. Crush three bay leaves over the meat and wrap it in heavy-duty foil.

Place the meat in a preheated oven (350 degrees) and cook until the meat is just done. This usually takes about an hour.

Serve with broccoli or brussels sprouts. Baby green lima beans would be another good choice for a complementary vegetable. Set out French bread, Lea and Perrins sauce and your favorite beverage.

ELAINE'S OVEN BARBECUE

The front shoulders can be handled in two ways. You can bone them for ground meat, or cook a whole shoulder as an oven barbecue. My wife prepared a whole shoulder this way:

Wrap the meat in heavy aluminum foil and cook it at 350 degrees until the meat starts to separate from the bone.

Drain off the broth but leave about two thirds of a cup. Salt the meat lightly and pour a commercial sauce over it. We suggest either Kraft's Regular or French's Ranch Style Sauce. Put the meat back into the oven for another 35 to 45 minutes.

When done, lay the shoulder flat and slice very thin. I like to use an electric knife for this purpose. This meat also makes good sandwiches.

CLEMENTS BUTTERFLY STEAKS

If you stripped the muscle layers from one ham, as mentioned in the chapter dealing with butchering, the strips can be made into fine butterfly steaks. My friend Bill Clements has a special knack for cooking them. Here's how he does it:

Lay the meat strip out flat and make a cut three fourths of the way through the meat about one half inch in from the end. The next cut will be one half inch from that and all the way through. You'll wind up with a steak an inch thick but cut almost all the way in the center; the two flaps held together at the bottom. That's where the "butterfly" description comes from.

Cut more steaks the same way. Figure on three steaks per person.

Prepare a batter of two thirds of a cup of milk, two eggs and two thirds of a teaspoon of sweet basil.

Pound each steak with a mallet, then drop them in a sack containing flour and coarse ground black pepper and shake well.

Heat the fat in a deep fryer about 350 degrees and drop a test steak in gently. Be careful not to burn the batter. Cook until done and salt lightly as it drains. Check the steak to see if it's done to your liking. Then duplicate or adjust cooking time accordingly with the remaining steaks.

Butterfly steaks are a treat on any occasion. They taste great in deer camp. Serve with baked beans, french fries, light bread, sweet purple onion and choice pickles. Very cold sweet milk or hot coffee complement this meal.

A venison roast in aluminum foil.

VENISON HAM IN FOIL

A venison ham goes well at an office party or a family gathering. A lot of people don't get to taste venison during the year and this is a nice treat.

As with preparing all venison, start by trimming away all white fat and muscle sheath. Apply a generous amount of coarse ground black pepper.

Wrap the ham in heavy-duty aluminum foil and cook in a 350-degree oven for five to six hours, until the meat starts to separate from the bone. About halfway through the cooking (three to four hours) drain off the excess broth.

Set up your smoker for a medium-hot smoke. When the ham is done in the oven take it out and sprinkle it lightly with salt and finish it off in the smoker. A thin crust will form on the meat.

I use an electric knife to slice the ham lengthwise. Serve the slices on a preheated platter, and offer your guests a choice of a good barbecue sauce or a cherry sauce to top it off. I'm sure they will enjoy venison ham.

GROUND VENISON PATTIES

The neck, forelegs and ribs are often boned for ground meat. Along with the ground flanks, this ground meat can be cooked in several ways. Before grinding, all white fat and muscle sheath should be removed. However, a certain amount of animal fat is needed for patties. Substitute fresh pork.

Grind up three pounds of boned venison. Add one pound of lean ground round beef. Add one pound of ground fresh pork.

This makes a lot of patties. If it's too much for your needs, cut down on the ingredients, but keep the proportions the same.

Add a moderate amount of coarse ground black pepper and salt lightly as you blend the venison, beef and pork. I use a regular saucer to shape the patties. Make them about 3/8 inch thick.

We prefer our venison hamburgers seared in peanut oil on a hot iron grill. Go ahead and charcoal grill your beef hamburgers but I suggest using a solid iron grill for venison patties.

Serve each pattie on a large sesame seed bun and put out garnishes for individual tastes.

VENISON RIB BARBECUE

If you saved the ribs instead of boning them out for ground meat, here's how to make a delicious barbecue:

Trim off all visible white fat. Put on a heavy application of coarse ground black pepper. Wrap the ribs in heavy-duty aluminum foil and cook in a 350-degree oven for approximately four hours.

Prepare a hot baste of apple cider vinegar, salt and a dash of French's mustard. Paint the ribs with the baste and finish the ribs over a low charcoal fire to brown them.

Cut the ribs into individual portions. Serve them with a good barbecue sauce, green salad, French bread, natural cut french fries and your choice of beverage. Put out dishes of pickles, olives, garlic butter and sliced sweet onions as relishes.

DELORES HOGUE CHILI

Delores Hogue keeps our bowhunting group supplied with chili, and we love it. Here's her recipe:

One pound ground venison.

3/4 pound of ground round beef.

1/4 pound of commercial pork sausage meat.

One medium chopped onion.

Mix the ingredients thoroughly, brown in a skillet and drain.

Next, add two No. 2 cans of tomatoes.

Add three small cans of tomato sauce.

Sprinkle on one tablespoon of chili powder.

Add one tablespoon of cumin.

Add one shake of garlic salt.

Add two cans of Bush's Mexican Hot Style Chili Beans.

Stir regularly and simmer for two hours.

HOGUE VENISON SWISS STEAK

Delores Houge also makes a great Swiss steak out of venison. She uses the stripped ham muscles for this dish.

Mix 1/4 cup of flour, 3/4 tablespoon of salt, and a dash each of cayenne pepper, thyme and nutmeg. Add three to four sticks of clove.

Pound the seasoned flour into three pounds of venison slab, then cut the meat into one-inch cubes. Brown the chunks in a heavy stew pot. Slice three onions very thin and add to the meat.

When the meat is well browned add in two cups of canned tomatoes, 1½ tablespoons of Worcestershire sauce and 1½ cups of dry red burgundy wine. Add another stick of clove and half of a small garlic pod.

Cover the pot and set it in a 325-degree oven for two and a half hours. Add salt and pepper to taste. Bring to a boil over direct heat and stir in one light cup of sauteed mushrooms. Serve with wild rice.

SMOKED VENISON JERKY

Drying is an age old method of preserving meat. There are several methods but they all involve removing the moisture from the meat. People living in hot, arid climates often let the sun do the drying. The meat is not actually cooked, but cured. Many people do not think of jerky as uncooked meat, but it is.

Jerky can be prepared in a smoker, using just enough heat to keep the smoke around the meat fairly hot and moisture free. We like to use pecan wood chips because their smoke imparts a delightful flavor to the jerky.

Start with a marinade. Blend the following:

One cup of white distilled vinegar, four tablespoons of soy sauce, one tablespoon of coarse ground black pepper and one tablespoon of plain table salt (non-iodized).

The muscles from the ham make good jerky. Be sure and remove all the muscle sheath and white fat. Cut 1/8-inch thick slices lengthwise.

Soak the slices in the marinade for four to six hours in the refrigerator. Use a glass or ceramic bowl — not a metal bowl. Then drain the slices, pat them dry with paper towels and let them air dry before putting them in the smoker. This is important.

Hang the strips of venison in your smoker and smoke them for four to six hours. Test a sample after four hours. They may require more exposure to the smoke, depending on thickness and your taste preferences. We store our jerky in tightly sealed fruit jars.

CLEMENTS WILD TURKEY BREAST

My old bowhunting buddy, Bill Clements, prepares a wild turkey in a different way, and it comes out delicious. Even tough toms provide tender eating when cooked in this fashion.

Start with a boned out turkey breast. Cut the meat into 1/2-inch thick slices and pound them with a mallet. Soak the pieces overnight in butter in the refrigerator.

The next day make a dip using 3/4 cup of milk, two beaten eggs and 1/2 teaspoon of sweet basil. Stir and blend well.

Coat each piece of turkey with the egg dip and drop it into a paper bag containing flour and shake well.

Fry them in medium-hot (350 degrees) grease. Test a small piece first. The grease should be hot but not enough to burn the batter. Figure frying time at about five minutes. Remove and drain the slices and salt lightly.

FRIED RATTLESNAKE BACKSTRAP

Every so often we come across a canebrake rattlesnake. The snakeskin can be used for a hatband, plus the snake itself provides the makings of an unusual meal.

Shoot the snake through the head. Pin the head to the ground and cut it off. Bury it deep. Never touch a rattler's head with your hand or foot. A reflex action could result in snakebite, even from a severed head.

Slit the skin lengthwise along the underside and peel the skin off. Remove the backstrap from a large rattlesnake by boning each side of the backbone. You will have two strips of meat as wide and thick as your first two fingers, and between two and three feet long. Cut the lengths into three-inch sections.

Dip the pieces into a simple milk and egg batter and drop them into a sack holding pepper-seasoned flour.

Fry the sections in medium-hot (350 degrees) peanut oil until done in about five minutes.

ARKANSAS CITY DISTILLATE

If you like a peppy barbecue sauce with a real kick, try this. It's no sweet, delicate sauce. It may make you stamp your foot, run rabbits and bark at the moon.

Blend four tablespoons each of salt and sugar into four cups of hot water.

Blend four tablespoons each of chili powder and coarse ground black pepper into four cups of apple cider vinegar.

Mix the seasoned water and seasoned vinegar together in a one gallon Dutch oven with a lid. Add four cups of high quality catsup. Stir in one finely chopped onion.

Let the covered mixture simmer outside for three to four hours. A Coleman camp stove is handy for this purpose. As the sauce simmers you will have neighbors come visiting that you haven't seen in a long time. You can add more salt or sugar near the end of the simmering if desired.

Chapter 12
Bowhunting Hazards

Bowhunters consider themselves the safest of hunters, yet some will be injured each season. During my research I queried all the fish and game commissions. One of the questions asked dealt with bowhunting injuries. Their answers were similar. In summary, they replied: "Bowhunter injuries are very few, minor in severity, mostly involving minor cuts and falls. Usually these injuries are self-inflicted and we suspect most are not reported."

The potential for serious injury is certainly present. Unfortunately, some bowhunters have been severely, even fatally, injured.

It should be obvious that climbing trees and handling sharp broadheads is a dangerous combination. When we first begin bowhunting we are very much aware of these facts and we exercise extreme caution. However, it's only human nature to ease off and treat equipment and climbing a bit more casually after we've been hunting for a few seasons.

That old saying, "Familiarity breeds contempt," is very true. This is the reason behind a lot of accidents. A striking example comes to mind.

When my son Travis and I were traveling the archery tournament trail, a young archer accompanied us to the 1972 National Field Archery Tournament. His name was Dave and he was a very good and enthusiastic archer and bowhunter. Dave was a college student and worked part time in construction. He had good natural balance and didn't care if he was working on the ground floor or setting framework up ten stories high. Height held no fears for Dave. He moved around with the sureness and agility of a squirrel.

That year, while setting up a tree stand, Dave fell just 15 feet and suffered compound fractures of both legs. It took the sheriff's department all afternoon to transport Dave out of the woods and to a hospital. It was six months before Dave could return to school and his job.

Falling from elevated tree stands is the major cause of serious bowhunting accidents. Bowhunters can fall while climbing or descending. They've been known to fall asleep and tumble off their seats.

Sometimes it's not their own doing. Stand support systems can break or come unbolted, especially with homemade seats. Another common cause

The case for a good safety belt when hunting from a tree stand cannot be overemphasized. It could save your life.

Here are some safety belt rules:

• Never use a slip knot to secure a safety rope or belt to your body. A tightening rope or strap could choke off your breath.

• Never wear any belt or rope that will make escape difficult when under tension from a fall.

• Keep safety belt slack between your body and the tree to a minimum. There will be less shock in the event of a fall.

Another potential bowhunting hazard is the permanent tree stand, usually erected on private land. These stands tend to be ignored except during deer season. They are exposed to the elements and wildlife all year long. Many of them are jerry-built to start with. After all, they will only be used a few days out of the year so why bother with top quality materials, is the misguided thinking of many hunters.

As a result, ladder rungs become weakened, supports rot and seats tilt and loosen. The unsuspecting hunter climbs up to one of these dangerous

of falling is attempting an awkward shot and losing your balance.

The use of a good safety belt while up in a stand, and common sense while climbing would seem to be a simple answer. The same thing applies to driving an automobile, yet how many people still refuse to use their seat belts? There is no simple solution. It's up to the individual. Know your equipment thoroughly and think about what you're doing every step of the way up or down. Only then can accidents be avoided.

Too many bowhunters improvise safety belts, using a rope around their bodies and tied to the tree. Little do they realize that an unexpected drop of just a few inches can cause serious problems. A sudden fall and a tightening rope around the waist or chest can interfere with breathing, sometimes severely.

A rope is better than nothing, but make sure it doesn't become a noose. Anticipate what would happen if you fell suddenly, and tie the rope in such a way that it would not become a hazard. Also be sure that you can free yourself if necessary after your fall has been arrested.

Buy and use a good commercial safety belt. These belts have been studied and tested. Your safety is certainly worth the small investment. Total Shooting Systems and Baker both make excellent safety belts.

Avoid these stands. Too high, too rickety, too dangerous.

Improvised rope safety belt and slip knot can be deadly.

tion that a little forethought when putting up a stand can reap big dividends.

Holding an arrow with a broadhead point is like holding a shaft with a bunch of pointed razor blades at one end. The potential danger should be obvious. I have seen and experienced cuts to hands and legs inflicted by broadheads. One state reported that one of its bowhunters sat on a broadhead. Fortunately, the wound was not too serious.

A broadhead belongs in a quiver or encased in a protective sheath until ready for use. Some hunters feel that they must walk or slip through the woods with an arrow on the string. When stalking, always carry an arrow in a manner providing complete control of that arrow in the event of a slip or fall. Some very serious injuries have resulted from bow-hunters falling on arrows.

Never carry an exposed arrow when walking in a group. Someone is likely to get cut.

Never use a bow quiver without a protective hood covering the broadheads. These exposed bow quivers have ruined many pairs of hunting pants and slashed a lot of legs, too.

I once saw a child with a nasty cut on his face. The boy had run into the nock of an arrow sticking into a target butt at the Little Rock City Range.

Another child had his hand mangled when he reached inside the strings on his father's compound bow just as the bow was fired.

Young children and archery don't mix. Your child is a source of distraction while you are trying to concentrate on accurate shooting. Make absolutely certain that any children keep a safe distance from the shooting line, and never allow them to run toward the target butts to retrieve your arrows. You can take them by the hand and walk up if they insist on helping.

perches only to have it give way without warning. Any permanent stand must be checked regularly and maintained. The hunter should be out before the season scouting for deer sign. That's a good time to inspect the stand for soundness. Parts may have to be replaced, or the whole thing rebuilt. If it's that bad do the work several weeks preceding opening day so the animals have a chance to get used to the new wood.

The experienced bowhunter avoids most hazards just by exercising good hunting procedures. He keeps his stand and climbing equipment in good repair. Heavily traveled game trails and other game sign clue him in on where to expect game and its direction of approach. Experience helps him choose the best stand site. A good scent station helps guide the deer into position for a sure shot with a minimum of archer's body movement up in the stand. If he can draw and aim comfortably he will make an accurate shot. There's no ques-

Improved rope belt with a harness snap as a means of escape, and knots to keep it from constricting the chest.

The Total Shooting Systems safety belt. Note the wide web belting and the two quick escape buckles.

Injuries to bowhunters can come from unexpected sources. In my home state of Arkansas several bowhunters have been shot by squirrel hunters. How can any hunter mistake a human for a squirrel, you might ask. Bowhunters feel secure up their tree stands, confident that they can spot any approaching figures and alert them with a low whistle.

I felt the same way until the day we decided to conduct a little experiment. I had my son take up a position in a tree stand while I moved away out of sight. Knowing exactly where he was, I attempted to "stalk" him. Keeping cover between us, I stayed out of sight. He didn't see me but the first glimpse I had of him was his shoe moving slightly. To a trigger-happy squirrel hunter that would have been enough for him to send a load of high base sixes skyward. Now I have a better understanding of how such accidents happen.

It goes against traditional bowhunting camouflage, but a strip of blaze orange wrapped around the tree below the stand may be a good idea if the woods are full of squirrel hunters. Bowhunters don't have exclusive use of the woods on public lands. Of course, where the seasons don't overlap, the danger is minimized.

I personally know of two incidents where humans were mistaken for deer. During the mid-1950s a commercial fisherman was shot by a bowhunter at Jack's Bay in the White River National Wildlife Refuge. The arrow wound was not fatal but it could have been. Luckily, medical help was nearby and quickly administrated. The victim did not realize that he had been hit. He knew something had happened but was not sure until he saw blood running down his leg. The two-bladed broadhead arrow passed through his left buttock. This accident occured in bad light at gray dawn.

I know both the fisherman and the hunter involved. The shooter was a very experienced archer but had a limited bowhunting background.

The second incident was a near miss by a man experienced in bow and gun hunting. Both shooters were positive they were aiming at deer. The common denominator was poor light conditions. This should tell us something about being positive of our game before drawing. Hasty shots at assumed game can prove tragic. Patience, deliberation and positive identification will reward bowhunters with better opportunities at game and add an immeasurable safety factor.

Obviously, the same care should be taken around livestock. They can and do get through fences and wander. Those crunching leaf sounds coming down the trail may be the landowner's prize Jersey heifer, or someone out looking for her.

Closeup of a quick release buckle on a safety belt.

Two large cottonmouths. Poisonous snakes are a potential danger, but reasonable caution will minimize the threat.

for information about receiving this training. Your ability to help yourself or a friend could save a life.

Studies of American Industry have shown that all accidents are a reflection of unsafe habits and allowing unsafe conditions to exist. If you ask yourself the question, "How can I get hurt?" and take proper precautions, chances are you'll be all right. A careful person in one activity will take those instincts into new activities and soon develop safe habits and eliminate unsafe conditions.

Here are a few general bowhunting safety tips:
- Never shoot a damaged arrow. Look for bent shafts, cracked nocks, loose points, cracked shafts and loose fletching.
- Don't shoot in areas where arrows may be deflected.
- Never shoot a weak (under-spined) wooden arrow from a heavy bow. It could literally explode on a bow. Break and safely discard all damaged wooden arrows. This also applies to aluminum arrows.

Bowhunting is a physically demanding sport. Climbing, long walks and dragging out deer have caused strains and pulled muscles. All this unaccustomed exertion can also cause a heart attack. It's always safest to hunt with a partner in case of emergencies and to share the work.

The usual woodland nuisances such as ticks, biting insects and snakes face bowhunters. Normal precautions and repellants should be used. Watch where you put your feet and hands. Bowhunting generally takes place in the fall before poisonous snakes have denned up for winter. As a rule snakes stay out of your way but a stalking hunter moving very quietly could surprise one. But that danger is minimal, considering the odds.

Allergic reactions to certain tree bark, poison ivy, oak and sumac have ruined many bowhunts. These plants have kept susceptible people from hunting and enjoying other outdoor sports. The use of Kerodex Cream, made by Averst Laboratories, before exposure has proved to be effective in many cases.

Another product worth considering is Ex-Nolo-Thylene, made by Bethurum Laboratories, It has been field tested and marketed as a new treatment for exposure to poison ivy, oak and sumac. It is also used on Portuguese man-of-war and jellyfish stings. I have not used either product, but they are endorsed by various outdoor organizations, according to my information.

All outdoorsmen should know first-aid techniques. Contact your local chapter of the American

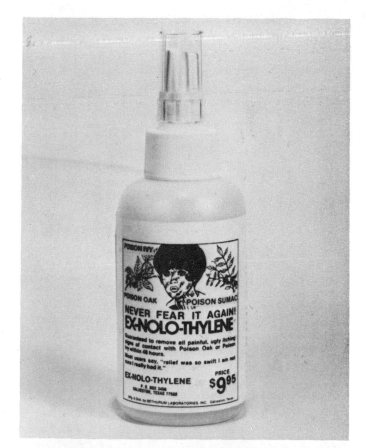

Ex-Nolo-Thylene is a new and effective treatment for poison ivy, poison oak or poison sumac from Bethurum Laboratories.

One of the largest mule deer ever taken by a modern bowhunter. The Utah buck's antlers scored 196 3/8 points, Pope and Young.

A five-point bull elk from Colorado. Elk are huge compared to deer, but are still susceptible to well-placed broadheads.

- Keep bowstrings and cables in good shape.
- Make routine examinations of tree stands and other related equipment.
- Protect all cutting edges.
- Don't carry a flashlight equipped with a magnet holding device. It can affect your compass needle bearing dramatically.
- Never climb or hunt without someone else being nearby, or at least knowing where you are and when you expect to return.
- Do not approach downed game closely until you've determined that it is dead. Never attempt to dispatch a wounded animal with a knife. Shoot it again. Wounded deer have injured and even killed hunters.
- Carry a first-aid kit, including the usual items, plus a snake bite kit, and any tablets or medication needed to counteract the effect of insect stings and bites, if you're allergic to them.

Bowhunting is the safest way to hunt big game, but it can be made even safer by using common sense and a few preventive measures.

Using a bow quiver without a protective hood is hazardous.

Chapter 13
Game Management

A regulated hunting season is necessary for the survival and continued propagation of the nation's game herds. Sport hunting is an essential game management tool. Wild game cannot be manipulated and culled as we do with domestic livestock. Some game can be live-trapped for examination, tagging and transport to other areas, but the vast majority of game animals roam at will. When their population grows to exceed the carrying capacity of their habitat, or when the animals' activities conflict with human interests, a crisis develops.

But before the situation gets that critical the surplus animals should have been removed to keep the herd in balance with its living space and food supply. The most practical method of harvesting wild animals is through sport hunting.

Our sport has drawn criticism and lawsuits from a growing number of people operating through various organizations presenting themselves as "The True Friends of Wildlife." These groups condemn sport hunting and intend to stop it. Their premise is that if animals were left completely alone some form of natural Utopia would exist. Wrong. Nature doesn't work that way.

The elimination of sport hunting would be catastrophic to our harvestable wildlife and countless non-game species as well. Why? The answer involves economics — money — money to hire trained biologists, support scientific research and provide law enforcement protection. Money is also needed to staff the regulating agencies that coordinate and direct wildlife management programs on both the federal and state levels. Sportsmen provide these vital functions.

The U. S. Fish and Wildlife Service is funded by an appropriation from Congress. It also receives revenue from the sale of Migratory Bird Hunting and Conservation Stamps (duck stamps), and other fees.

Most state fish and game agencies are funded by the proceeds from the sale of hunting and fishing licenses, and funds returned under the Dingell-Johnson Act and the Pittman-Robertson Wildlife Restoration Programs.

Some state conservation agencies receive additional revenue from taxes on their mineral, oil and timber resources. One gets some money from a sales tax. But as a general rule the bulk of the money to support state wildlife agencies comes from the sportsman's pocket when he buys a hunting and fishing license.

The Dingell-Johnson Act imposes a ten percent excise tax on sport fishing equipment at the manufacturer's level. These funds are used to improve fish management techniques, provide protection for aquatic habitat, provide for public access to fishing waters and aid in construction of new fishing lakes. Dingell-Johnson funds are returned to the local level on a three federal dollars to one state dollar ratio for approved projects. Since 1950 an average of $11.3 million per year has been returned to state agencies.

The Pittman-Robertson Federal Aid To Wildlife Restoration Program assists in land acquisition, habitat improvement and wildlife research. It is funded by a ten to 11 percent excise tax on sporting firearms, ammunition and archery equipment. A ten percent excise tax is also imposed on handguns.

Pittman-Robertson funds are returned to the state agencies according to a formula based on the number of licensed hunters, land area and population. Funds are allocated for use on approved projects. Usually P-R funds cover approximately three fourths of the costs of state initiated, federally approved projects. Since 1937 this program has provided more than one billion dollars to restore and propagate this country's harvestable and non-game wildlife.

Monies collected under these two federal acts go into special separate funds and are administrated by the U. S. Fish and Wildlife Service. These acts are both "pay as you go" programs. No one can accuse them of contributing to the federal deficit or of being inflationary.

May I point out that the Pittman-Robertson Program was enacted by wise and far-sighted sport hunters while this country was in the depths of the Great Depression and a dollar was very scarce.

The anti-hunter cries that any necessary harvest should be carried out by professional hunters for humanitarian reasons. Who are those professional hunters? Where will they come from? Without sport hunting, who is going to pay their wages? Who is going to provide and maintain wildlife habitat in the face of an ever increasing population and land use demand? What politician would allocate general funds for wildlife in the face of necessary increases for social and defense spending? The plentiful wildlife of today would soon be a thing of the past without sport hunting.

Many game management policies established by our grandparents were good in their day. However, what worked years ago to establish game herds has often succeeded in defeating it's purpose once the herds were established.

An effective game management agency should be free from political support and sport association pressures to manage wildlife efficiently with both long range and immediate programs. It should be free to restrict and build, or free to harvest as need arises.

One of the first management failures due to a wildlife agency's legal inability to move was on the Arizona Kaibab Plateau. Mule deer were completely protected and they flourished. By the time the legal blocks preventing a harvest had been removed, there was no need for a harvest. The mule deer had not only depleted their food supply and starved to death, they also destroyed their habitat. Many years went by before the Kaibab herd was able to recover.

The White River National Waterfowl Refuge in eastern Arkansas was established in 1934-35. It was created and managed for migratory waterfowl. Other species of wildlife benefited indirectly.

My family and I hunted White River before the refuge was formed, and I well remember the forest of giant oak, pecan, hackberry and rock elm. This was squirrel country at its best — all big timber, a completely clear forest floor, no underbrush and not a deer anywhere. One of the first things the new administrators did was to arrange to have the mature timber logged off, possibly to help pay off the cost of acquiring the land.

With the "umbrella" trees gone, sunlight reached the forest floor and browse erupted. The white-tailed deer moved in and thrived.

The refuge was bordered by agricultural lands and the deer were quick to discover free lunch counters. The grumblings of the unhappy farmers were reaching both federal and state agencies, and a very restricted bow season was opened in 1955. During the following seasons hunting restrictions were relaxed as it soon became apparent that bowhunting was safe and provided recreation for many sportsmen. The White River Refuge gained a reputation as "the place" to bowhunt.

In the spring of 1958 the deer herd problem on the refuge came to a head. Rising water from the White and Mississippi rivers forced many of the deer off the refuge and onto freshly planted farmland to face angry farmers. The state fish and game department was powerless to help. All they could say was, in effect, "If you shoot it for crop depredation, let it lay."

An overpopulation of animals, exceeding the carrying capacity of their habitat, can have tragic results. The number of animals must be kept under control for their own good. Sport hunting is an effective and economical management tool.

The .270's and .30-06's cracked loud and clear. There were many heated arguments between farmers whose lands bordered on the refuge and those who lived farther away, the latter claiming that the deer were being slaughtered. It was a terrible situation.

That summer the refuge deer herd was dealt another blow when a die-off occurred in the lower half of the refuge. A commercial fisherman friend told told me of counting 28 dead deer within sight of the road leading to his camp. Both state and federal wildlife officials were trying to cope but bureaucracy plods slowly, especially when forced to overcome many legal stumbling blocks. In the meanwhile, shooting deer for crop depredation continued.

During the spring of 1959 a friend told me of flying over an 80-acre field and counting 121 dead deer rotting on the ground. Shortly after that flight, I met another friend in a Little Rock sporting goods store. He had just bought ten boxes of .270 ammunition because his local store in De Witt was sold out. My friend, Duane Holloway, took me for a ride on his soybean farm. He pointed to a field and said, "Roger, the deer moved in yesterday."

The young soybeans had been about four inches high and you could see where deer had straddled the rows of beans like four-legged power mowers. In one night they wiped out 33 acres of soybeans.

That same spring, Sedgewick Watson, now retired former Chief Forester for the White River Refuge, took Bill Clements, Lewis Rush and me to a refuge owned farm near Ethel, Arkansas. "Fellows," he said, "you're looking at more than 1,500 deer and a bear, and you could see more deer walking around out there if the grass wasn't so high." This experience clearly highlighted the enormity of the problem the farmers were facing.

Finally, in the fall of 1961, a gun hunt was initiated on the refuge. Over 6,000 deer were harvested. Since then the White River herd has been managed so that sportsmen can remove surplus animals annually. The overall number of deer has been reduced to a reasonable level. During a recent season over 1,200 whitetails were taken by hunters.

Shooting deer for crop depredation has stopped. The animals are no longer nuisances and a threat to crops. The herd now lives in harmony with its neighbors.

The U. S Endangered Species Act is a fairly recent piece of legislation with a very restrictive cap on the top end. Lately we've been reading of the strong comeback of alligators in some regions, and the practicality of reestablishing legal harvest quotas. We've also noted reports of alligator attacks on domestic animals and even humans. The toothy reptiles are not about to take over Florida or Louisiana but there's a good indication that their numbers may have grown too large in places.

Feral animals that have turned truly wild can also cause problems for themselves and other wildlife in the vicinity. I'm speaking of wild horses and burros in the West. They are looked on as romantic reminders of western history by most people. But just ask a rancher who's trying to raise livestock on the same land and you'll get another story. The mustangs and burros compete with cattle, sheep and horses for food and water, and also compete with desert bighorns, elk and mule deer where their ranges overlap.

Various groups demand that mustangs and burros be protected, insisting that live-trapping and transporting a few for adoption will solve the problem. The trouble is that there aren't enough eager adopters to make a difference. Trapping and transporting these large animals is also very expensive.

The mustangs and wild burros are rapidly eating themselves out of a food supply, and when that's gone, starvation is inevitable. Meanwhile, the condition of the range deteriorates to the detriment of all concerned.

The human population of this country is increasing steadily. Many people now live in cities or suburbs far removed from nature and the world of hunting and fishing. Some never feel anything but asphalt or concrete beneath their feet. They have no personal knowledge of what hunting and fishing are all about. All they know is what they see on television and read in the newspapers. For some reason, it seems that all news directors in metropolitan areas, regardless of the media, are anti-hunting. They seldom miss an opportunity to show hunting in a bad light.

This adds fuel to the fires of the anti-hunting groups who find a naive and susceptible audience ready to accept emotional pleas to protect the animals from the "bad guys," the hunters.

Each year more people question our privilege to hunt for sport. And it is a privilege, not a right, subject to state and federal law. Each year our image as safe, law-abiding sportsmen becomes more difficult to maintain, our language more important and our activities more vital to sport hunting and to America's wildlife.

Our fish and game departments set minimum power standards for both gun and bowhunting. These standards are established based on proved field experience. No wildlife agency is going to allow the use of inadequate or inhumane weapons. Nor will they ever consider opening a season on any species whose numbers are in doubt. Remember that only a handful of wildlife species may be hunted and those game species are constantly monitored for any change in population figures.

We should point with pride at the many accomplishments of wildlife biologists. Take the re-establishment of the wild turkey for example. The big bronze birds have been introduced into their old habitats nationwide, and into many new areas where they never existed before. Through wise, modern and efficient trapping and transporting methods the birds are more widespread now than ever before in history. American wild turkeys have been stocked in West Germany, and are doing well.

Non-game species get their share of attention too. The bald eagle and peregrine falcon restoration projects are noteworthy. Artificially reared birds have been successfully released into the wild and are now breeding naturally. More will be released. Sportsmen's money pays for these programs. Who benefits? Everyone.

The general public has seen enough people shot on television shows to associate firearms with instant death. Such is not the case in real life, as any hunter knows. An animal may be dead on its feet yet run off a surprising distance before falling. An arrow is considered as cruel or inhumane by some people because the animal doesn't drop stone dead instantly. It doesn't matter to them that the deer expires within seconds.

They see hunting only as killing, not as part of game management.

Some of these people will never admit that hunters play an important role. Others will listen to reason when presented with the biological truths about wildlife.

One of these inescapable truths is that wildlife cannot be stockpiled. When this country was settled and land cleared any natural balance that may have existed between animals, predators and habitat was disturbed forever. Some animals such as the timber wolf and grizzly bear could not adapt to their changing environment, and since they preyed on livestock, their numbers were reduced drastically.

White-tailed deer, on the other hand, benefited from the clearing of forests. Browse grew thick and deer multiplied. Pioneers shot deer the year-round and the animals became scarce in some settled areas. Game laws were enacted to protect them and the science of wildlife management was born. Between the two, deer populations flourished again. It is estimated that today there are far more whitetails in America than there were when the first settlers stepped ashore.

We've already seen what happens when populations of hardy, adaptable, prolific animals are left to expand unchecked. Nature reaps its own harvest through disease and starvation. These are far crueler deaths than a hunter's bullet or broadhead.

So far we haven't touched on the recreational and economical aspects of sport hunting. Millions of people go deer hunting each year. Only a small percentage take a deer but they all welcome the challenge.

Hunters contribute to the economy. They buy licenses, gas, food, lodging, clothing and equipment.

Then there's the venison. Surely it's better to utilize this great renewable natural resource rather than let the animals starve and rot in the woods. Wildlife is a natural resource — a "crop" of nature, so to speak, and there is no justifiable reason why an annual harvest should not take place. Quite the contrary, as we've attempted to explain here.

A mallard duck shot in full flight with an arrow from Ben Pearson's bow.

To Roger
Best Wishes
Ben Pearson

Chapter 14
Bowhunting Regulations

As part of my homework in preparing this book I sent questionnaires to the appropriate wildlife agencies in all 50 states, the District of Columbia, Guam and Puerto Rico.

I asked various questions about the status of bowhunting, history, regulations and restrictions, number of bowhunters, hunter success, bowhunting related accidents and an opinion about anti-hunting efforts in their state, to name a few.

Most questionnaires were completed and returned promptly. Others took a while to get back to me. A couple were so full of bureaucratic jargon it would have taken a Philadelphia lawyer to decipher them. Puerto Rico did not reply.

During the course of conducting this survey it became apparent that a number of states were reluctant or hesitant in answering the question dealing with anti-hunting group activities. I have the feeling that answering this question would be like giving aid to the enemy.

There is very real opposition by the anti-hunting groups. They are well funded, organized and vocal. It will take cool heads, logic, facts, organization and top caliber leadership to contain this threat to sport hunting.

Our conduct in public as hunters and our statements about hunting will contribute to the success or failure of the anti-hunting movement.

The bow was a legal weapon in 18 states before World War II. Some early state records are sketchy about exactly when special archery seasons were established.

Arkansas, California, Michigan, Minnesota and Wisconsin are probably the only states with "archery only" seasons prior to 1941. The rapid growth of bowhunting created a popular demand for these archery hunts. By 1969 every state had established special regulations for bowhunters.

You could probably hunt some form of big game with the bow almost the year-round in Alaska. Arkansas and Rhode Island seem to be vying for the longest bow season for deer. Maryland and Delaware also have very long bowhunting seasons. Arkansas allows you to hunt turkey gobblers with the bow for six months plus a week.

Very long bow seasons do not mean a proportionate increase in hunter success or total kill. Bowhunting is primarily a fall warm weather sport. Long seasons do, however, stimulate interest and increase the number of licenses sold, adding revenue to fish and game coffers. There has been a general tendency among states to establish more special area bow hunts and to lengthen seasons.

Only 34 states require a separate bowhunting license in addition to a regular hunting license. Iowa and Kansas do not permit non-residents to hunt deer or turkeys. North Carolina offers a general Sportsman's License which entitles the holder to all hunting privileges in the state, on public land only, of course. Several other states are considering similar measures.

Personal bowhunting tags are considered a nuisance by some hunters, yet recognized as a means of increasing revenue by others. Some state bowhunting organizations have requested that the separate tags be required. Bowhunters like to pay their own way. Undoubtedly, budget conscious game commissions look favorably on sporting activities that pay their own costs and pose no threat to game herds.

Draw weight requirements vary from state to state, with 40 pounds at 28 inches being the norm for deer hunting. Some states require a heavier bow for big game larger than deer.

To be legal in several states, a bow must be able to cast a broadhead hunting arrow a specified distance. This is a good way to establish meaningful criteria for the many types of bows in use today.

Broadhead width requirements range from 3/4 inch to 1 inch minimum. If a minimum length is specified it is generally 1½ inches; or they want three inches of cutting edges combining all blades. States having additional requirements normally specify two or more steel cutting edges on a barbless point design. Several states have a maximum broadhead width limit of 1½ inches.

Minimum weight requirements for broadheads are low and all modern 125-grain heads will exceed them, and be legal.

All modern arrow shaft materials are legal. Wyoming requires a minimum 400-grain arrow for deer, and a minimum 500-grain arrow for elk, moose and grizzly bear. South Dakota and Tennessee require that a hunting arrow measures at least 24 inches; and New Mexico has a 25-inch minimum length. There was no mention of these minimum lengths including the broadhead or not. Check your current state regulations.

New Hampshire, Rhode Island and Texas require that your name and address be printed on the arrow with a non-water soluble substance.

Bowsights are legal in every state. The use of magnifying or telescopic bowsights are not legal for bowhunting in Arkansas.

There are several devices designed to hold a bow at full draw. Thirty-four states reported that these devices are illegal; with two other states undecided.

Massachusetts, Nebraska, Ohio, Utah and Vermont ban the hand-held mechanical release.

When hunter success figures are given they pertain to the number of bowhunters pursuing a specific species, not the total number of bowhunters in that state. For example, 10.5 percent of the bowhunters in Wyoming who went after pronghorn were successful — not to mean that 10.5 percent of all Idaho bowhunters bagged an antelope.

There were several states reporting a success figure of over 20 percent on deer. Louisiana noted an amazing 35 percent success on whitetails. Wyoming responded that 46.7 percent of the bowhunters trying for moose were successful. But, very few moose permits were issued, so don't be mislead by that high percentage.

Generally, a young hunter must be accompanied by a licensed adult and be of minimum age before he can hunt in most states. Twenty states require a young hunter to pass a Hunter Safety Course before he can get his first license. Maryland requires that everyone have a Hunter Safety Certificate, or a recent out of date hunting license, before a new license can be issued.

Various amounts of blaze orange are required in 33 states for some or all deer hunting with a gun. Blaze orange is needed to hunt on some public lands and wildlife management areas, but hunters make their own decisions about using the bright color on private lands. Blaze orange is usually not required of bowhunters unless they are hunting with a bow during the firearms season. Some states did not answer the question concerning blaze orange. Some require it on all big game hunts. Others have a minimum requirement. Check your own state laws.

As to accidents, the most common injuries are self-inflicted such as falls and cuts. My survey turned up 22 states reporting "mistaken for game" injuries. Sixteen of these were fatal. Some were inflicted by other bowhunters, and some by gun hunters who mistook bowhunters for game.

One death in Mississippi involved a bowhunter with a drug pod-equipped arrow in possession; one bowhunter fatally injuring another. One questionnaire listed a drowning when a bowhunter went into a lake to retrieve a wounded deer.

Temporary, portable tree stands are legal in all states. Most states specify that the stands do no

Hunters should not overlook water to help in bringing out big game. This black bear was arrowed in Quebec's canoe country.

BOWHUNTING REGULATIONS

If not badly spooked, some young bucks will often stop and look back giving the alert hunter time for a quick shot.

permanent damage to the tree, or no visible damage, depending on the terminology and state. Permanent stands on private land are usually not regulated. Minnesota said they have a six-foot maximum stand height restriction.

The total number of bowhunters in the United States is difficult to judge accurately because not all states have complete data, but the figure appears to be close to 1.75 million.

More important, all states but two reported that the sport was growing. Louisiana, with its high bowhunter success on deer, described bowhunting interest as "stable," and California simply said "no" without further explanation.

As far as I know, my survey is the most current one nationwide. Statistics fluctuate, of course, but the numbers given here are sufficient for comparison and discussion purposes.

For complete, up-to-date details of bowhunting regulations refer to the game laws in your home state, or the state in which you plan to hunt.

Department of Conservation and Natural Resources Division of Game and Fish
Montgomery, Alabama 36130

Bowhunting has been legal in the state since the early 1950s. A separate bowhunting tag is not required. Alabama does not require a Hunter Safety Certificate, but anyone under 16 years of age must be accompanied by a licensed adult while hunting on Wildlife Management Areas.

There is a 144-square-inch blaze orange requirement on Wildlife Management Area gun deer hunts.

No figures were available on hunter success.

A legal broadhead must have a 7/8-inch minimum width and two or more cutting blades.

Alaska Department of Fish and Game
Bow 3-2000
Juneau, Alaska 99802

Bowhunting has been legal since 1959. An archery license is not required. A legal hunting bow shall pull at least 45 pounds. Alaska has no other tackle restrictions. They do not require a Hunter Safety Certificate or the wearing of blaze orange.

It is estimated that there are 1,400 bowhunters, representing approximately two percent of the state's licensed hunters. It is very possible that Alaska has more non-resident bowhunters than resident bowhunters. There are no success figures available.

Arizona Game and Fish Department
2222 West Greenway Road
P.O. Box 9099
Phoenix, Arizona 85068

Arizona sportsmen have enjoyed bowhunting privileges since 1969. A regular hunting license is required, along with a free archery permit.

A legal hunting bow pulls at least 40 pounds at 28 inches draw. A broadhead must measure 7/8 inch minimum width, with two or more metal cutting edges.

Arizona does not require a Hunter Safety Certificate, or blaze orange. The minimum age for hunting with gun or bow is ten years old.

The state's approximately 10,000 bowhunters represent about five percent of all licensed hunters.

Bowhunter success ratio runs about three percent on deer, ten percent on elk and 23 percent on javelina.

Bowhunting in Arizona is on the increase.

Arkansas Game and Fish Commission
2 Natural Resources Drive
Little Rock, Arkansas 72205

Bowhunting in Arkansas has a long history, beginning in 1938. Razorback bowmen enjoy special game seasons, along with the longest archery season in the nation.

A legal hunting bow shall weigh at least 40 pounds at 28 inches, or during the draw length of the bow, and shall shoot a 7/8-inch minimum width broadhead. Telescopic or magnifying sights are not legal.

A Hunter Safety Certificate is not required, but a blaze orange vest and hat are required during any gun season.

Arkansas has approximately 36,000 bowhunters, with about ten percent of the state's licensed hunters using the bow.

There has been a five percent annual increase in the number of bowhunters. The success ratio averages a bit less than four percent.

State of California
Department of Fish and Game
1416 Ninth Street
Sacramento, California 95814

Bowhunting has always been legal in California. It could be considered the birthplace of the sport in America.

A special archery license is not mandatory. A legal hunting bow must be able to shoot a broadhead hunting arrow at least 130 yards horizontal distance. A broadhead must measure 7/8 inch minimum width, with two or more metal cutting edges.

A Hunter Safety Certificate is required of all resident gun or bowhunters. Blaze orange is not required. The minimum age limit to hunt deer or bear with gun or bow is 12 years old.

There are approximately 40,000 bowhunters in California. About seven percent of all licensed hunters hunt with a bow. State officials feel the level of bowhunting activity is static at present.

Bowhunter success is low, with only two percent bagging deer. A few bears are also taken, that success ratio averaging three percent.

Colorado Division of Wildlife
Department of Natural Resources
6060 Broadway
Denver, Colorado 80216

There have been special archery seasons since 1961. An archery license is required for deer, elk or antelope.

A legal hunting bow must pull at least 40 pounds for deer, and 50 pounds for elk. A legal broadhead will measure 7/8 inch minimum width, having at least two cutting edges.

A Hunter Safety Certificate is required for gun only for both residents and non-resident first time hunting license applicants. Blaze orange is required during any gun deer season.

Bowhunter success figures are not available. Recent archery license figures indicate 21,000 bowhunters, with six percent of the state's licensed hunters using the bow. Bowhunting is on the increase.

State of Connecticut
Department of Environmental Protection
State Office Building
Hartford, Connecticut 06115

Bowhunting in Connecticut has been legal on privately owned land since 1947, and on state owned land since 1957. A bowhunting permit is required for deer and turkey hunting. The only tackle requirement is that a bow must be capable of shooting a broadhead arrow 150 yards.

First-time license buyers must have a Hunter Safety Certificate. The minimum age limit for hunting with a gun is 12 years old, and 16 years old for bowhunting. Blaze orange is required for any gun deer season.

Survey figures show a little over seven thousand bowhunters. They represent slightly more than ten percent of the state's total number of licensed hunters.

Bowhunting in Connecticut is on the increase.

Department of Natural Resources and
** Environmental Control**
Division of Fish and Wildlife
Post Office Box 1401
Dover, Delaware 19901

Bowhunting has been legal since 1956. An archery tag is not required. A 7/8-inch minimum width broadhead is Delaware's only tackle requirement.

A Hunter Safety Certificate is required of residents under the age of 18 years. Blaze orange is required during any firearm deer season.

A mail survey indicates approximately 3,000 bowhunters, and the sport showing a slow yearly increase. About 11 percent of the state's licensed hunters use the bow, with one percent being successful on deer.

Florida Game and Fresh Water Fish Commission
Farris Bryant Building
Tallahassee, Florida 32301

Bowhunting has been legal since the early 1950s. A special archery permit is required. There are no tackle restrictions.

A Hunter Safety Certificate is not required. Blaze orange is required in specified Wildlife Management Areas.

There were 22,120 bowhunters at the time of the survey. About eight percent of the state's licensed hunters use the bow. Success figures are not available. Bowhunting is on the increase.

State of Georgia
Department of Natural Resources
270 Washington Street, S.W.
Atlanta, Georgia 30334

Georgia has had legal bowhunting since 1963. A separate, special archery license is issued.

Legal tackle calls for a hunting bow to pull at least 40 pounds at 28 inches draw length, with a 7/8-inch minimum width on broadheads.

A Hunter Safety Certificate is required for residents and for non-resident applicants. Blaze orange is stipulated for gun deer hunting.

Our survey showed nearly 31,000 bowhunters in Georgia, which is about eight percent of all licensed hunters. There has been a steady increase in bowhunting activity.

Bowhunters do well, with an 11 percent success figure.

Division of Aquatic and Wildlife Resources
Department of Agriculture
P.O. Box 23367 GMF
Guam M. I. 96921

Bowhunting has been legal here since 1964. The principal game is deer and wild pigs.

A legal bow must pull at least 40 pounds, and a broadhead must be 7/8-inch wide or more, with two or more cutting edges.

A Hunter Safety Certificate is not required. The minimum age limit for hunting with a gun or bow is 14 years old. Blaze orange is not necessary, except on military lands.

There are only about 25 archers on Guam and their success is fairly low. Authorities reported increasing interest in bowhunting.

State of Hawaii
Department of Land and Natural Resources
Division of Forestry and Wildlife
1151 Punchbowl Street
Honolulu, Hawaii 96613

Bowhunting is legal and they do not require an archery permit. A legal hunting bow shall pull at least 45 pounds for a straight bow, 30 pounds for a compound and 35 pounds for a laminated full recurve bow. There are no broadhead restrictions.

A Hunter Safety Certificate is not mandatory, but they do have a minimum age requirement for gun hunting. Blaze orange is required during any gun hunt.

Bowhunting is on the increase and it is possible that Hawaii has a larger number of non-resident bowhunters than resident. The success figures on deer, pigs and goats are unavailable.

State of Idaho
Department of Fish and Game
600 South Walnut Street, P.O. Box 25
Boise, Idaho 83707

Idaho has seen legal bowhunting since the 1950s. The first special archery permits were issued in 1975. Idaho bowhunters have a variety of big game available to them.

To be legal, a hunting bow must pull at least 40 pounds at 28-inch draw. A legal broadhead must measure at least 7/8-inch wide.

A Hunter Safety Certificate is required for young hunters under 15 years of age. The minimum age limit for hunting with both gun and bow is 12 years old.

Blaze orange is required for firearms big game hunts.

Bowhunting is reported to be on the rise in Idaho for deer, elk, pronghorn antelope and bear.

Illinois Department of Conservation
Lincoln Tower Plaza
524 South Second Street
Springfield, Illinois 62706

Bowhunting has been legal in Illinois for many years. A special archery license is required. A legal bow must pull at least 40 pounds within the archer's normal draw length. A legal broadhead must be of barbless construction.

A Hunter Safety Certificate is required for young hunters under the age of 16 years. Blaze orange is required for any gun deer hunts.

The number of bowhunters has been increasing steadily. Their success ratio is a very respectable 14 percent on deer.

State of Indiana
Department of Natural Resources
State Office Building
Indianapolis, Indiana 46204

Bowhunting has been legal since 1951. They do not require a special archery license. A legal hunting bow shall pull at least 35 pounds. There are no broadhead restrictions.

A Hunter Safety Certificate is not required. Blaze orange is required for gun and for bow during the combination muzzleloading and archery hunt.

There are approximately 40,000 bowhunters, with 11 percent of the state's licensed hunters using the bow. Bowhunting is on the increase. Indiana's bowhunters have a 10.2 percent success on deer.

Iowa Conservation Commission
Wallace State Office Building
Des Moines, Iowa 50319

The bow has been legal for small game since 1934. The first archery deer season was 1953. An archery license is required for bowhunters. A non-resident cannot hunt deer in Iowa. There are no restrictions on the bow or arrow; however, any device that will hold a bow at full draw is illegal.

A Hunter Safety Certificate is not required. Blaze orange must be worn during any gun deer season. In recent years Iowa has issued over 17,000 archery licenses annually. This is almost six percent of all licensed hunters in the state.

Iowa bowhunters scored very high in percentage of success, averaging 26 percent on deer.

Kansas Fish and Game
Pratt Headquarters
Bow 54A, Rural Route 2
Pratt, Kansas 67124

Bowhunting has been legal in Kansas for many years. A special permit is required for hunting deer, in addition to a hunting license. Non-residents may not hunt deer or turkeys in Kansas.

A legal bow must pull at least 45 pounds at 25-inch draw. To be legal a broadhead must have metal cutting blades and a metal or high impact plastic ferrule.

A Hunter Safety Certificate is required of resident gun hunters. The minimum age for gun hunting is 16 years old, and 14 years old for bowhunting. One hundred square inches of blaze orange is required for gun hunts.

There are approximately 16,000 bowhunters, with nearly seven percent of the state's licensed hunters using the bow.

Bowhunting is showing an increase. Late figures indicate nearly a 30 percent success on deer, and 20 percent success on pronghorns.

State of Kentucky
Department of Fish and Wildlife Resources
Frankfort, Kentucky 40601

Bowhunting has been legal for over 25 years. There is no special license required. The only tackle restriction is for a 7/8-inch minimum width broadhead with two blades.

A Hunter Safety Certificate is not required. Blaze orange must be worn during any gun deer hunts.

Kentucky is a very active bowhunting state. It has 42,000 or more bowhunters, with 13 percent of the state's licensed deer hunters using the bow. Bowhunting is definitely on the increase with a seven percent hunter success ratio on deer.

Louisiana Department of Wildlife and Fisheries
P.O. Box 4004
Ouachita Station
Monroe, Louisiana 71203

The bow has always been legal, with special seasons starting in 1957. A special archery license is required. A legal bow must pull at least 30 pounds at 28-inch draw length. A legal broadhead must have a 7/8-inch minimum width.

A Hunter Safety Certificate is not required, but blaze orange must be worn during gun deer hunts.

Louisiana has 14,000 bowhunters with about four percent of the state's licensed hunters using the bow. It is felt that bowhunting is not increasing but remaining stable. There is a 35 percent hunter success ratio on deer. This is an extraordinarily high figure and confirmed by state officials.

Maine Department of Inland Fisheries and Wildlife
284 State Street
State House Station 41
Augusta, Maine 04333

Bowhunting has always been legal. An archery permit is required. A legal hunting bow must shoot a 7/8-inch minimum width broadhead arrow at least 150 yards.

A Hunter Safety Certificate is not required. The minimum age limit for hunting with a gun is ten years old, and 12 years old for bowhunting. Blaze orange is required for gun deer hunts.

Maine issues about 4,400 archery tags annually. Interestingly, Maine bowmen bag more black bears than deer.

Bowhunting is on the rise here.

Maryland Wildlife Administration
Tawes State Office Building
Annapolis, Maryland 21401

Maryland does not require an archery license. A legal hunting bow must pull at least 30 pounds at full draw. A legal broadhead measures 7/8-inch minimum width.

A Hunter Safety Certificate is required. Blaze orange is required during any gun deer season.

There are about 17,500 bowhunters and it is felt that the sport is gaining in popularity. Bowhunters harvested 1,749 deer in a recent season.

Massachusetts Division of Fisheries and Wildlife
Field Headquarters
Westboro, Massachusetts 01581

Bowhunting has been legal since 1957. No special archery license is required.

A legal bow must pull at least 40 pounds at 28-inch draw. Massachusetts places minimum and maximum limits on broadheads. The point width may not exceed 1½ inches, or be smaller than 7/8 inch. Mechanical releases are not legal.

A Hunter Safety Certificate is not required. The minimum age limit for hunting with either a gun or a bow is 12 years old. Blaze orange is required for gun deer hunts.

About ten percent, or 11,500, of the state's licensed hunters use the bow. Bowhunting is increasing, but the success ratio remains low; only about two percent of the archers bagging deer.

Michigan Department of Natural Resources
Box 30028
Lansing, Michigan 48909

Bowhunting has been legal since 1937. An archery permit for deer is required. There are no minimum tackle restrictions.

A Hunter Safety Certificate is required for those between the ages of 12 to 16 years. Blaze orange is required for firearm deer hunting.

There are 215,000 bowhunters, with nearly 19 percent of the state's licensed hunters using the bow. Bowhunting is on the increase with 13.7 percent of the hunters being successful on deer. There are no available figures for black bear.

Minnesota Department of Natural Resources
Centennial Office Building
St. Paul, Minnesota 55155

Bowhunting has been legal since 1929, with special archery seasons beginning in 1943. A special archery permit is not required.

A legal bow pulls at least 40 pounds at or before full draw. Minnesota goes into detail about its broadhead requirements. A legal broadhead is one inch wide for a two-blade point. A three-blade head must have a three-inch circumference encompassing the cutting edges. There is a minimum broadhead weight limit of 110 grains. The blades must be made of high carbon steel and kept sharp.

Non-mechanical string releases are legal.

A Hunter Safety Certificate is required for those under 16 years old. The minimum age limit for hunting with a gun or bow is 12 years old. Blaze orange is required during any gun deer season.

Approximately 55,000 sportsmen, or ten percent of the state's licensed hunters, use the bow. Ten percent are usually successful on deer, and 22 percent regularly bag bears.

Mississippi Department of Wildlife Conservation
Southport Mall P.O. Box 451
Jackson, Mississippi 39205

Bowhunting has always been legal in Mississippi. A special archery license is required. There are no tackle restrictions.

A Hunter Safety Certificate is not required, but they do require blaze orange during firearms deer seasons.

There are 37,500 bowhunters, with 13 percent of the state's licensed hunters using the bow. Mississippi has a 28.7 percent success on deer. Bowhunting is on the increase.

Missouri Department of Conservation
P.O. Box 180
Jefferson City, Missouri 65102

Bowhunting has been legal for over 35 years. An archery permit is required. There are no minimum tackle requirements.

A Hunter Safety Certificate is not required, but blaze orange is required for firearms deer hunts.

There are over 46,500 bowhunters currently, with about ten percent of the state's licensed hunters using the bow. For the last several years eight percent of Missouri's bowhunters have bagged a deer, and .87 percent have taken a turkey. Bowhunting is on the increase.

State of Montana
Department of Fish, Wildlife, and Parks
1420 East Sixth Avenue
Helena, Montana 59620

Montana authorized special archery seasons and issued its first bowhunting licenses in 1968. The state has no restrictions on bow draw weight or on broadheads.

A Hunter Safety Certificate is required. Young hunters must be at least 12 years old to hunt with either gun or bow. Blaze orange must be worn during big game hunts.

A recent season saw 15,400 bowhunters licensed in Montana. About 13 percent of them are successful on whitetails, mule deer, elk and pronghorns.

Bowhunting is on the rise in this state.

Nebraska Game and Parks Commission
District II
P.O. Box 508
Bassett, Nebraska 68714

Nebraska issues an "archery only" license. No other hunting license is required of resident bowhunters.

A legal bow must pull at least 40 pounds at 28-inch draw. A legal broadhead width limit is 7/8 inch minimum, and the cutting edges must total three inches.

The arrow must be drawn, held and released by hand without the aid of any mechanical release.

Young hunters under age 16 cannot apply for an archery permit unless they have a Hunter Safety Certificate. The minimum age for big game hunting is 14 years old. Blaze orange is required for big game gun hunts.

Nebraska has about 11,500 bowhunters, with six percent of the state's hunters using the bow. Hunter success runs about 21 percent on deer and four percent on pronghorn antelope. About 11 percent of the bowhunters who go after turkeys are successful in the spring, as against 28 percent in the fall.

Nevada Department of Wildlife
P.O. Box 10678
Reno, Nevada 89520

Bowhunting has been legal for over 35 years. A special archery license is not required.

A legal hunting bow must be capable of shooting a 400-grain arrow 150 yards over level terrain. A legal broadhead must be no less than 3/4 inch wide.

A Hunter Safety Certificate is required of both residents and non-residents. The minimum age limit for hunting with either the gun or bow is 12 years old. Blaze orange is not required.

Two percent of the state's licensed hunters, or 1,600 sportsmen, use the bow. About 15 percent of them are successful on deer.

Bowhunting is increasing slowly in Nevada.

New Hampshire Fish and Game Department
34 Bridge Street
Concord, New Hampshire 03301

Bowhunting has been legal since 1949. A special archery license is not required. A legal hunting bow shall pull at least 40 pounds. A legal broadhead shall measure not less than 7/8 inch or more than 1½ inches wide.

A Hunter Safety Certificate is required of first time license applicants — both resident and non-resident. Blaze orange is not required.

The number of bowhunters in New Hampshire is small, about 8,500. They represent ten percent of all the licensed hunters. Six and a half percent are successful on deer, and 10.5 percent on black bears.

State of New Jersey
Department of Environmental Protection
Division of Fish, Game and Wildlife
CN 400
Trenton, New Jersey 08625

Bowhunting has been legal for over 27 years. A special hunting license is required. A legal hunting bow must pull at least 35 pounds and cast a hunting arrow 150 yards. A legal broadhead shall measure 3/4 inch minimum width and 1-3/8 inches minimum length, and have metal cutting edges.

A Hunter Safety Certificate is required for residents and non-residents. Blaze orange is required during any firearm deer season.

A tree stand is legal but must be at least 300 feet from any type of bait.

There are 38,800 bowhunters, with 29 percent of the state's licensed hunters using the bow. About 15 percent of the bowhunters are successful on deer. Bowhunting is on the increase.

New Mexico Department of Game and Fish
State Capitol
Santa Fe, New Mexico 87503

New Mexico does not require a special archery deer tag. A legal hunting bow is required to shoot an arrow with a sharpened steel broadhead more than 160 yards.

A Hunter Safety Certificate is required for young hunters under the age of 18 years old. Blaze orange is not required. Additional information was not provided on the questionnaire reply.

New York State Department of
Environmental Conservation
Albany, New York 12233

New York's first archery hunting licenses went on sale in 1948. To hunt big game with a bow the hunter must have a regular big game license plus a bowhunting stamp, or junior archery stamp for young hunters 14 and 15 years old.

A legal hunting bow must be capable of shooting an arrow with a 7/8-inch minimum width broadhead at least 150 yards.

A Hunter Safety Certificate is required for both residents and non-residents to hunt with either gun or bow.

There is a minimum age limit of 14 years old for small game hunting with a gun, and 16 years old for big game hunting with a gun. The minimum age limit for hunting both large and small game with a bow is 14 years old.

About 12 percent of all the state's licensed hunters use the bow. These approximately 94,000 bowhunters have a five percent success ratio on deer.

Bowhunting is a growing sport in New York.

North Carolina Wildlife Resources Commission
Archdale Building
512 N. Salisbury Street
Raleigh, North Carolina 27611

Bowhunting has always been legal in North Carolina. A special archery license is required unless a hunter buys a Sportsman's License which also covers the primitive weapon requirement. A legal hunting bow must pull at least 45 pounds. There are no broadhead restrictions.

A Hunter Safety Certificate is not required, nor is blaze orange for any hunting.

Exact figures on bowhunters' success ratio were not supplied.

North Carolina bowhunters hunt deer and black bear.

North Dakota Game and Fish Department
2121 Lovett Avenue
Bismark, North Dakota 58505

Bowhunting has been legal since 1954. A special archery license is required. A legal hunting bow will cast a hunting arrow complete with broadhead at least 130 yards. The arrow must be at least 24 inches long. A broadhead must be all metal with point specifications of 3/4 inch minimum and 1½ inches maximum.

A Hunter Safety Certificate is required for big game firearm hunting, but not for bowhunting. The minimum age limit for gun big game hunting is 14 years old, but not for bowhunting. Blaze orange is mandatory for gun big game hunting.

About 9,700 hunters in North Dakota use the bow. Their success averages 15.5 percent on deer.

Bowhunting is on the increase in this state.

Ohio Department of Natural Resources
Division of Wildlife
Fountain Square
Columbus, Ohio 43224

The bow has been a legal hunting weapon since 1857 in conjunction with gun hunting. There have been extended bowhunting seasons for deer since 1953. An archery license is not required. There are no bow or broadhead restrictions. Hand-held string releases are not legal.

The Hunter Safety Certificate requirements and minimum age restrictions are incomplete in this survey. Blaze orange is not required for big game.

There are over 30,000 bowhunters with approximately six percent of the state's licensed hunters using the bow. Bowhunting is on the increase with ten percent of bowhunters being successful on deer.

Oklahoma Department of Wildlife Conservation
P.O. Box 53465
Oklahoma City, Oklahoma 73152

Bowhunting has been legal here for over 30 years. A special archery license is required.

A legal hunting bow must pull at least 40 pounds. Broadhead requirements are a 7/8-inch minimum width, and 1½ inches minimum length. The point must be of metal construction.

A Hunter Safety Certificate is not required. There is a 500-square-inch blaze orange requirement for firearms deer hunting.

Oklahoma has approximately 29,000 bowhunters, with ten percent of the state's licensed hunters using the bow. Hunter success runs about five percent.

Bowhunting is increasing.

Oregon Department of Fish and Wildlife
506 South West Mill Street
P.O. Box 3503
Portland, Oregon 97208

Bowhunting has been legal for 38 years. A special archery license is required. A legal hunting bow shall pull at least 40 pounds for deer, and 50 pounds for elk at your normal draw length. A legal broadhead shall measure 7/8-inch minimum width and be razor sharp.

A Hunter Safety Certificate is not required, nor is blaze orange. There is a minimum age limit of 12 years old for gun or bowhunting.

There are about 27,700 licensed bowhunters in Oregon, representing almost seven percent of all hunters. They do very well. Bowhunter success is around 28 percent on deer, and 14 percent on elk.

Bowhunting is on the increase.

Pennsylvania Game Commission
P.O. Box 1567
Harrisburg, Pennsylvania 17120

Bowhunting has been legal since 1929. An archery license is required for special deer bow seasons only. There are no tackle requirements.

A Hunter Safety Certificate is required for a resident and non-resident first time license purchaser if under the age of 16 years. Blaze orange is required for gun deer hunting. There is a minimum age limit of 12 years old for gun or bow hunting.

There are more than 267,000 bowhunters in Pennsylvania, with 20 percent of the state's licensed hunters using the bow. Bowhunting success averages around three percent on deer.

Bowhunting is on the increase.

State of Rhode Island and Providence Plantations
Department of Environmental Management
Division of Fish and Wildlife
Washington County Government Center
Tower Hill Road
Wakefield, Rhode Island 02879

Bowhunting has been legal since 1956. A special archery license is required. A legal hunting bow must pull at least 40 pounds at the archer's draw length. A legal broadhead is 7/8-inch minimum width with two or more cutting edges.

A Hunter Safety Certificate is required for a first time license. There is a reciprocal agreement with other states. The minimum age limit for hunting with either a gun or bow is 12 years old. Blaze orange is required for any gun deer hunt.

Rhode Island has about a thousand bowhunters, representing roughly seven and a half percent of the state's licensed deer hunters. Bowhunter success is about ten percent.

Bowhunting is on the increase.

South Carolina Wildlife and Marine Resources
 Department
P.O. Box 167
1000 Assembly Street
Columbia, South Carolina 29202

The bow has always been legal in South Carolina. A special archery license is not required. There are no tackle restrictions.

A Hunter Safety Certificate is not required. Blaze orange is required for gun deer seasons.

There are about 8,200 bowhunters, or nearly four percent of the state's licensed hunters using the bow. Hunter success figures were not given.

Bowhunting is on the increase.

South Dakota Department of Game, Fish and Parks
Anderson Building
Pierre, South Dakota 57501

South Dakota held its first archery season in 1956. A special archery license is required for residents. A legal hunting bow must pull at least 40 pounds and shoot a legal hunting arrow 125 yards. The arrow must be at least 24 inches long and the broadhead requirement is a 7/8-inch minimum width and 1½ inches minimum length.

A Hunter Safety Certificate is required for residents 12 to 16 years of age either gun or bow.

Persons under 12 years old are not allowed to hunt with gun or bow. Blaze orange is not mandatory.

There are over 9,400 bowhunters in the state. This is roughly six percent of all licensed hunters. Hunter success on deer runs around 22 percent annually.

Bowhunting is on the increase.

Tennessee Wildlife and Resources Agency
Ellington Agricultural Center
P.O. Box 40747
Nashville, Tennessee 37204

Bowhunting has been legal since the early 1960s. A special resident archery license is required, but non-residents are exempt. A legal hunting bow must be able to cast a legal broadhead-equipped arrow 150 yards. An arrow must be at least 24 inches long. The broadhead must be at least 7/8 inch wide with two or more cutting blades. The point design must be barbless. The broadhead must weigh at least 100 grains and be of sharpened steel.

A Hunter Safety Certificate is required for youngsters ten to 16 years of age on special Juveniles Only hunts on Wildlife Management Areas. Tennessee has a group of special hunts for young hunters and women only for both gun and bow. Blaze orange is required on gun deer hunts.

There are about 43,000 bowhunters, with over seven percent of the state's licensed hunters and 40 percent of the licensed big game hunters using the bow. About eight percent are successful on deer. Figures on wild boar and black bear were not available.

Bowhunting is on the increase.

Texas Parks and Wildlife Department
4200 Smith School Road
Austin, Texas 78744

Texas has had special archery seasons since 1959. An archery license is required.

A legal bow must be capable of shooting a legal arrow a minimum of 130 yards. A broadhead must measure between 7/8 inch minimum and not wider than 1½ inches to be legal. The hunter's name and address must be printed on each arrow with a non-water soluble substance.

A Hunter Safety Certificate is not required, nor is the wearing of blaze orange during firearms seasons.

There are about 37,000 bowhunters in Texas, representing about four percent of the state's licensed hunters. Hunter success averages between eight and ten percent on deer.

Utah Division of Wildlife Resources
1596 West North Temple
Salt Lake City, Utah 84116

Bowhunting in Utah has been legal since 1942. A special archery license is required. A legal hunting bow pulls at least 40 pounds at the archer's draw length. A legal broadhead must be at least 7/8 inch wide. Hand-held string releases are not legal.

A Hunter Safety Certificate is required for residents under 21 years old; non-residents are exempt. Blaze orange is required during any gun deer season.

There are about 23,500 bowhunters in Utah; nearly ten percent of all the state's licensed hunters using the bow. Bowhunting success is around 15 percent on deer, and nine percent on elk.

Bowhunting is on the increase.

Vermont Agency of Environmental Conservation
Fish and Game Department
Montpelier, Vermont 05602

Bowhunting has been legal since 1950. A special archery license is required. The only tackle requirement is that a broadhead measure a minimum of 7/8 inch wide and have two or more cutting edges. Mechanical releases are not legal.

Vermont requires a Hunter Safety Certificate before a hunting license can be issued. Blaze orange is not required.

There are about 27,000 bowhunters, and that number is thought to be stable. About 20 percent of the state's licensed hunters use the bow. Hunter success runs about five percent, or slightly less.

Commonwealth of Virginia
Commission of Game and Inland Fisheries
P.O. Box 11104
Richmond, Virginia 23230

Bowhunting has been legal since 1954. An archery license is not required. A legal bow must be able to shoot a legal arrow at least 125 yards. The broadhead requirement is a minimum width of 7/8 inch.

A Hunter Safety Certificate is not required, nor is the wearing of blaze orange.

There are approximately 40,000 bowhunters, with nine percent of all the state's licensed hunters using the bow. Bowhunting success is about ten percent annually.

Bowhunting is on the increase.

Washington Department of Game
600 North Capitol Way
Olympia, Washington 98504

Bowhunting has been legal for over 30 years. A special archery stamp is required. A legal bow must weigh at least 40 pounds at 28-inch draw. A broadhead must measure a minimum of 7/8 inch and be of barbless design.

A Hunter Safety Certificate is not required, nor is the wearing of blaze orange.

There are approximately 20,000 bowhunters, with six percent of the state's licensed hunters using the bow. Hunter success runs about 20 percent on deer, seven percent on elk and 30 percent on goats. No figures were available for black bears.

Bowhunting is on the increase.

State of West Virginia
Department of Natural Resources
Charleston, West Virginia 25305

Bowhunting in West Virginia dates back to the late 1940s. The state does not require a resident archery tag, but non-residents may purchase an archery only tag.

The only tackle requirement is that broadheads be a minimum of 3/4 inch wide. Youngsters under age 15 may hunt if accompanied by an adult. A Hunter Safety Certificate is not required, nor is the wearing of blaze orange.

There are approximately 45,000 bowhunters; with 14 percent of the state's licensed hunters using the bow. Hunter success averages ten percent on deer.

Bowhunting is increasing.

State of Wisconsin
Department of Natural Resources
Box 7921
Madison, Wisconsin 53707

Bowhunting has been legal since 1931. There is a separate archery license, but you are not required to buy a regular hunting license. A legal hunting bow must pull at least 30 pounds at full draw. The broadhead must measure between 7/8 inch minimum to 1½ inches maximum, and be well sharpened and of metal construction.

A crossbow permit can be issued to a disabled person.

A Hunter Safety Certificate is not required. The minimum age limit for hunting with either gun or bow is 12 years old. Blaze orange must be worn during gun deer hunts.

There are approximately 173,800 bowhunters in Wisconsin; with almost 23 percent of the state's licensed hunters using the bow. Hunter success runs 15-20 percent on deer. Figures on black bears were not available.

Bowhunting is definitely increasing.

State of Wyoming
Game and Fish Department
5400 Bishop Boulevard
Cheyenne, Wyoming 82002

Wyoming has a wide variety of small and big game and issues three different special archery licenses, in addition to regular resident and non-resident hunting licenses.

Big game archery covers deer, elk, pronghorns, moose, bighorn sheep and mountain goats.

An archery license for trophy game covers black bears and mountain lions.

There is a separate archery license for small game and birds.

A legal bow of 40 pounds minimum draw weight must be able to cast a 400-grain arrow over 160 yards for most big game hunting. When hunting elk, grizzly bears or moose the bow must pull a minimum of 50 pounds and cast a 500-grain arrow more than 160 yards. A legal broadhead is one inch wide or more.

A Hunter Safety Certificate is required of anyone born after January 1, 1966. The minimum age limit for hunting with either gun or bow is 14 years old.

A recent survey showed over 7,000 bowhunters; with less than four percent of the state's licensed hunters using the bow. Success figures are for hunters specifically seeking those species: mule deer, 18 percent; white-tailed deer, 15 percent; elk, 11 percent; moose, 46.7 percent; black bears, six percent; and antelope, 33 percent. For example, six percent of the hunters after black bears were successful.

Bowhunting is gaining in popularity.

District of Columbia
Metropolitan Police Department
Washington, D.C. 20001

All wildlife in the District is protected and as a result all hunting is prohibited. There is a provision for wildlife depredation. The wildlife control is administered by the Chief of Police.

NUMBER OF BOWHUNTERS	Approx.
Alabama	40,000
Alaska	1,400
Arizona	10,000
Arkansas	36,000
California	40,000
Colorado	21,000
Connecticut	8,900
Delaware	3,000
Florida	22,000
Georgia	31,000
Guam	25
Hawaii	3,000
Idaho	15,000
Illinois	29,000
Indiana	40,000
Iowa	17,000
Kansas	16,000
Kentucky	42,000
Louisiana	14,000
Maine	4,400
Maryland	17,500
Massachusetts	11,500
Michigan	215,000
Minesota	55,000
Mississippi	37,500
Missouri	46,500
Montana	15,400
Nebraska	11,500
Nevada	1,600
New Hampshire	8,500
New Jersey	38,000
New Mexico	6,000
New York	94,000
North Carolina	9,000
North Dakota	9,700
Ohio	30,000
Oklahoma	29,000
Oregon	27,700
Pennsylvania	267,000
Rhode Island	1,000
South Carolina	8,200
South Dakota	9,400
Tennessee	43,000
Texas	37,000
Utah	23,500
Vermont	27,000
Virginia	40,000
Washington	20,000
West Virginia	45,000
Wisconsin	173,800
Wyoming	7,000

Typical of the many fine items of equipment now available to bowhunters is this adjustable pin bowsight.

ARCHERY SUPPLIERS

Here is a listing of archery suppliers, archery magazines and archery organizations as sources of additional information.

A

Accra 300
805 South 11th Street
Broken Arrow, Oklahoma 74012
BOWSIGHTS and ACCESSORIES

Acme Wood Products Co.
P.O. Box 636
Myrtle Point, Oregon 97458
PORT ORFORD CEDAR ARROW SHAFTS

Adaptive Instruments Corp.
1930 Central Avenue
Boulder, Colorado 80301
"ARROWMETER" CHRONOGRAPH

Allen Original Compound Bow
201 Washington Street
Billings, Missouri 65610
**COMPOUND BOWS, RELEASES and
  ACCESSORIES**

Amacker Products, Inc.
P.O. Box 1432
1011 Beach Street
Tallulah, Louisiana 71282
TREE STANDS

Ambusher Co.
2007 West 7th Street
Texarkana, Texas 75501
PORTABLE LADDER TREE STANDS

Anderson Archery Corp.
Box 130
Grand Ledge, Michigan 48837
ARCHERY SUPPLIES

Archery Discount Co.
P.O. Box 324
Youngwood, Pennsylvania 15697
ARCHERY SUPPLIES

Archery Electronics Co.
7822 Myers Lake Avenue
Rockford, Michigan 49341
ELECTRIC SIGHT PINS

Archery Sights and Products
9724 East 55th Place
Tulsa, Oklahoma 74145
BOWSIGHTS

Arrow Manufacturing, Inc.
1365 Logan Avenue
Costa Mesa, California 92626
ARROW MAKING EQUIPMENT

Arrowhead Manufacturing Co.
12890 25 Mile Road
Utica, Michigan 48087
PORTABLE TREE SEATS

B

Baker Manufacturing Co.
P.O. Box 1003
428 North Street
Augustine Road
Valdosta, Georgia 31601
TREE STAND EQUIPMENT

Barner Release Co.
Box 382
Bozeman, Montana 59715
RELEASES and ARROW RESTS

Barrie Archery Co.
717 Fifth Avenue, S.W.
Waseca, Minnesota 56093
"ROCKY MOUNTAIN RAZOR" BROADHEADS

Bear Archery
Rural Route 4
4600 Southwest 41st Boulevard
Gainesville, Florida 32601
ARCHERY and BOWHUNTING EQUIPMENT

B (Cont'd.)

Bethurum Laboratories, Inc.
P.O. Box 3456
Galveston, Texas 7752
MANUFACTURER OF A POISON IVY TREATMENT

Bighorn Bowhunting Co.
Lafayette, Colorado 80026
RECURVE BOWS

Bohning Adhesives Co., Ltd.
Box 140
Route 2
Lake City, Michigan 49651
ARROW MAKING SUPPLIES and ACCESSORIES

Bowhunter's Discount Warehouse, Inc.
Box 158
Wellsville, Pennsylvania 17365
ARCHERY SUPPLIES

Bowing Enterprises, Inc.
P.O. Box 6076
Arlington, Virginia 22206
"TREBARK" CAMOUFLAGE CLOTHING

Brownell and Company, Inc.
Moodus, Connecticut 06469
BOWSTRING MATERIALS and ACCESSORIES

Browning
Route No. 1
Morgan, Utah 84050
ARCHERY and SPORTING EQUIPMENT

Buck Knives
P.O. Box 1267
El Cajon, California 92022
CUTLERY

Burnham Brothers
P.O. Box 100
Marble Falls, Texas 78654
GAME CALLS

Butterfield Custom Products, Inc.
Box 14
Cornell, Wisconsin 54732
"BUTTERFIELD BRUTE" BROADHEADS

C

Calmont Archery Co.
P.O. Box 207
Inverness, Mississippi 38753
TARGET BUTTS

Camo Clan Corp.
154 Howell Street
Dallas, Texas 75207
CAMOUFLAGE CLOTHING

Carroll's Archery
59½ South Main Street
Moab, Utah 84532
RECURVE and COMPOUND BOWS

Chek-It Killian
P.O. Box 38
Onalaska, Wisconsin 54650
BOWSIGHTS

Cobra Bow Sight
P.O. Box 667
16609 South Sheridan
Bixby, Oklahoma 74008
BOWSIGHTS

Crosman Airguns
980 Turk Hill Road
Fairport, New York 14450
TREE STANDS

Custom Archery
6505 Wakefield Drive
Little Rock, Arkansas 72209
ARCHERY SUPPLIES

Custom Long Bows
Angel Rock Road
Moab, Utah 84532
LONGBOWS by DON STURGES

D

Deer Me Products Co.
Box 345
Anoka, Minnesota 55303
TREE STEPS

Deer Run Products, Inc.
166 Granite Springs Road
Yorktown Heights, New York 10598
GAME SCENTS

Jim Dougherty Archery
4304 East Pine Place
Tulsa, Oklahoma 74115
ARCHERY SUPPLIES

E

James D. Easton, Inc.
7800 Haskell Avenue
Van Nuys, California 91406
ALUMINUM ARROW SHAFTS

Easy Climbers, Inc.
3900 60th Street
Kenosha, Wisconsin 53142
TREE CLIMBING EQUIPMENT

F

Feline Archery, Inc.
220 Willow Crossing Road
Greensburg, Pennsylvania 15601
ARCHERY SUPPLIES

Fine-Line, Inc.
6922 North Meridan
Puyallup, Washington 98371
BOWSIGHTS and STRING PEEPS

Jim Fletcher's Archery Aids
P.O. Box 218
Bodfish, California 93205
RELEASES

G

Game Tracker
5265 West Pierson Road
Flushing, Michigan 48433
GAME FINDING DEVICE

Gateway Feathers, Inc.
Route 2
Box 165
Holmen, Wisconsin 54636
TURKEY FEATHERS

Gerber Ledgendary Blades
14200 SW 72nd Avenue
Portland, Oregon 97223
CUTLERY

Gilmore Sporting Glass, Inc.
Box 469
Spencer, Iowa 51301
FIBERGLASS and GRAPHITE ARROW SHAFTS

Golden Eagle Archery, Inc.
P.O. Box 310
Creswell, Oregon 97426
COMPOUND BOWS

Gordon Plastics, Inc.
2872 South Santa Fe Avenue
Vista, California 92083
FIBERGLASS and GRAPHITE ARROW SHAFTS

Gorman's Design
Box 21102
Minneapolis, Minnesota 55421
ELECTRONIC SIGHT PINS

Graham Archery Sales
425 Faith Road
Salisbury, North Carolina 28144
TREE STEPS

Graham's Custom Bows
P.O. Box 1312
Fontana, California 92335
"DYNABO" BOWS

H

Hiawatha Archery, Inc.
228 Bridge Street
East Syracuse, New York 13057

"MAGNUM" BROADHEADS

Himalayan Industries, Inc.
P.O. Box 5668
Pine Bluff, Arkansas 71611

OUTDOOR CLOTHING

Stanley Hips Targets
17499 Blanco Road
San Antonio, Texas 78232

TARGETS

Howard Hill Archery
219 Blogett Camp Road
Hamilton, Montana 59840

ARCHERY EQUIPMENT

Jack Howard Hunting Bows
Nevada City, California 95959

RECURVE BOWS

Hoyt Archery Co.
11510 Natural Bridge
Bridgeton, Missouri 63044

RECURVE and COMPOUND BOWS

Hunter's Choice Products
Rt 5 W310 S0049
Highway 1
Mukwonago, Wisconsin 53149

CAMO SOAP

Hunter's Comfort
3668 Skyora Road
Cleveland, Ohio 44105

PORTABLE TREE SEAT

I

Impact Industries, Inc.
904 Sumner Street
Wausau, Wisconsin 54401

LADDER TREE STAND

Indian Archery Co.
817 Maxwell Avenue
Evansville, Indiana 47717

BOWS AND ACCESSORIES

J

Jennings Compound Bows
P.O. Box 1750
Gainesville, Florida 32601

COMPOUND BOWS

K

Kolpin Manufacturing, Inc.
P.O. Box 231
Berlin, Wisconsin 54923

ACCESSORIES and OUTDOOR EQUIPMENT

Kwikee Kwiver Co.
7292 Peaceful Valley Road
Acme, Michigan 49610

BOW QUIVERS and ACCESSORIES

L

Loc-On Co.
Route 1, Box 711
Summerfield, North Carolina 27358

TREE STANDS

M

Martin Archery, Inc.
Route 5, Box 127
Walla Walla, Washington 99362

ARCHERY and BOWHUNTING EQUIPMENT

Martin Manufacturing Co.
1742 Brown Road
Hepzibah, Georgia 30815

TREE STEPS and MINERAL SALT SUPPLEMENT

N

New Archery Products Corp.
370 North Delaplaine Road
Riverside, Illinois 60546

"RAZORBACK" BROADHEAD SYSTEM

Nirk Archery Co.
Potlach, Idaho 83855

ARROW NOCKS

North River Products, Inc.
806 DeSale Street
Vienna, Virginia 22180

ARCHERY RELEASES

Norton Co.
16624 Edwards Road
Cerritos, California 90701

SHARPENING STONES

O

Ole Norm's, Inc.
Hwy. 93 and 123
P.O. Box 966
Clemson, South Carolina 29631

SIGHT PIN LIGHTS

P

Patsco
Route 1
Box 499c
Sylacauga, Alabama 35150

TREE STANDS

Ben Pearson, Inc.
P.O. Box 7465
Pine Bluff, Arkansas 71611

ARCHERY and BOWHUNTING EQUIPMENT

Potawatomi Products
16683 West 6th Road
Plymouth, Indiana 46563

BOW SQUARES

Precision Shooting Equipment, Inc.
P.O. Box 5487
Tucson, Arizona 85703

ARCHERY and BOWHUNTING EQUIPMENT

Pro Line Co.
1843 Gun Lake Road
Hastings, Michigan 49058

ARCHERY EQUIPMENT

R

Range-O-Matic Archery Co.
35572 Strathcona Drive
Mount Clemens, Michigan 48043

BOWSIGHTS

Ranging Measuring Systems
90 Lincoln Road North
East Rochester, New York 14445

RANGE FINDING DEVICES

Rapid-Vance Technology
P.O. Box 5457
Willoughby, Ohio 44094

ARROW HOLDERS

Roger Rothhaar
Box 35
Oceola, Ohio 44860

"SNUFFER" BROADHEADS

S

Safariland Archery Corp.
P.O. Box NN
McLean, Virginia 22101

**SCENTS, COMPOUND BOWS, CLOTHING,
  AFRICAN TRIPS**

Saunders Archery Co.
Box 476
Columbus, Nebraska 68601

ARCHERY ACCESSORIES

Savora Archery Co., Inc.
P.O. Box 594
Kirkland, Washington 98033

"SAVORA" BROADHEADS

Schrade Cutlery Corp.
Ellenville, New York 12428

CUTLERY and SHARPENING STEELS

Sherwin Industries Inc.
100 Sherwin Drive
Port Richey, Florida 33568

"SATELLITE" BROADHEADS

S (Cont'd.)

Skunk Skreen
P.O. Box Drawer CB
College Station, Texas 77841.
SCENTS

Smith's Whetstones
1500 Sleepy Valley Road
Hot Springs, Arkansas 71901
ARKANSAS WHETSTONES

Stuart Manufacturing Company
P.O. Box 718
Rockwell, Texas 75087
TOURNAMENT and HUNTING RELEASES

Swede Seat
P.O. Box 471
Pelican Rapids, Minnesota 56572
PORTABLE TREE STANDS

T

Texas Feathers, Inc.
Box 1118
Brownwood, Texas 76801
TURKEY FEATHERS

Tomar Corporation
Industrial Park Drive
Harbor Springs, Michigan 49740
ARROW POINT TOOLS, BOW STABILIZERS

Total Shooting Systems, Inc.
419 Van Dyne Road
North Fond Du Lac, Wisconsin 54935
"QUADRAFLEX" BOWS, ARCHERY EQUIPMENT

Trueflight Manufacturing Co., Inc.
Manitowish Waters, Wisconsin 54545
TURKEY FEATHERS

Twilite Products Inc.
7400 Africa Road
P.O. Box 295
Westerville, Ohio 43081
ELECTRONIC BOWSIGHTS

V

Vogl-Schultz, Inc.
2245 Mt. Hope Road
Okemos, Michigan 48864
TREE CLIMBING EQUIPMENT

W

Wasp Archery Products
P.O. Box 760
Bristol, Connecticut 06010
BROADHEADS

L.C. Whiffen Co., Inc.
923 South 16th Street
Milwaukee, Wisconsin 53204
ARCHERY ACCESSORIES

Wilson Brothers Archery
Route No. 1
Box 142-2
Elkland, Missouri 65644
"BLACK WIDOW" BOWS, TABS, ARROW RESTS

Winn Archery Equipment Co.
410 North Shore Drive
South Haven, Michigan 49090
WRIST-SUPPORTED RELEASES

Winona Sportswear, Inc.
904 East 2nd Street
Winona, Minnesota 55987
CAMOUFLAGE CLOTHING

Wolverine Manufacturing
811 South Center Road
Saginaw, Michigan 48603
PORTABLE TREE SEATS

Woods and Water, Inc.
8301 West Calumet Road
Milwaukee, Wisconsin 53223
TREE STANDS

Y

York Archery
Woodcraft Equipment Co.
P.O. Box 110
Independence, Missouri 64051

ECCENTRIC CAM COMPOUND BOWS

Z

Zwickey Archery Co.
2571 East 12th Avenue
North St. Paul, Minnesota 55109

**"BLACK DIAMOND" BROADHEADS and
"ZWICKEY ZUDO" SMALL GAME POINTS**

NATIONAL ARCHERY PUBLICATIONS

Archery World
Winter Sports Publishing, Inc.
715 Florida Avenue South
Minneapolis, Minnesota 55426

Bow and Arrow
P.O. Box H H
Capistrano Beach, California 92624

Bowhunter
3808 South Calhoun Street
Fort Wayne, Indiana 46807

Deer and Deer Hunting
114 West Glendale Avenue
Appleton, Wisconsin 54912

Western Bowhunter
P.O. Box 511
Squaw Valley, California 93646

NATIONAL ARCHERY ORGANIZATIONS

American Archery Council
200 Castlewood Drive
North Palm Beach, Florida 33408

Archery Manufacturers Organization
200 Castlewood Drive
North Palm Beach, Florida 33408

National Archery Association
1750 East Boulder Street
Colorado Springs, Colorado 80909

National Field Archery Association
Route 2
Box 514
Redlands, California 92373

Professional Archery Association
731 North Cliff Avenue
Sioux Falls, South Dakota 57103

Professional Bowhunters Society
2533 TR192
Coshocton, Ohio 43812

The Fred Bear Sports Club
Rural Route No. 4
4600 Southwest 41st Boulevard
Gainesville, Florida 32601